DION BOUCICAULT
A Biography

DION BOUCICAULT

A BIOGRAPHY

Richard Fawkes

QUARTET BOOKS
LONDON MELBOURNE NEW YORK

First published by Quartet Books Limited, 1979
A member of the Namara Group
27 Goodge Street, London W1P 1FD
Copyright © 1979 by Richard Fawkes
Foreword copyright © 1979 by Donald Sinden
Designed by Roy Trevelion
ISBN 0 7043 2221 8
Made and printed in Great Britain by
The Garden City Press Limited
Letchworth, Hertfordshire SG6 1JS

FOR
CHRISTOPHER CALTHROP
WHO FIRST INTRODUCED ME
TO HIS GREAT-GRANDFATHER

CONTENTS

ILLUSTRATIONS

ix

Charles Kean *(Calthrop Collection)*
Scene from *The Octoroon (Calthrop Collection)*
Scene from *Arrah-na-Pogue (author's collection)*
Babil and Bijou (Calthrop Collection)
Two cartoons by Alfred Bryan, 1880, 1876 (and back of jacket) *(Calthrop Collection)*
Cartoon by Sem *(National Portrait Gallery)*
Nina Boucicault as Peter Pan *(Radio Times Hulton Picture Library)*
Dot Boucicault in *Her Husband's Wife (Radio Times Hulton Picture Library)*
Boucicault advertising cigarettes *(Andrew Eliot)*
Boucicault and Louise Thorndyke *(Calthrop Collection)*

Playbills
All playbills are from the Calthrop Collection or the author's collection except *Lodgings To Let* (page 26), Stephen Smyth, and *London Assurance* (page 38), British Library.

FOREWORD
by Donald Sinden, C.B.E.

IN 1970 I was touring Australia in the Royal Shakespeare Company's production of *Twelfth Night* when I received a copy of Boucicault's *London Assurance* from Trevor Nunn, asking me to look at the part of Sir Harcourt Courtly. I have always been particularly interested in Victorian drama and had been suggesting various nineteenth-century plays to Mr Nunn for some time, but this was one I didn't know. I knew of Boucicault, of course, and of the Boucicault family, and as a young actor I had read such plays as *The Colleen Bawn* and *The Poor of New York* because so many Victorian actors I had known had told me I had to. My reaction had been to wonder if such plays really had been put on!

I read *London Assurance* and found it very funny. Once home I did some research and discovered that it had been put on originally in 1841 by Charles Mathews and his wife Madame Vestris at Covent Garden, and that Mathews had played the part of Dazzle. If Mathews, the manager, had played Dazzle, the obvious leading role, why was I being asked to look at Sir Harcourt Courtly? I checked the original cast and found that he had been played by William Farren. I remembered that Farren had retired by 1841, so his appearance would have been the equivalent of bringing someone of the stature of Alfred Lunt out of retirement – and only a marvellous part would have brought him out. If it was good enough for Farren, I thought, it was good enough for me.

During rehearsals for a play, the most important aspect for the actor is that of exploration: exploration of his character and his character's relationships with others. In a period drama that means understanding how people behaved, how they spoke, stood, walked and sat, what they ate and what they wore – the sort of knowledge which helps an actor acquire period atmosphere and is one of the layers of experience he needs. I always consult my elders about period plays, about the problems they found and how they overcame them. Although our designer had decided 1841 was too drab a period and had set the play back twenty years to 1820, to give it a Regency air (which was, I think, more in keeping with the spirit of the play), I couldn't find a single actor who had appeared in a contemporary play of 1820 to 1840, in contemporary costume. Nor could I think of a single play of that period which was not a historical romance or costume drama. And so came our first problem with *London Assurance*: where could we find out about patterns of behaviour? What was it like theatrically to be an actor at that time? How did people behave on stage? What innovations were there? We do know that *London Assurance* was the first play with a box set, and that, from an actor's point of view, must have been electrifying. No actor living at that time had ever made an entrance through a door; he had always entered through the wings, just walking on and off. Suddenly he was faced with a set containing doors and you can hear him muttering, 'Damned doors! What are they doing to us? You can't make an entrance through a door!' Now, of course, it's the reverse; an actor cannot get on stage unless he has one. But one can imagine how irritating it must have been for the original actors, especially an old one like Farren who had never entered through a door on stage in his life, to have to use a real door, to have real furniture and real carpets to trip over.

Another interesting point emerged from talking to the actor Robert Atkins. He had never done a play of that period, but he advised me to remember that it was not until 1904 that Gerald du Maurier had become the first actor to face another actor when he spoke to him. Before that, an actor listened in profile while the other actor faced the audience and spoke his lines. We actually tried this with *London Assurance* and it worked superbly.

One of the most exciting single moments in my life occurred during rehearsals for the play. Christopher Calthrop, Boucicault's great-grandson, knowing of my interest in theatrical history, tele-phoned to ask if I would like to see some Boucicault material in his possession. I jumped at the idea and he showed me various prints, playbills, programmes and letters, and then suddenly he produced the manuscript of *London Assurance*. There I was, three weeks into rehearsal, holding the original! We had already hit several problems with the printed text, in the version we were using, and even in my own, which had been printed in 1841. For instance, my character was down as Sir Harcourt Courtly and yet, within the text, for some reason we could not work out, people called him Billy. The answer lay in the original: several of the characters had different names; Sir Harcourt Courtly was known as Sir William Dazzle, his son as Charles Dazzle, and the character we now know as Dazzle was called Ignatius Mulfather, a good Irish name. We had never before considered the possibility of Dazzle being Irish, but the more we thought of him as Irish, the more sense he made as a character, for, quite simply, Dazzle is a leprechaun. One could see what had happened. The play had been sent to Covent Garden in the days when an actor-manager bought a script and then put it right. Mathews and Vestris had liked it and thought they could do some-thing with it, but Mathews, who wanted to play the part of Ignatius Mulfather, refused to be lumbered with the name. Instead he looked at the cast list and chose the name Dazzle, leaving Boucicault to find a new name for the Dazzle character. Eventually, because it sounded right, he picked Sir Harcourt Courtly. So, although the names had been changed, the actors failed to change them in the text and Sir Harcourt Courtly, fomerly Sir William Dazzle, remained Billy.

Another interesting point to emerge from the manuscript was that Grace Harkaway's two great arias do not appear. Once again, it would have been a question of Madame Vestris, who was playing Grace, asking for her part to be built up and of Boucicault having to write another couple of speeches for her. I've always maintained that the works of Shakespeare in the Folio are as the actors left them after they'd been tightened up and made theatrical, and that is what I think happened with *London Assurance*. One wouldn't know that it is the work of a young playwright, and I don't think it is. It is very much as Mathews and Vestris left it. They were vastly experienced and told Boucicault what would or would not work, where they needed another line or another laugh. Boucicault was learning his trade and the differences between the manuscript and the printed version show just how much he learned.

The reason why I like nineteenth-century drama so much is that plays then were written for actors. Some plays were, of course, literary – the better the writer the more literary they were – but they were not written to be literary masterpieces. Boucicault wrote for actors and his writing is, above all, theatrical. He knew how to use words and he knew the possibilities of a scene. His dialogue, like that of those other Irishmen, Wilde and Shaw, is beautifully speakable; it falls off the tongue. A play like *London Assurance*, for the actor especially, is great fun to do.

I played in *London Assurance* for eighteen months, in one of the happiest engagements of my career. It is a play I consider to be the equal of *The Importance of Being Earnest*, and I, for one, am very grateful that the Royal Shakespeare Company rediscovered it. Boucicault is clearly one of the major figures, not just of British theatre but of world theatre, and his work ought to be better known. He is indeed long overdue for reassessment, both as a working dramatist and as a theatrical phenomenon. There has until now only ever been one full biography of him, and that was published over sixty years ago and then only in the United States. A book like Richard Fawkes's *Dion Boucicault* would have been invaluable to me at the time I was working on *London Assurance*. Not only does it gather together all the known facts about Dion Boucicault (and reference books are a mass of contradiction, I discovered), but the author has, I feel, succeeded in placing Boucicault in the perspective of his time. He stresses Boucicault's importance in theatrical history while, at the same time, taking account of his virtues and faults (which could be equally vivid) and the changes in taste which led to his eclipse. I hope, above all, that this book will inspire some of our metropolitan and provincial managements to delve into the archives, blow the dust off some of Boucicault's more rewarding plays and put him back where he belongs: on the stage.

INTRODUCTION

I<small>T WAS</small> a chance meeting at a party that first got me interested in Dion Boucicault. I had seen the Royal Shakespeare Company's hugely enjoyable production of *London Assurance* but knew nothing about the playwright other than what was contained in the programme note; I didn't even know how to pronounce his name (Boo-see-ko).

Then I met Christopher Calthrop, Boucicault's great-grandson. He began to tell me the story of a remarkable man whose birth was shrouded in mystery, who ran away to become an actor and was a successful playwright before he was twenty-one; who wrote, adapted or doctored more than 200 plays, many of them highly influential; who made and lost fortunes, was involved in scandal, was considered to be one of the wittiest men of his age – 'None but the brave deserve the fair, and none but the brave can live with some of them' was an often-quoted comment – and was for fifty years the most important single figure in the theatrical life of both Britain and America. I was hooked, and out of that fascination came a radio play and now this biography.

Boucicault was a man of immense energy and drive. He was not only a prolific playwright but was instrumental in establishing copyright for dramatists in America, was the first writer to obtain a royalty from a play instead of a flat fee (a move that was to have far-reaching effects) and contributed decisively towards the establishment of both the run and the touring production. As a manager he abolished the custom of admitting audiences for half-price after nine o'clock, cut the length of performances from several pieces lasting several hours to one full-length play, was credited with introducing the matinee, and made many technical innovations including the introduction of fire-proof scenery. He was an accomplished teacher and stage director, demonstrating how crowd scenes should be handled long before ensemble playing became fashionable. He encouraged and promoted such talents as Henry Irving, Harry Montague, Joseph Jefferson and Henry Miller. He was a skilful actor, considered by many to be great, especially in the Irish roles he created for himself. During the third quarter of the last century he was the most prolific, most prosperous and most widely imitated playwright of the English-speaking stage. And yet, today, Boucicault is almost completely unknown except to a handful of actors, enthusiasts and academics.

Why should this be? Partly it has to do with fashion. Boucicault was the supreme melodramatist and melodrama has never enjoyed a substantial revival, at least not on stage. Hollywood, of course, thrives on melodrama (which is, after all, only drama with music) and many of Boucicault's plays were turned into films in the early days of the cinema. His writing, even though it was done some years before the cinema was born, shows such an awareness of cinema techniques that had he lived fifty years later I am sure he would have been a screenwriter. However, the arrival on stage of such 'realistic' writers as Ibsen, Zola, Strindberg and Shaw, sounded the death-knell for Boucicault's style of play. It is ironic that the man whose pioneering work in bettering conditions for dramatists allowed such writers to make a living from the theatre was Boucicault!

Partly the reason for his eclipse has to do with his personality and private life. Boucicault never cared whom he offended and he had enough enemies happy to do him down. After his bigamous marriage to Louise Thorndyke even his friends decided to ostracise him, at least publicly. It cannot be an accident that although he knew virtually everyone in the Arts worth knowing, Boucicault's name appears in very few autobiographies until some ten or fifteen years after his death. It is as if there was a conspiracy to ignore his existence until he was safely out of the way.

Apart from being a fascinating man, Boucicault is, I believe, a far more important playwright than is often recognized. His comedies bridge the gap between those of the Restoration, Goldsmith and Sheridan, and those of Wilde, Shaw, Synge and O'Casey, all of whom were influenced significantly by Boucicault. Asked how one could learn about drama, Shaw replied that the only way was to study the masters – and went on to include Boucicault on his list. And it was O'Casey who remarked, 'Shakespeare's good in bits, but for colour and stir give me Boucicault'. Among the hundred or so of Boucicault plays which survive today there are a significant number which are extremely good and would repay close attention. His plays may not always 'read' well but the R.S.C's production of *London Assurance*, the Abbey Theatre's production of *The Shaughraun*, and the occasional repertory or amateur productions of the other Irish dramas prove that his plays are still very powerful on the stage.

Boucicault was born Dionysius Lardner Boursiquot. He adopted several spellings for his surname before settling on the one we use today. For the sake of clarity I have, except when quoting, always used this final spelling. The name Boursiquot is used when referring to his father or mother.

It is surprising that there should be so many mysteries and questions about a man who spent the best part of fifty years in the public eye, whose many activities were chronicled in newspapers. And yet mysteries there are. One of the major problems with Boucicault's life is that so many references to him are wrong: biographical dictionaries, for example, manage five different birthdates between them. And reference books have not been helped by the fact that Boucicault himself was an inveterate romancer and distorter of the truth! As far as possible every date in this book has been checked. Many people have given me invaluable assistance in carrying out this work, and as well as thanking the librarians and staff of those libraries which helped me (listed in a separate section), I would like to offer my deep gratitude to the following for their patience, advice and, often, very hard work on my behalf: Jennifer Aylmer of the Theatre Museum, London, Kathleen Barker, Reginald Bioletti, Susan Conradi, Elizabeth Cuthbert, deputy registrar of the Royal Archives, Windsor, Alfred Emmet, Raymund FitzSimons, John Hadley, Alan Hankinson, Michael

Hardwick, Robert Hogan, Arthur Jacobs, Jeanne T. Newlin, curator of the Harvard Theater Collection, David Phillips, Louis A. Rachow of the Player's Club, New York, Terence Rees, Jack Reading, George Rowell and Julius H. Tolson. I must single out for special mention two people whose researches and generosity made my task so much easier: the late Dr Albert E. Johnson and Professor F. Theodore Cloak. Dr Johnson, who had been working on Boucicault for the past twenty-five years, even though he was seriously ill when I started this book, found time to answer my questions and allowed me to see part of his research. His untimely death robbed the world of a fine scholar and man. Professor Cloak, who has himself spent the past forty years researching Boucicault's life, also gave me freely and unselfishly of his time and extensive knowledge. He very kindly agreed to read my manuscript and corrected some of the more glaring errors, for which I am indebted to him.

No formal acknowledgement of the people who have helped me would be complete without mention of Christopher Calthrop, to whom this book is gratefully dedicated. It was his enthusiasm and his willingness to share that enthusiasm which first encouraged me to start writing, and without him I would certainly not have finished. To Diana Sinden, who introduced us, a special thank you.

Finally I would like to thank Peter Ford and Janet Law for their advice, encouragement and constant interest, and my wife Cherry, who has had to live with Boucicault in the house for a long time, for reading the manuscript in all its stages with an unfailingly critical – and helpful – eye.

1

BIRTH AND SCHOOLDAYS

O N THURSDAY, 4 March 1841, the curtain of the Theatre Royal, Covent Garden, rose on a new five-act comedy by a young Irishman calling himself Lee Moreton. The house was half-full. It was pouring with rain and not even an outstanding cast, headed by Charles Mathews, Madame Vestris, Louisa Nisbett and William Farren – probably the strongest London was able to muster at that time – could persuade the public to venture out on such a night for a play by a writer of whom they'd never heard.

During the performance the woe-begone author wandered about the corridors of the house, for he had been warned off the stage by Madame Vestris, who said his presence would make the actors nervous. So he crept up to a back seat in the upper boxes, and there listened to his play. Oh, how slow it seemed! how bald. The first act provoked a little laughter here and there, and then he drew a breath. The beautiful stage-setting of the second act elicited the first round of applause. As the play proceeded he discovered Mark Lemon, Douglas Jerrold, and Gilbert à Beckett seated together in the front row of an adjacent box. He crept into the row behind them and tried to overhear their opinions of the piece. When the situation arrived at the end of this act,

Jerrold turned to his companions. 'That is fatal,' he observed. 'He has reached his climax too early in the play. Nothing will go after that.' The public had, indeed, greeted the scene with the wild enthusiasm an English audience alone are capable of displaying. Wellington never awaited the arrival of the Prussians at Waterloo with the pale anxiety that the appearance of *Lady Gay Spanker* and *Dolly* in the third act was waited for by that young dramatist. Nisbett came, she spoke, and conquered. She outranked herself. The hunting speech carried the house by storm. Jerrold, Lemon and à Beckett rose in their seats and cheered. The pit seemed to boil over. Nothing was heard for several minutes. The author left the house. Up and down Covent Garden Market, back and forth, he paced, not sensible where he directed his steps, until he found himself on Waterloo Bridge, seated in a recess, trying to cool his face by pressing it against the wet stone balustrade. It was raining, but he did not know it. Then there crept over him a dread that the end of the comedy might change the tide of success. He rose and crept back to the theatre; the fifth act was on; there was an ominous silence. Hush! who was speaking?

Sir Harcourt – Charles, who is Mr Dazzle?

Charles – Dazzle? Well, I don't exactly know who he is. I say, Dazzle, excuse an impertinent question.

Dazzle – Oh, certainly!

Charles – Who are you?

Dazzle – I have not the slightest idea!

The house shook with peal after peal of laughter at the inimitable manner of Mathews. And every fibre of the young author quivered responsively. In a few moments after this the curtain descended. The actors had responded again and again to the enthusiastic calls and recalls of the public, when a strange uproar commenced – a din amidst which it seemed impossible to discern what the audience wanted. In the midst of all this the author felt himself being seized by some one, who cried, 'Mr Mathews is searching for you, sir, everywhere; please follow me at once'; and presently he found himself behind the scenes, standing at the prompt entrance. 'Come,' said Mathews, 'don't you hear the public? They are calling for you!' 'For me?' he stammered. 'What for?' Mathews caught the boy by the arm; Bartley pushed him forward, and he found himself suddenly in the presence of the audience.[1]

That was how, in an article written nearly fifty years later, Dion Boucicault (Lee Moreton was a pseudonym) was to recall the first night of *London Assurance*, the play with which he established his reputation. Although prone to exaggeration and romanticizing, Boucicault's memory served him well on this occasion, for the evening was undoubtedly the sensation he remembered. During the performance, news of the play's reception had travelled quickly along the theatrical grapevine. Lester Wallack, the American actor-manager, was backstage at the Haymarket when someone burst in to say that Covent Garden had a hit on its hands. 'The third act is over,' he gasped, 'and it is tremendous. If the other two acts go in the same way it is an immense go.'[2] And an immense go it was. The play 'met with the success it deserves', reported the critic of the *Observer*. 'It gives promise of forming something like a new era in our drama.' 'The audience shook the house with applause at the fall of the curtain,' wrote another, 'and had on Mr Lee Morton, the author, to receive their congratulations. The triumph was complete.'[3]

For Dion Boucicault the triumph was indeed complete. At the age of only twenty he had written a play that was to become not just the hit of the season, running for three months, but one that would remain in the repertory of theatres throughout Britain and the United States until the turn of the century. It was a fairy-tale start to a glittering career for the man who was to become one of the most powerful, potent and influential forces in the theatre on both sides of the Atlantic during the next fifty years.

Boucicault was born in Dublin, at 28 Middle Gardiner Street, on 27 December 1820. There has always been controversy surrounding the place and date of his birth, and his parentage. At least five different dates have been suggested, and Boucicault himself always claimed to have been born in

1822, no doubt because of a typical actor's desire to be thought younger than he really was. And how much better it seemed to be able to claim that *London Assurance* was written when he was only eighteen. Boucicault's word is not to be trusted, however. Registration of births in Ireland did not become compulsory until 1864, and in the absence of a birth certificate or baptismal records (which, if they ever existed, were almost certainly destroyed in the 'Troubles' of 1916–22) to provide conclusive proof, there is only circumstantial evidence to go on. And all such evidence points towards 1820, not 1822, as being the correct year.

Boucicault's mother was Anna Maria Darley, a sister of the poet George Darley and the Reverend Charles Darley, first Professor of English Literature at Queen's College, Cork. The Darleys were a well-known Irish Protestant family, related to the Guinness brewing family by marriage, and it was from them that Boucicault claimed to have inherited whatever literary talent he possessed. Both his uncles were minor playwrights. George's blank-verse drama, *Thomas à Becket,* one of the earliest attempts to dramatize the life of the martyr, was produced in London in 1840, while Charles's play, *Plighted Troth* (which was so bad it earned itself the nickname *Slighted Broth*), was seen at Drury Lane in 1842.

In 1813, when she was eighteen, Anne (as she was always known) married Samuel Smith Boursiquot, a Dublin wine merchant of Huguenot extraction, twenty-six years her senior. Samuel may have been Boucicault's father, but it seems much more probable that the honour should be given to Dr the Reverend Dionysius Lardner, a lecturer at Trinity College, Dublin, who was Anne's lover, gave his name to the boy and became his guardian, paying for most, if not all, of his education.

Lardner was an interesting man. Born in Dublin in 1793, he graduated from Trinity (where his lecture on the steam engine, his greatest passion after women, won him a gold medal and was later published) with degrees in logic, mathematics, ethics, metaphysics and physics. In 1827 he was awarded a doctorate in Divinity, but never practised Holy Orders, preferring instead to devote himself to writing and scientific experiment. He was best known for his 134-volume reference work, *The Cabinet Cyclopedia*, to which Mary Shelley was a contributor, and for his frequent public disputes with distinguished engineers and inventors. He was ambitious, talented and prolific (qualities shared by Boucicault), and yet, also like Boucicault, there was an air of spuriousness surrounding much of his work, which led to William Makepeace Thackeray satirizing him as Dr Dionysius Diddler. In Newcastle, in 1836, he delivered an extravagant eulogy of George Stephenson, referring to him as 'the Father of the Locomotive', a phrase which has passed into English folklore. And yet only four years earlier, in an anonymous article in the *Edinburgh Review*, he had savagely attacked the directors of the Liverpool and Manchester Railway for becoming so 'fascinated' by Stephenson that the man had obtained an unassailable monopoly whereby all other talent and all rolling stock not built by his son had been excluded from the project. When Isambard Kingdom Brunel proposed, in 1834, building a box tunnel two miles long on the Great Western Railway outside Bath, it was Lardner who appeared to damn the scheme. He demonstrated that, should the train's brakes fail while it was in the tunnel, it would emerge at not less than 120 m.p.h. and all the passengers would be asphyxiated. Two years later, when Brunel was building an iron steamship to provide a regular passenger service across the Atlantic, it was Lardner who again popped up to prove it would never work. No steamship built to Brunel's specifications, argued Lardner, could possibly carry enough fuel to get it across the Atlantic; once coal stocks had been exhausted, any passengers foolish enough to have sailed on such a voyage would be doomed to drift engineless until they perished. On both occasions, Brunel in practice confounded Lardner in theory, and yet, despite Charles Dickens's description of him as 'that prince of humbugs' and inventor Samuel Hall's denunciation of him as 'an ignorant and impudent empiric', Lardner managed to maintain an aura of scientific respectability. His downfall was brought about not by being proved a scientific fraud, but by scandal. In 1840, he eloped to Paris with the wife of Captain Richard Heaviside, a director of the

London and Brighton Railway. Heaviside sued him for alienation of affections and was awarded the massive sum of £8,000 damages. Lardner's career in Britain was effectively finished. He set up home in Paris with Mrs Heaviside, whom he later married, and died in Naples in 1859.

Much less is known about Samuel Smith Boursiquot. A man of medium height, well read and an accomplished musician, he was forty-four when he married eighteen-year-old Anne Darley at St Thomas's Protestant Church, Dublin, on 29 July 1813.[4] In 1814 their first child, Mary, was born. Three years later they had a son, William, and in 1819, twin boys, George and Arthur. Whatever their feelings for each other may have been at the start of their relationship, by 1820 the marriage had run into serious difficulties.[5] Samuel had inherited the Boursiquot family wine business, but he was no businessman and under him the family fortunes went into a sharp decline. He withdrew more and more from reality, becoming an unhappy, disillusioned daydreamer. He was convinced (quite erroneously) that he was descended from the French aristocracy, and that a noble ancester, whose advice, if taken, would have altered the course of the battle and given victory to the French, had fought at Agincourt. In fact his family came originally from Taillebourg, in the Charente region of France, where they were salt merchants. His great-grandfather had fled to Ireland following the 1685 revocation of the Edict of Nantes, and had, after a spell in the army (a brother, who joined with him, was killed at the Battle of the Boyne in 1690), settled in Dublin, married another French refugee and opened the wine shop that was the foundation of the business Samuel inherited. Samuel was equally certain (though on what grounds no one knew) that he would one day inherit Branksea Castle, the home of his cousins, the Smiths.[6] The gradual realization that he would never become the owner of Branksea Castle, coupled with his failure as a businessman, made Samuel deeply aware that he could never live up to the ancestry he claimed for himself, that his family would never be able to occupy the position in Dublin society he felt was its due. He became increasingly withdrawn and reticent. By 1820, when he was fifty-one, he was finding it very difficult to make ends meet. His daughter Mary had been born with a spinal complaint (from which she died in 1831) and needed constant care and attention, and with three young boys to support as well, it took all Samuel's time and energy just to keep a roof over their heads. He had little time to spare for his much younger wife. Anne, still only twenty-five, attractive, vivacious and strong-willed, began to look elsewhere for the attention she lacked at home.

She had known Lardner since childhood. Their families had been close friends and they had grown up together. Even though they went their separate ways in marriage (Lardner married Cecilia Flood in 1815) they remained friends and were frequent visitors in each other's home. Lardner was only two years older than Anne. He was a witty, amusing companion who enjoyed spending his money on his lady-friends – the exact opposite of the dour, elderly Boursiquot. In 1820, Anne persuaded her husband that it was essential for their children's health and well-being that they should spend the summer by the sea, so Samuel rented a small cottage at Bray where she could stay with them while he remained in Dublin, visiting them at weekends and occasionally during the week if he could get away. Living only a few miles away, at Black Rock, were Lardner, his wife and two daughters. They saw a lot of one another.[7]

Exactly when the relationship between Anne and Lardner developed into an affair isn't known, but by midsummer they were definitely lovers. She was seen letting him into her cottage on nights when Samuel was in Dublin; he was overheard calling her 'My love'; and, one morning, he was spotted creeping out of the back door before straightening his clothes and presenting himself at the front as if he'd just arrived.

Cecilia Lardner may not have had proof of her husband's infidelity but she certainly had strong suspicions. For almost two years she had been growing increasingly irritable with Lardner, picking fights with him on the smallest provocation. His relatives could never understand why he didn't adopt a firmer line with her and keep her in her place, putting it down to his over-generous nature. In all probability, he felt too guilty to want to run the risk of antagonizing her further and so suffered her outbursts in silence.

In October 1820 her patience finally gave out. One evening at the Black Rock cottage, when they had guests for dinner, Cecilia, much to everyone's embarrassment, refused to serve coffee or tea after the meal, ordered the maid to clear the tray from the room, and launched into a bitter denunciation of her husband. She accused him of being unfaithful to her and making her a laughing stock in the neighbourhood; she intended leaving him and wanted her dowry back. Lardner could only silence her by picking her up and bodily carrying her from the room. That night she left his house never to return. The following evening, after she had taken one of her children to see a doctor in Dublin, Anne Boursiquot arrived, and stayed for several days.

At the end of October, Anne and her children left their summer cottage in Bray and returned to their Dublin house at 28 Middle Gardiner Street. At the same time, Lardner (who was suffering from a nervous complaint brought on by Cecilia's tantrums and had been advised by his doctor not to live on his own) gave up the Black Rock cottage and moved in to Middle Gardiner Street as the lodger. If Samuel Boursiquot was aware of the relationship that existed between his wife and the new lodger, he said and did nothing.

By the beginning of December, Anne was pregnant. She went into labour on 22 December, and was confined to bed in the front attic bedroom on the third floor, where a son was delivered on the 27th. It was a difficult and painful birth, and Anne went down with milk fever, which forced her to stay in bed for another eight weeks. Since the birthdates of her other children are known, this son must have been Dion Boucicault. This account of his birth came to light twelve years later when Lardner sued Cecilia for divorce in the Dublin Ecclesiastical Court.[8] After Cecilia had walked out on him in October 1820 she had gone to stay in Dublin with a family called Murphy. She and Mr Murphy became lovers and had a daughter. Lardner did not find out about the child until 1829 but as soon as he did, he started divorce proceedings. Unable to deny the charge of adultery, Cecilia counter-charged Lardner with adultery, naming Anne Boursiquot as co-respondent.

Although Lardner and Anne denied the charge, and Lardner won his case, it is clear from the evidence offered by both sides that something had been going on between them, certainly during the summer by the sea in 1820, and Cecilia's tantrums for two years before that would seem to indicate that the affair had started some time before. If Lardner was not Dion Boucicault's natural father, the shrewd Anne did a good job of persuading him that he was. Not only was the child named Dionysius Lardner Boursiquot after him, but she also managed to get him to agree to pay for the boy's education. Lardner may have enjoyed spending money but he was not rich. He had two daughters of his own to support and he was making regular contributions to support his mother and sisters. It hardly seems likely that he would have agreed to finance someone else's son, however well he got on with the mother, had she not been able to convince him that the boy was his responsibility. The rumour of illegitimacy was to dog Boucicault all his life. In 1841, before he had acquired enough enemies wanting or prepared to find as much scandal about him as they could, a reviewer of *London Assurance* noted that the play was 'the effort of a youthful author – the son, we are told, of Dr Lardner'.[9] Although he spent much of his life denying the rumour, Boucicault, particularly in his youth, was not averse to using Lardner's name if he thought it would be useful, especially to obtain credit.

There is one other vital piece of evidence to support 1820 as the year of Boucicault's birth. In 1841, shortly after the successful opening of *London Assurance*, Boucicault went into a tailor's shop in Regent Street and bought £300-worth of clothes for which he offered a bill of exchange. When the bill became due for payment, he refused to honour it and John Hart, the tailor, took him to court, winning his case. Boucicault immediately issued a writ of *coram nobis* (a writ to right a wrong caused by a mistake of the court), claiming that since he was under age at the time of the default, he could not be sued by an attorney. His mother was called as a witness and swore, under oath, that her son had been born on 7 December 1820. The discrepancy in the day was probably due to a typographical error in the newspaper report of the case, but since Boucicault would still have been under age had he been born in 1822 (the year he always gave) there is no reason to doubt that his mother gave the correct month and year.[10]

Once Anne Boursiquot had recovered from the effects of the milk fever brought on by Boucicault's difficult birth, the family moved to 47 Lower Gardiner Street. With them went Dr Lardner. This time he was much more than the lodger: he paid the rent and paid for all the repairs the new house needed. In 1824 they all moved home again, to Mount Pleasant. It was here that Anne's cousin Maria came to stay from Paris. Anne and Samuel were sleeping in separate rooms, though for the sake of propriety Lardner also had his own quarters. What went on in there filled Anne with the greatest concern. Maria was an attractive seventeen and soon caught the eye of the doctor. Anne took to hiding about the house, including in the coal cellar, in order to spy on them but she never managed to catch them together. She heaved a sigh of relief when Maria's ten-month visit was over and she returned to Paris.

It was in this strange atmosphere of intrigue, possessiveness and moral hypocrisy that Boucicault grew up. He was devoted to his mother and she was equally devoted to him. But what was he to make of the two men in her life? His father Samuel, old, sullen, weighed down by the cares of his failing business and crumbling marriage, remains a shadowy figure in the background, filling his young son with romantic stories of an ancestry that did not exist. He must have seemed more like a grandfather to Boucicault than a father. Then there was Lardner, of whom he saw as much as his father and whom he never really liked, who took his father's place in almost every aspect of the family's life. It was a confused, lonely child who trudged off every day to the school on St Stephen's Green run by the Reverend Richard Wall.[11]

In 1827, the Boursiquot family fortunes reached their lowest ebb. Samuel's wine business finally folded and he moved from Jervis Street to new premises in Batchelor's Walk to begin again as a general merchant. Lardner, on the other hand, was starting to do well for himself. In July it was announced that he had been appointed to the first chair of Natural

Philosophy and Astronomy at the newly created University College of London, and although the college was not due to open its doors to students until October 1828, he immediately left Dublin for London to take up his post.

Anne wasn't going to let him get away so easily. She persuaded Samuel that it was in the children's best interests for them to be educated in London, and since his new business had failed to get off the ground, he might just as well try his luck there. At the beginning of 1828 she travelled to London and stayed with Lardner at his lodgings in Golden Square while looking for a suitable house for her family. She found one conveniently close to Lardner in Tavistock Street, and in February sent to Dublin for the children. Only Mary, the twins and Dion joined her. With money being an acute problem, the eldest boy, William, was left in Dublin in the care of one of Anne's brothers. As soon as he had finished sorting out his business affairs, Samuel followed them, but the move was not profitable. He was growing old (he was nearly sixty), he knew no one and he couldn't settle. He remained in London for only a year and then decided to return to Dublin. Anne refused to go with him. Dion and the twins were at school and Mary required constant nursing. She was not prepared to jeopardize their future for an uncertain life back in Ireland, so Samuel left on his own. He couldn't settle in Dublin either, and in 1830 decided to visit Italy to see if he could make money in Florence and Naples, but that move also proved to be a dismal failure. Dispirited and alone, he returned to Ireland and went to Athlone where some old friends, the Robinsons, gave him a job in their family brewery. He died there in 1853 at the age of eighty-four. His marriage to Anne had been over in all but name for many years, and although they never divorced, after the year in London they never even made the pretence of living together.

For Boucicault, London meant school. Details of his schooling are sketchy. There were in London and the suburbs, at that time, hundreds of small schools, run in private houses by ageing academics, which took only a handful of pupils who attended erratically and stayed for short periods. On the recommendation of Lardner, Boucicault went to several such small establishments and his education followed an irregular pattern. Many years later he was to write:

> The life of a man does not begin at the moment of his birth. For a few years he is a vegetable. Then he becomes an animal, and at last – as the grub turns into the fly – his mind unfolds its wings and he lives under the sun. My first experience of life was at a school at Hampstead, then a rural village three miles from London, now swallowed into the metropolis. There were seven or eight of us. I was the stupidest and worse of the lot. In vain the patient, gentle old man tried to find some way into my mind; it was a hopeless task. It was not there. It was wandering into day-dreams and was not to be confined in a bare room, a pile of grammars and slates. Oh, how I hated Latin! The multiplication table was a bed of torture.[12]

As well as spending time at the Hampstead school run by Dr Hessey, father of the Master of Merchant Taylors' School and a dignitary of the church, Boucicault also attended Zion House School in Margate, and may even have gone for a time to Bruce Castle, the progressive school in Tottenham, North London, run by Thomas Wright Hill, whose brother Rowland introduced the penny post to Britain and was a friend of Lardner. They were far from being the happiest days of Boucicault's life. His mother moved house at least a dozen times during the first four years of their stay in England, spending time in Margate, Ramsgate and Brighton as well as London, and although Boucicault was probably sent to most of his schools as a boarder, he certainly accompanied her to Margate.[13] He was rarely given a chance to settle down before being moved on to his next school. He was desperately lonely. His father had left them, his sister Mary died in 1831, and although he spent his holidays with Lardner, his mother's long affair with the doctor was drawing to a close, which must have placed an additional strain on his formative years. He may have been only twelve in 1832 when his mother was called to give evidence in Lardner's divorce case and her relationship with Lardner became public knowledge, but

Boucicault must have had some inkling of what had been going on and may even have been teased at school for being Lardner's son. He was a strong-willed, high-spirited boy, whose ready temper was always getting him into fights, invariably with boys bigger than himself. He resented authority, hated studying, and most of the time came bottom of his class. Not that he wasn't bright. He was quickwitted and clever, and Lardner sent him to some of the most progressive schools in the country in which the staff believed in letting a child express himself and matching the curriculum to a pupil's capability. He read voraciously (his favourite book was *The Seven Champions of Christendom*), had a retentive mind, and gained a solid grounding in French which was to stand him in good stead when he was older. He was introduced to the plays of Shakespeare and eighteenth-century drama, and skimmed wide areas of knowledge so that 'his general information on every conceivable subject was quite remarkable'.[14]

In February 1834, when he was thirteen, Boucicault was sent by Lardner to University College School, where he boarded first with a Mr Hazlewood in Gower Street, then with the Reverend Henry Stebbing in Euston Square.[15] A grammar school within the walls of the university, University College School was not part of the university. Boucicault, in fact, never went to university. He had no interest in an academic career nor in the Church, the other main occupation for which a degree would have fitted him. He much preferred to daydream and write, scribbling poems and articles for the school magazine. In spite of being an outsider, as much from the Irish accent he never lost throughout his life as through his fiery temper, Boucicault was popular with his fellow students. His biting wit, often at the expense of his teachers, and his ability to mimic them, were highly appreciated even if they frequently got him into trouble. At the University College School there was a small, bare room, known as the 'black hole', which was kept especially for disobedient boys. Boucicault and a class-mate, Charles Lamb Kenney (who was to become a life-long friend), vied for the honour of occupying this room and Boucicault spent his many hours in it covering the walls with libellous poems about the staff which he signed with Kenney's name.[16]

His friendship with Kenney was to have an important effect upon Boucicault. Kenney's father, James, was a well-known dramatist, and through him Kenney had a ready access to all the major London theatres. He loved the theatre and went frequently, and every time he did, he took his friend Boucicault. Boucicault was captivated by what he saw. There was a romantic world of the imagination in which his story-book heroes came to life, in which he could escape from his family problems and personal loneliness. The Reverend Stebbing, with whom they both boarded, was also keen on the theatre and allowed them to go as often as they wished, encouraging their interest by discussing the plays they saw, analysing performances and suggesting other plays they ought to see or read.

For some unknown reason, Boucicault missed the first two terms of the academic year 1834–5, but returned to the school for a final term in June 1835. He left University College School at the end of 1835 and went for a year to a Collegiate School in Brentford, Middlesex, run by a Dr Jamieson. It was there that the fifteen-year-old Boucicault decided what he wanted to do with his life. In the summer of 1836 the boys put on an end-of-term production of Sheridan's play *Pizarro* in which Boucicault was given the part of Rolla. It was his first experience of acting. 'For the first time,' he recalled later, 'my mind seemed to soar. I wanted to play every part in the piece myself but had to content myself with teaching all the rest how their parts should be given.' Following the custom of the professional theatre, the school decided to perform *Pizarro* with an afterpiece. 'I offered to write one,' remembered Boucicault, 'and I wrote the little sketch (afterwards played at the Princess's Theatre, London) called *Napoleon's Old Guard*. The success attending this exhibition settled my mind. I would be an actor and nothing else.'[17]

It is tempting to see *Napoleon's Old Guard*, the first play of an impressionable schoolboy, as being autobiographical, at least in attitude. In the story, Henry Lefebre, the hero, is the adopted son of Lord Beauville. He falls in love with the girl

Lord Beauville is trying to seduce, rescues her from his clutches, and is revealed as being the son of the honourable General Lefebre and heir to a fortune. Could Lord Beauville, the villain of the piece, be Dr Lardner? Could Henry Lefebre be Dion Boucicault hoping that his own father would one day turn up with a fortune and rescue him from his guardian? Certainly Lefebre resents Lord Beauville in much the same way as Boucicault resented the man who had always come between him and his father and who had caused doubts to be cast on his legitimacy even while at school.

That same year, 1836, Anne Boursiquot's affair with Lardner came to an end and she returned to Dublin, taking Boucicault with her, to open a boarding house. There he entered his final year of schooling at Dr Geoghegan's Academy on St Stephen's Green, where, among his fellow pupils, were General Sir Henry de Bathe, a pageboy at Queen Victoria's coronation, whose son Hugo married Lillie Langtry, Richard Boyle, an engineer who led the defence of Arrah during the Indian Mutiny, and William Howard Russell, *The Times* war correspondent. Russell remembered Boucicault as

a very cantankerous boy, though unquestionably plucky. I remember he fought a big fellow named Barton – who, by the by, became a famous advocate in India . . . – with one arm tied behind his back, and took a licking gallantly. He was always considered a very clever fellow; but, oh! how he used to romance.[18]

Although he had set his heart on a career in the theatre, Boucicault had to put up with considerable opposition from his family. His literary uncles, who might have been expected to encourage him even if they didn't help him, did neither. For them the theatre was not a career – it was a toy to be played with by people who had steady, respectable jobs, and acting was certainly not considered to be respectable. Boucicault and his mother, surrounded as they were by the taint of scandal and illegitimacy, were a constant source of embarrassment to the upright Darleys. They wanted nothing to do with them, and in their opinion the least Boucicault could do would

15

be to find a solid, comfortable occupation in which he would cause the family no further distress.

Once more it was Lardner who came to the rescue. He had resigned his chair at University College in 1831 to concentrate on scientific experimentation, mostly connected with railways, and the writing of his cyclopedia. Boucicault was dispatched to London and apprenticed to Lardner as a civil engineer, helping, according to family tradition, to lay the first railway line between London and Harrow (the London and Birmingham line, the first section of which, to Boxmoor, was opened on 7 July 1837). But civil engineering was not for him; he loathed the work almost as much as he loathed Lardner. Persuading his guardian to give him a quarterly allowance, Boucicault turned his back on engineering and London, and at the beginning of 1838 set off to the provinces to make a career for himself as an actor.

2

LEE MORETON, ACTOR AND DRAMATIST

JUST THREE months after his seventeenth birthday, towards the end of March 1838, Boucicault, calling himself Lee Moreton (he didn't want his family to know where he was, nor did he intend using his real name until he was successful), presented himself at the stage door of the Theatre Royal, Cheltenham, and asked for a job. Charles Hill, the manager, was used to stage-struck young men turning up and wanting to act, and gave him the usual polite rejection. But Moreton wasn't to be dismissed so easily. Day after day he waited for Hill outside the theatre, begging him for a part, any part, in which he could show what he could do. Impressed by his persistence, Hill decided to give him a chance.

It was Hill's custom, as a way of thanking local dignitaries who had subscribed to the season or given him help, to put on occasional amateur performances with them in leading roles. On 2 April, Colonel Charritie, a well-known Gloucestershire eccentric, was due to appear as Richard III, and Hill offered Lee Moreton the part of the Duke of Norfolk. His acting did not go unnoticed. 'The little which fell to the lot of the Duke of Norfolk to do was really well done,' commented the reviewer of the Cheltenham *Looker-On*, 'but, notwithstanding, the character was rendered ludicrous by the brogue of the representative.'

Hill, who also had the management of the Theatre Royal, Gloucester, for the season, was clearly impressed not just with his acting but his enthusiasm, for Moreton had not only learnt the part of Norfolk but also that of Richard. Four days later, on 6 April, Moreton appeared as Richard in another amateur performance for Hill in Gloucester. The following night he played the leading role in *Teddy the Tiler*, an Irish character tailor-made for his natural Irish charm and the brogue that had so disconcerted the critic of the *Looker-On*. On 18 and 20 April, he again appeared at the Theatre Royal, Gloucester, as Iago in *Othello*, and then returned to Cheltenham to play Sir Giles Overreach in Massinger's *A New Way to Pay Old Debts* on 24 April.

> For ourselves [wrote the critic of the *Cheltenham Journal*] we are free to confess that we were far from anticipating so excellent a performance as it turned out to be; because of the extreme youth of the gentleman . . . coupled with the information we had received that he never saw the part played by anyone appeared to us to weigh heavily against him . . . It is not our custom to analyse amateur performances for reasons we have given before; but there are peculiarities in this instance which warrant we think a deviation from this rule . . . Mr Lee Moreton convinced us by general correctness of his ideas of the parts, and his originality in some particulars, that he has within him that which would, under judicious guidance, lead him on to the highest rank in the art . . . Mr Moreton terminated his wonderful performance by one of the most striking scenes we ever witnessed: it was in all respects worthy of the elder Kean, and stamped indelibly in our opinion the conviction that he may, if he chooses, contest the honour of succeeding that Prince of Actors with any one the stage in England now possesses.

This was remarkable praise indeed for a young amateur, without training, making his second appearance in Cheltenham and his seventh on a stage anywhere (if we include his performance at school in Brentford). In fact, the review is so fulsome that one wonders how much Boucicault had to bribe the journalist to write it. Clearly, however, even if these reviews were meant to persuade Hill to take him on permanently, Boucicault possessed a considerable talent and was popular with the audiences. Charles Hill, who rarely made money from his theatrical ventures, may have been happy to keep casting in leading roles an amateur whom he didn't have to pay, but there's no doubt the public would not have let him get away with it more than once had they not enjoyed the performances.

Boucicault's appearances continued with the title role in *Rory O'More*, and then, on 8 May, he was persuaded, at the earnest request of J. Peart, Esq., 'to attempt the arduous character of HAMLET'.

> After what we saw in Sir Giles Overreach, we were prepared for something good, [reported the *Journal*], and our expectations have not been disappointed. Mr Moreton's conception and delineation of the noble creation of Hamlet were truly surprising. That a youth of 17 should fully enter into the intellectual depths of such a character, and that he should forcibly and effectively embody his conceptions the first time of performing (for we believe it was the first), must convince every reflecting mind that genius has taken him by the hand.

A week later he returned to Gloucester to play Henry Fitz-herbert in *The Handsome Husband*, and the following night was back in Cheltenham for what was announced as his final appearance of the season, playing Rory O'More. For the *Journal*, he could do no wrong. 'With respect to the high estimation we have felt and expressed of the talents of Mr Moreton, we have had the gratification of hearing our opinion confirmed . . . ,' declared its critic. 'One gentleman in particular, who had the advantage of studying under the great John Kemble . . . has pronounced Mr Moreton to be the most promising youth he ever saw appear upon the stage, whether as a professor or an amateur.' So popular was he with local audiences that he was asked to take the role of Sir Edward Mortimer in *The Iron Chest* for the final night of Hill's management, and so ended Boucicault's first taste of life as an actor. Even allowing for the fact that he may well have bribed the local critics, it was a remarkable début. In a period of two months, before he was seventeen and a half, Boucicault had appeared in two leading provincial theatres, playing eight different roles including three of the most formidable on the English-speaking stage.

In June, Charles Hill left the West Country and moved to Brighton to take over the management of the Theatre Royal. Boucicault went with him. Hill had decided that Lee Moreton possessed enough talent to become a permanent member of his company and had agreed to take him on as his protégé. He lodged with Hill and his family at Rutland House, Marine Parade, and when he made his Brighton début on 30 July, as Sir Giles Overreach, he was billed as Hill's pupil. Judged as a professional and unable to bribe the critics, his performance did not receive the acclaim it had in Cheltenham.

Of Mr Lee Morton [sic] we do not feel willing to say overmuch. He is a very, very young man, and has therefore plenty of time before him if he seriously intends to study for the stage. At present his acting ranks with that of a clever school-boy at a boarding school on breaking-up night.[1]

This gentleman certainly possesses good courage to make such a part his first appearance [declared another critic]. He labours under the disadvantage of a bad stage voice . . . He is a young man of promise, though his first appearance certainly presented us with many of those defects which are almost inseparable from so young an actor. Some of the speeches were spoken with rather over-studied effect, and the gentleman has a constant bad habit of stooping at making points. Time and practice, however, will do much for him.[2]

He was a handsome young man, brimful of confidence, and there must have been much of the precocious conceit of Dion Boucicault already in evidence in Lee Moreton, for he was singled out for a very firm put-down by a third critic.

Mr Moreton, we presume, is labouring under the peculiar and unfortunate malady commonly expressed by the phrase of being 'stage-struck': he is a young man, and this renders the circumstances more excusable. His friends, too, have doubtless persuaded him that he has talent, and the mere suspicion of this has been sufficient to induce many a wiser and older man to 'walk the plank' of public judgement. [His performance] did not fail from a want of that confidence and knowledge of the business of the scene which are the usual stumbling blocks in the way of a young actor. He was perfectly at home and trod the stage with a firmness that betokens a full confidence in his own powers and a long course of study . . . On the whole, it is evident to us that Mr Moreton's friends have very much overrated his powers.[3]

Ten days later, on 9 August, Boucicault made his second Brighton appearance, as the Irishman Tom Moore in *The Irish Lion*. One critic was impressed, particularly by his accent, which he did not seem to know was genuine, but from the others Boucicault drew an angry fusillade of abuse, directed as much towards him personally as to his acting.

We have now a word or two to say respecting a young gentleman whom we did not expect to behold on the stage a second time [sneered the reviewer of the *Brighton Guardian*]. From *Richard* to *Scrub* was a bold step even for Garrick, from *Lear* to *Abel Drugger* was equally bold for the elder Kean, and from Lady Macbeth to Nell in *The Devil To Pay* was great and daring for Mrs Siddons. Mr Lee Moreton, it appears, aspires at the very commencement of his career to rival the venturous achievements of these great actors in their zenith; and after reciting the dialogue of Sir Giles Overreach a week or two ago, has now come forward to repeat the words of Tom Moore in *The Irish Lion* . . . We feel the less compunction in speaking our mind openly of Mr Moreton's appearance, because, to judge from the self-assurance and perfect unembarrassment of his deportment on the stage, we do not feel ourselves wounding by our remarks a very timid or susceptible novice; but to say the least, in hopes that it may be the last, we may observe that whereas many serious passages of his Sir Giles Overreach were comic enough for Tom Moore, many of the comic parts of his Tom Moore were serious enough for Sir Giles.

The *Brighton Patriot* also joined the attack:

> We never saw a gentleman on the stage more uncon- strained. If Mr Lee Moreton were bashful or awkward we should take it as a good augury, and an indication of improvement; but his confidence in himself is complete, and his acting is *finished* acting. What he does now he will always do. It will be his fate to act tragedy without making people weep, and comedy without making them laugh; to seek applause without exciting emotion, and admiration without receiving honour; to act continually without improvement, and to grow old without amendment.

The tone of these attacks is remarkably similar in its animosity to those Boucicault was to receive throughout his career, but in later times he was famous and a legitimate target for the hostility of a press of which he was always contemptu- ous. In Brighton, in 1838, a minor player without a repu- tation, at the start of his career, would hardly have merited such scathing condemnation had there not been something in his personality which marked him out for attention. This hostility had little effect on him other than momentarily to dent his pride. He loved adulation but he cared nothing for the estimation of provincial critics, who would, he knew, still be small-town journalists while he was making his mark on stages around the world.

He was as arrogant and assured off stage as he was on. Although only seventeen, he was already showing signs of the dandy personality he would effect once he had made his name in London, spending his allowance from Lardner and the pittance he received from Hill on expensive clothes, imported fruits, cakes and sweetmeats, smoking the finest Havana cigars and entertaining his friends lavishly.[4] In 1853, an anonymous writer in the American *The Spirit of the Times* recalled Boucicault's Brighton début.

> It was announced that a dramatic comet, in the shape of an amateur, a Mr Lee Morton, was about to appear in the temple dedicated to Thespis . . . Rumor . . . was busy – strange stories of distinguished parentage and mysterious incognito . . . Nor was the general excitement diminished by the appearance on the esplanade of a youthful, downy-moustached, *homme blasé*, his taper fingers protected by lemon-coloured kids, holding white silken reins, which directed the movements of a pair of cream-coloured ponies, harnessed to what was styled in England in those days a 'Park Chair' . . . From that moment Lee Morton was the rage . . . His single-breasted white coat, with its jaunty cape, made the fortune of tailors; while the would-be *distingués* solicited, as an extreme favour, the address of the scientific architect who built his sky-blue trousers, over his then novel patent boots. The eventful day approached for his début as 'Sir Giles Overreach,' – but ere it came, I went.

Allowing for exaggeration, this was a true picture of the impression Boucicault tried to create throughout his career and would explain the hostility he met from the Brighton critics. No wonder they sought to find fault with his acting. Hard though he worked to perfect his dandy image, Boucicault worked even harder in the theatre. Hill had decided to capitalize on his Irish accent and gave him a series of Irish characters to play, including Rory O'More, the role he had done in Cheltenham. Whether his acting improved or he managed in some way to mollify his critics, the reviews became kinder. 'We have now seen this gentleman in several Irish assumptions,' wrote the one man who seemed to be permanently ignorant of Boucicault's birthplace and who still marvelled at his ability to sustain an Irish accent for a whole evening, 'and we feel emboldened in saying it is a line for which he appears to possess many natural qualifications; and should his particular attention be devoted to the study of the same, we doubt not that the result might prove to his advantage.'[5]

In addition to socializing, rehearsing and performing, Boucicault was busy writing and completed at least two plays during his stay in Brighton. Neither *A Lover by Proxy* nor *A Legend of Devil's Dyke* was performed, though the daydreaming playwright filled in the *dramatis personae* of *A Legend* with a cast drawn from the Brighton company and even gave it a fictitious first night – 1 October 1838 – on which he was actually appearing in *Rory O'More*.[6] *A Legend of Devil's Dyke* is a four-act comic melodrama, with a perfunctory plot and many improbable situations. It contains some good moments and some lively dialogue, particularly in the comic sub-plot dealing with the antics of the servants and Teddy Rodent, the Rat-catcher (the part Boucicault gave to himself in his cast list). In a parody of the main plot, Teddy, Bessy (the girl he is in Brighton to marry) and Tim Terrier, a footman, dress up and gatecrash a ball, Teddy masquerading as Bessy's wealthy aunt and managing to hook a fortune-hunting fop. But these moments were not sufficient to have persuaded a manager of Hill's experience to stage the play without considerable rewriting. His response when Boucicault took him these early offerings was encouraging: he could see considerable potential in them, and if Boucicault would rewrite along the lines he suggested, Hill would certainly consider them for production. Boucicault, however, was too impatient for success to contemplate the chore of revision. Deciding, after only five months with Hill, that he was getting nowhere in Brighton, he packed his bags and left. He made his way back to Cheltenham, where a fellow actor from the Brighton company had recently taken over the management of the Theatre Royal, and was engaged to appear in the parts he'd played in Brighton as well as several new ones, including Sir Benjamin Backbite in *The School for Scandal* and Sir Lucius O'Trigger in *The Rivals*. Cheltenham's enthusiasm for the young Lee Moreton had cooled considerably and his performances were not much liked, so at the end of December he moved to neighbouring Bristol for the opening of the Theatre Royal's new season, under the management of Mrs McCready, stepmother of the great tragedian.

Boucicault made his Bristol début on 26 December, the day

before his eighteenth birthday, as Mantilini in an adaptation of Charles Dickens's *Nicholas Nickleby*. It was while he was at Bristol that he had his first play performed professionally. This was *Lodgings To Let*, a one-act farce, which was given as an afterpiece on 18 February 1839, to *Married Life*, a play starring Benjamin Webster, the manager of the Haymarket Theatre in London. Boucicault played Tim Donaghue, the male lead.

It is one of those plotless bagatelles which serve to make us laugh for half an hour, and then wonder for an hour afterwards at what it is we've been laughing [reported the critic of the Bristol *Mercury*]. In a word it is a tolerable vehicle for many bad jokes, some good ones – a few new, still more old; and, above all, for Lover's charming song of 'Rory O'More', arranged for the *first*, and we trust, the *last* time as a duet. The whole weight of the piece rests on the shoulders of Mr Lee Moreton and Miss Le Batt, who, to do them justice, worked hard, and were as frolicsome and amusing as the wildest Tipperarians ever imported into this country.

Officially the author of this afterpiece, written expressly for the Bristol Theatre, was anonymous, but Boucicault had tipped off enough friends in the gallery for the name Lee Moreton to be shouted enthusiastically at the end. He came forward, admitted that the play was his and announced it for repetition the following night to great applause. 'It is,' admitted the *Mercury*, 'a trifle not without merit, but we venture to prophesy that both the pruning knife and polishing brush must be liberally applied to it before it will become a popular farce, as, notwithstanding the noise of the *clacqueurs* in the gallery, we saw a disposition to somnolency pretty evidently manifest itself in the pit and boxes.'

The play was given two further performances during February, and for the first time Boucicault tasted the sort of success he really wanted. Whether it was his idea, or that of Webster hoping the piece might repeat its success in London, Boucicault decided the time had come to try his luck in the

THIRD NIGHT OF MR.

WEBSTER'S

ENGAGEMENT.

First Night of a highly interesting Drama, produced with the most unqualified success, entitled

The Maid of Croissey.

On Wednesday Evening, February 20th,

Will be presented the Drama of

The Maid

OF CROISSEY,

Or, Theresa's Vow.

Serj. Austerlitz	- - - - - -	Mr. WEBSTER
Francis ....Mr. W. CHAPLIN	Walter ....Mr. SUTER
Villagers—Messrs. DOUGHTY, JAMES, WILLIAMS, &c.
Theresa ....Mrs. C. POPE	Maria ....Miss LE BATT

A Favourite PAS SEUL,

By Miss G. LE BATT.

To be followed by the

LOTTERY TICKET.

Wormwood - - - - - **Mr. WEBSTER**

Capias............Mr. MULFORD | Charles............Mr. ARTAUD
Mrs. Corset............Mrs. JEPHSON | Susan............Miss LE BATT

To conclude with the Original Farce, so enthusiastically received on its First Representation, written by
MR. LEE MORETON, entitled

LODGINGS TO LET.

Old Higgins, a retired Cheesemonger, Emigrant from the Seven Dials, ...Mr. MACNAMARA
Mons. Millefleurs, a French Emigrant........Mr. SILVER
Cassio Forrest, Nephew to Old Higgins, just returned from the Continent............Mr. H. E. STEVENS
Tim Donoghue, an Irish Emigrant, and a Genius of the first rate....Mr. LEE MORETON
Bill Quickset, an Old Bailey Emigrant, and unrivalled Pick-Pocket......................Mr. WILSON
Mr. Spooner, a Gentleman from the Country............Mr. CLARKE

Mr. Dummy		Mr. LODGE
Master Augustus Dummy	} A Family in want of Lodgings	Master SOMERTON
Master Scipio Dummy		Master JAMES
Master Napoleon Dummy..........		Master WILLIAMS

Policemen......................... Messrs. HOWARD & DOUGHTY
Mrs. Higgins, an Aristocrat and Emigrant from the Seven Dials,......................Mrs. JEPHSON
Katty, a Tipperary true Connaught Breed, from Green Erin....Miss LE BATT
Mrs. Dummy............Mrs. LODGE | Miss Anastatia Dummy............Miss G. LE BATT
Miss Zenobia Dummy......Miss EARNSHAW | Miss Boadicea Dummy........Miss SOMERTON

On Thursday the Popular Comedy of a LESSON FOR LADIES ; Gibolette, Mr. WEBSTER.
To conclude with a New Piece, in which Mr. WEBSTER will perform.

Somerton, Printer, Mercury-Office, Broad-Street, Bristol.

The second performance of the one-act farce, Lodgings To Let,
20 February 1839. It was the eighteen-year-old Boucicault's first
play to be performed professionally. He also starred (under his
pseudonym, Lee Moreton).

capital. He threw in his hand with Mrs McCready and left Bristol on 2 March. A week later, on 9 March, *Lodgings To Let*, with Boucicault repeating his performance as Tim Donaghue, opened at the Haymarket. It came to nothing. The more sophisticated theatregoers of London did not take to his schoolboy pranks and the play lasted just one night.

Although *Lodgings To Let* was given three further performances at the Strand Theatre in May, Boucicault had failed to make any impact as a writer and he was forced to find work as an actor in order to live. He managed to land a few engagements in minor London theatres, mostly playing Irish characters, but the parts were none in which he could really shine or make a name for himself, so when Mr Hooper, who was assembling a company of London artists for a season at the Theatre Royal, Hull, offered him a contract, he was only too pleased to accept.

The Hull engagement followed the pattern of a typical provincial season, with Boucicault playing a different part every night. Billed as 'Mr Lee Moreton, from the Theatre Royal St James's' (where he had appeared for one night in May), Boucicault opened in Hull on 2 December, playing his familiar role of Tom Moore in *The Irish Lion*. The following night he appeared as Trip in *The School for Scandal*, and the night after as Osric in *Hamlet*. With him in *The School for Scandal* on 3 December, making his first appearance on any stage, was his brother George, who also changed his name to Moreton to continue the deception. When Boucicault first contacted his family to let them know what he was doing is not known. It may have been to witness his night of glory at the Haymarket, when *Lodgings To Let* had its one and only disastrous performance, though he was in constant touch with Lardner, who was continuing to pay him a quarterly allowance. He was delighted to see his brother again after a gap of nearly four years, and they spent every available moment in each other's company, drinking, chasing women and gossiping. One afternoon they were in a coffee house and became so engrossed in conversation that neither realized the time. They were both due to appear that evening in *The School for Scandal*, but missed the curtain up and two other actors had to go on in their places.[7] George didn't stay with the company for long. He wasn't cut out to be an actor, and at the beginning of 1840 he and his twin, Arthur, sailed to Australia, where they became journalists and eventually newspaper proprietors, George founding the Melbourne *Daily News* and Arthur the Rockhampton *Northern Argus*.

On 26 December 1839, the day before his nineteenth birthday, the Hull Christmas production opened. This was *Jack Sheppard*, Boucicault's first full-length play to be performed, adapted from Harrison Ainsworth's novel. Boucicault played Jack. The house was packed and the play was well received, although its morality and Boucicault's use of 'the lowest slang' disturbed some members of the audience. Despite the play's popularity, Hooper, the manager, was anxious not to offend his regular patrons and decided to shorten it from four acts to three, and to offer it as an afterpiece. Boucicault was outraged. He, in company with many of his fellow actors, was already highly critical of the way Hooper was managing the theatre and was unhappy with the parts he was being allocated. Hooper's high-handed action in tampering with Boucicault's undoubted success, even though he was within his rights as manager, brought Boucicault's grievances to a head. Following a blazing row, Hooper cancelled the benefit night he had promised Boucicault for 4 February 1840, tickets for which were already on sale. Boucicault retaliated by plastering Hull with posters explaining his side of the story and offering to refund money personally. On the night on which the benefit should have taken place, Boucicault crept unnoticed into a box and proceeded to harangue the audience before the performance could begin. Hooper appeared, furious, and had him thrown out. But the interruptions to the evening were not over. Shortly after the curtain had gone up, another actor, named John Herbert, who sided with Boucicault and had himself crossed swords with Hooper, appeared very drunk in the upper boxes. Hooper sent for the police to remove him, but Herbert wouldn't go and created such a commotion that Hooper finally had to turn out the gas lighting in the auditorium and ask the audience to leave.

It was the end of Boucicault's engagement in Hull, and the

following day he left town. He was probably pleased to be on his way for, apart from his disagreements with Hooper, he was beginning to find the daily routine of an actor's life irksome and was already contemplating entering management on his own.[8] There was, however, one major obstacle to his ambition – he was flat broke. He had missed out on his benefit (which would probably have brought him in about £50, enough to live on for four months), and had no job and, even more disconcerting, the quarterly allowance from Lardner, on which he relied to pay for his increasingly expensive tastes, suddenly stopped, for at the beginning of March his guardian carried out his elopement to Paris with Mary Heaviside, the wife of the colleague who was a director of the London and Brighton Railway. Heaviside, six feet six inches tall and athletic, followed them to Paris and traced them to an apartment in the rue Tronchet where he confronted the terrified doctor. Although the tiny Lardner sought refuge beneath the piano, Heaviside managed to snatch off Lardner's wig and throw it on the fire, and then proceeded to thrash those portions of his wife's lover that remained in view. He did not, however, succeed in regaining his wife, and it was in August that he was awarded £8,000 damages at Lewes Assizes for alienation of affections. Even if Lardner had wished to, he could no longer afford to subsidize Boucicault and he clearly considered his obligation to the boy had already been paid in full.

Where Boucicault went to from Hull is uncertain, but without money his plans to put on his own productions came to nothing. It seems most likely that he went back to Dublin to stay with his mother. There were records, now unfortunately missing, of him working as a clerk at the Guinness brewery at some time during 1840,[9] a position probably obtained for him by his mother's cousin, Arthur Lee Guinness. Arthur was a prominent member of the brewing family and although he was far from pleased to be closely associated with Boucicault and his mother, of whom most of the family had washed their hands, he was persuaded by Mrs Boursiquot to take an interest in her son. Many years later Boucicault claimed that Arthur Guinness had paid for him to complete his studies in London and had made him his heir.[10] This was almost

MISS KELLY'S
THEATRE,
DRAMATIC SCHOOL,
73, DEAN STREET, SOHO SQUARE,
Licensed by the Lord Chamberlain and under the Patronage of
HIS GRACE THE
DUKE OF DEVONSHIRE,
WILL BE OPEN TO THE PUBLIC
On MONDAY, May 25th, and during the Week.

THE PERFORMANCES WILL COMMENCE WITH

AN APPROPRIATE ADDRESS,
To be spoken by Miss KELLY.

After which will be presented a new Farce in One Act, to be called,

SUMMER AND WINTER

Mons. Girard,	(a French Emigrant,)	Mr. MORRIS BARNETT,
Henry Graham,	(his Protegé,)	Mr. PITT,
Nicholas O'Nib,	(a School Master,)	Mr. LEE MORTON,
Emily Somers,		Miss COOPER.
Patty,		Mrs. FRANKS.

After which, (First Time these Five Years, by Permission of S. J. ARNOLD, Esq.) BANIM'S popular Drama, called The

SERGEANT'S
WIFE.

Frederick Cartouch,		Mr. FRANKS,
Old Cartouch,		Mr. G. BENNETT.
Sergeant Lewis, Mr. YARNOLD,	Sergeant George, Mr. GRAHAM,	Denis, Mr. GRANT,
Gaspard,	Mr DE RANCE,	Robin, Mr. COLLIER,
Luelle,	(the Sergeant's Wife,)	Miss KELLY,
	(HER ORIGINAL CHARACTER.)	
Margot,		Mrs. FRANKS.

Soldiers, Villagers, &c.

The whole to conclude with the admired Drama of The

MIDNIGHT HOUR!

The General,	Mr. W BENNETT,	The Marquis, Mr. T. PARRY,
	Nicholas, Mr. COMPTON,	
Sebastian,	Mr YARNOLD,	Ambrose, Mr. RAY, Mathias, Mr SALTER,
Julia,	Mrs. GURNER,	Cecil, Mrs. STANLEY,
	Flora, Miss KELLY.	

Stage-Manager, **Mr. G. BENNETT.**
Leader of the Band, **Mr. HEALY.**

Under whose Direction will be performed a Variety of WELL SELECTED MUSIC at the Commencement and Between the Acts of the Entertainments.

The Doors to be Opened at Half-past Seven, Performances to commence at Eight o'clock precisely.

Tickets to the FIRST TIER of BOXES and STALLS, Seven Shillings each.
To the PUBLIC SEATS and FAMILY BOXES, Five Shillings each.

Private Boxes to be had Nightly at Mr MITCHELL, Royal Library, Old Bond Street, and at the Office of the Theatre, 73, Dean Street, Soho Square.

VIVAT REGINA!

The first show by students of Miss Fanny Kelly, 25 May 1840.
Boucicault, his pseudonym mis-spelt, appeared in *Summer and Winter*. In later life Fanny Kelly was immensely proud of her
protégé and often recalled his days as her pupil.

certainly a fanciful exaggeration, but there must have been some truth in it for the job in the brewery didn't last long and by mid-May Boucicault was back in London, enrolling as a student at the dramatic academy in Dean Street just started by Fanny Kelly, a famous, retired actress. On 25 May he appeared in the academy's opening production of a one-act farce called *Summer and Winter*. For a young man who had appeared, albeit briefly, in the West End in his own play, he must have been very piqued by the review he got from *The Times*.

It was to be wished that a better piece had been selected for the opening than a trifle called *Summer and Winter* which is exceedingly weak and tedious . . . The lover, and an Irish character intended to be comic, were played by two young men, who, from their novice-like mannerisms, appear to be pupils of the establishment.

That Arthur Guinness was paying for Boucicault's tuition does seem likely (though he may not have known exactly what he was paying for), for a young man of Boucicault's temperament would hardly have had the humility to return to school without some very strong financial inducement, and he had also acquired the money to indulge in high living. He booked himself into Long's Hotel in Newman Street, bought a horse and cab, and entertained his friends with frequent and lavish suppers. As soon as Arthur Guinness got to hear how his generosity was being abused, he stopped the allowance and, according to Boucicault, cut him off from the promised fortune.

For the second time that year Boucicault was penniless, without a job and with no real prospects. Pride would not allow him to run back to his mother in Dublin a second time. He was no longer interested in a career as an actor; what he wanted to be was a writer, a playwright. This time, he knew, he had to stay and prove himself. Pawning his watch and selling all but his most treasured possessions – a handful of books – he moved from one cheap lodging house to another, writing feverishly but unable to sell anything. His twin

31

brothers had left England earlier in the year for a new life in Australia and, as he sat in his drab rooms, without money for heating and barely enough for food, Boucicault began to wonder seriously if he shouldn't join them.[11] Three separate days' work as an actor at the Queen's Theatre in September decided him to stay, though the irony of the title of one of the plays in which he appeared, *Very Hard Up*, cannot have escaped him. As the winter of 1840 drew closer, he moved lodgings yet again to the fourth-floor attic, costing 4s. a week, of a house in Villiers Street. Living in the same digs was a fellow Dubliner, the actor John Brougham.

Brougham, six years Boucicault's senior, was a member of the prestigious Covent Garden company under the management of the husband-and-wife team, Charles Mathews and Madame Vestris. He and Boucicault spent hours together, reminiscing about Dublin, talking theatre and writing plays, and it was probably Brougham who first suggested that Boucicault should try his work with Mathews. Boucicault had three or four full-length plays finished, but he knew that the chances of persuading Mathews to read one, let alone put one on, were so remote that he decided to submit first a short piece. Quite which play it was, isn't certain. Boucicault always claimed it was *A Lover by Proxy*, the play Hill had rejected in Brighton, but John Webster, with whom Boucicault shared lodgings at the beginning of 1841, claimed at the time that it was a play called *Woman*.[12] Whichever it was, Boucicault took it to Covent Garden and left it at the stage door. Day after day he returned to see if there had been any reaction to it, but there never was, until one afternoon the stage-door keeper, glancing at his card, told him he was an hour late for his appointment. The man had misread the card and thought Boucicault was Maddison Morton, the writer of popular farces. The mistake was enough to get Boucicault into the theatre and up to Mathews's room, where the manager was sitting in front of the fire, his back to the door, reading a manuscript. He motioned Boucicault to sit down while he finished the page, and when he finally looked up was astonished to see, not Maddison Morton, but Lee Moreton. Boucicault was quick to explain the mix-up at the stage door and told Mathews he had been calling at the theatre regularly to find out about his play. Mathews had not even read it, but told him he would have the manuscript found and returned to him. What, he wanted to know, was the title? When Boucicault told him, Mathews couldn't believe it: it was the play he had been reading. He checked the cover and sure enough, instead of the M. Morton he expected to see, it read 'by L. Moreton, Esq.'. Mathews had been sufficiently impressed by the piece, and intrigued, to question Boucicault about himself, but finally the rejection came. 'I wish I could help you,' he said, 'but we are glutted with farces. What we want nowadays is a good five-act comedy of modern life. Now, if I could find such a part as you have sketched here in this farce, expanded in a modern comedy, there would be room for such a work.'[13]

Boucicault returned to Villiers Street. If Mathews wanted a five-act comedy, that is what he would get. He talked over ideas with John Brougham and set to work, writing day and night, completing the manuscript at 5.30 one morning. Thirty days after his first interview with Mathews he was back in the theatre with his new play. Mathews, bemused by the speed with which he had worked, promised to read it and give him a decision the following week. The next Monday the stage manager, George Bartley, summoned Boucicault to Covent Garden. His play had been read and liked; Mathews intended to put it on. Bartley, however, did not share Mathews's enthusiasm for the piece; it would require a great many alterations and Boucicault must be prepared to suffer many blows to his pride. A play on at Covent Garden! Boucicault was prepared to suffer anything.

Boucicault was fortunate in his timing. Covent Garden's new productions that season had been few and undistinguished, the Christmas pantomime had been a comparative failure, and Mathews and Vestris were on the look-out for something new. He was also fortunate in his choice of theatre, for Covent Garden possessed one of the very few managements that would, or could, give his play a sensitive production. The Theatre was, at that time, in a state of transition. There were still the 'major' and the 'minor' houses (Drury

Lane and Covent Garden did not lose their patents and the sole privilege of producing legitimate drama until 1843), and the vast majority of theatregoers preferred the minor houses. Audiences in the mid nineteenth century were largely middle or lower-class, and they demanded entertainment on the broadest lines: broad comedies, farces, melodramas and extravaganzas with spectacular effects, the bigger the better. Large barns of theatres were built to accommodate the huge numbers which flocked to see these shows, and actors broadened their styles to reach out to the distant galleries. An evening's entertainment, lasting anything up to six hours, would include a curtain-raiser, a main play, an afterpiece and possibly musical interludes. It was not a world in which subtle acting or sophisticated dramatic writing could flourish. Without the considerable encouragement of Mathews and Vestris, it is doubtful whether Boucicault's play would have got off the ground.

The first reading took place in the Covent Garden Green Room on 5 February 1841, and at the finish the assembled company, there to hear the play and be given their parts, broke into spontaneous applause. Madame Vestris warmly embraced the young writer. But, as Bartley had warned, his real work was only just about to begin. No one liked his first title, *Country Matters*, nor his second suggestion, *Out of Town*. It was Madame Vestris who finally christened the play *London Assurance*.[14]

It was not just the title which proved troublesome. The play was rewritten radically during rehearsal, scene after scene being handed to the actors with the ink still wet. It was cut, pruned, shaped and altered by Boucicault and the cast until each part fitted its interpreter like a glove, with much of the credit for the additions going to Mathews, who had given himself the role of Dazzle. 'It will not bear analysis as a literary production,' declared Boucicault in the preface to the published edition. 'In fact, my sole object was to throw together a few scenes of a dramatic nature; and therefore I studied the stage rather than the moral effect.'

The play is a hotch-potch of ideas borrowed from Restoration comedy, with strong echoes of Sheridan, Vanbrugh,

34

Congreve and Goldsmith, Boucicault's great idol. But for the fact that it was billed as a 'modern comedy', the setting could as easily have been the middle of the eighteenth century as in the nineteenth. The plot turns on a father failing to recognize his son, a dramatic device which must have seemed faintly absurd in modern dress, but Boucicault's keen ear for dialogue, his sharp eye for characterization, his warmth and sense of fun, make the incongruities unimportant. He was profoundly grateful to the cast for the help they gave him in making London Assurance a hit, but they, in their turn, had cause to be grateful to him for providing a vehicle in which they could all shine (with the possible exception of James Anderson, whose loud voice and stagey manner were ill-suited to the part of Young Courtly). Their playing, coupled with Madame Vestris's production, on which no expense was spared (the scenery alone was reputed to have cost £600),[15] contributed vitally to the play's success. Although it was not the first occasion on which box-sets had been used, it was the most important and it set a new standard in stage production. The use of real carpets, chandeliers, ottomans, windows and mirrors, drew gasps of astonishment and rounds of applause, and established a style that was to predate the realistic dramas of Tom Robertson by some twenty years.

While rehearsals for London Assurance were in progress, public interest in the play was whipped up by a quarrel between Mathews and William Macready, the senior tragedian of the London stage. Boucicault happened to mention to Mathews that Macready had turned down his play Woman because he had refused to take the main speech from the female lead and give it to the character Macready would have played. If Mathews, who loathed Macready, did not actively encourage the story, he certainly did nothing to stop it spreading, particularly since it implied that he, Mathews the comedian, was a greater encourager of new talent than Macready the tragedian. When the story reached Macready, as Mathews knew it would, the pompous actor exploded. He denied it completely, claiming he had never seen or heard of the play, and was so annoyed that he went to the trouble of seeking out Boucicault, offering a £5 reward to the man who would bring the young author to him. Learning that Boucicault was living in Leicester Square (where he was calling himself Belvedere Dion Boucicault), Macready couldn't wait, but jumped into a cab and hurried round to confront the perpetrator of the scurrilous slander. Somewhat lamely, Boucicault explained that he had given his manuscript to a friend, Roynon Jones, who had passed it on to Macready and returned with the account of Macready's reaction he had told Mathews. He denied telling Mathews anything other than the bare outline of the story; he had certainly not said that he had refused to rewrite. Macready barely accepted his account or apology, and forced him to sign a letter to Mathews retracting the allegations.[16] Two days later, Boucicault appeared at Macready's front door and asked to see him. 'For what I could scarcely understand,' wrote Macready in his diary, 'except to seek for pity somewhere; the whole Covent Garden tribe turn like curs upon him and yelp and bark in one cry, one note against him . . . I dealt kindly with him, and gave him some salutary advice.'

Boucicault's attempts to keep on the right side of Macready, who was then negotiating for the lease of Drury Lane (and who knows when Boucicault might need an entrée there?) didn't come off. Two weeks after the opening of *London Assurance*, Bulwer Lytton invited Macready to dinner to meet the new young playwright everyone was talking about, but the actor huffily declined. Nor did the incident endear Boucicault to Mathews, who had been made to look foolish in public. From that moment on, he and his wife viewed their young author with the deepest suspicion and mistrust – 'that young liar'[17] was how Madame Vestris frequently referred to him.

Green Room gossip convinced them they were right to be wary – and also added further interest in the production – by claiming that the play was not really Boucicault's at all, but had been written by John Brougham, who had conceived the role of Dazzle for himself. The two men had certainly discussed the play while it was being written, and Brougham had made suggestions, but the piece that was handed to Mathews and was then rewritten in rehearsal was undoubtedly the work of Boucicault not Brougham, as a close examination of the subsequent output of both clearly demonstrates. If anyone else had a right to claim a part in the authorship, it was Mathews, who was responsible for many of the alterations. The people who pushed forward Brougham's claim were those of his friends who had a vested interest in doing down Boucicault. Madame Vestris thought she had scotched the rumour at the time by making Boucicault pay part of his fee to Brougham for the help he had given, but she hadn't. It continued for many years afterwards, and nearly twenty years later Boucicault and Brougham met in the offices of solicitor George Lewis to sign a document stating exactly what contribution each had made to the play. This was supposed to put an end to the controversy, but unfortunately the papers were lost without their contents ever being divulged. Boucicault, as might be expected, always claimed to be the sole author, a fact that Brougham himself eventually confirmed. Shortly before his death in 1880, Brougham was asked for the truth about the play's genesis. 'The simple fact,' he replied, 'is that while living in London, Boucicault conceived the idea of the play and, just as you may fancy two friends would do in concert, he developed the plot and developed the dialogue, now and then availing himself of my suggestions. That's all there is about it, and it's the history of every play.'[18]

By the time the play opened on 4 March 1841, there were enough people who had taken a violent dislike to Boucicault for them to be prepared to believe anything bad about him. According to one malicious rumour, spread by James Anderson (who was the only member of the cast to receive a bad notice), both Brougham and Boucicault were waiting backstage to be brought on at the end, a dilemma that was solved by Madame Vestris banishing Brougham from the theatre. Another version of the story claimed that there was such an unholy row between Boucicault and Brougham that no author at all appeared. This was patently untrue, for every newspaper reported that Lee Moreton had acknowledged the cheers of the audience.

Convinced as he was of his own abilities, Boucicault was nevertheless overwhelmed by the play's success and his recep-

THEATRE 🛡 ROYAL
COVENT 🛡 GARDEN

UNDER THE MANAGEMENT OF

Madame VESTRIS.

The FREE LIST (the Public Press excepted) will will be suspended This Evening.

This Evening, THURSDAY, March 4th, 1841,

WILL BE PRODUCED, FOR THE FIRST TIME,

A NEW COMEDY

IN FIVE ACTS,

ENTITLED

LONDON ASSURANCE

The Scenery by Mr. GRIEVE, Mr. T. GRIEVE, and Mr. W. GRIEVE
The Decorations and Appointments by Mr. W. BRADWELL.

Sir Harcourt Courtly, Bart.   -   -   Mr. W. FARREN,

Max Harkaway, Esq.   Mr. BARTLEY,

Mr. Charles Courtly,   -   -   -   -   Mr. ANDERSON,

Mr. Adolphus Spanker,   Mr. KEELEY,

Mr. Dazzle,   -   -   -   -   Mr. CHARLES MATHEWS,

Mark Meddle,   -   -   Mr. HARLEY,

Cool, Mr. BRINDAL,   Isaacs, Mr. W. H. PAYNE,

Martin, Mr. AYLIFFE,   Simpson, Mr. HONNER,

James, Mr. COLLETT,   Servants, Messrs. IRELAND & GARDINER,

Grace Harkaway,   .. Madame VESTRIS,

Lady Gay Spanker,   -   -   -   -   -   Mrs. NISBETT,

Pert, Mrs. HUMBY,

The first night of *London Assurance*, 4 March 1841. It was followed by the Christmas Pantomime, *The Castle of Otranto*. Reported as being by Lee Moreton, it was not until 27 March that the bills announced 'by D. L. Bourçicault Esq'.

tion when he stepped out in front of the footlights. He stood mesmerized by the applause. When the curtain fell for the final time, he was led, still in a trance, to the Green Room, where he stammered his thanks to the cast and was showered with compliments. It didn't take long for him to recover his wits. Mathews had taken him over to where Madame Vestris and Louisa Nisbett were sitting. 'There,' he said, 'does not their presence inspire you to speak? What do you say to your heroines?' Boucicault looked from one to the other. 'Kiss me,' he said. And they did.[19]

3

ADAPTING TO
SUCCESS

'London Assurance was made to order, on the shortest possible notice,' wrote Boucicault in the preface to the
printed play, published three weeks after the first night. 'I
could have wished that my first appearance before the public
had not been in this out-of-breath style; but I saw my opportunity at hand – I knew how important it was not to neglect
the chance of production; the door was open – I had to run for
it – and here I am.'

And there he was, the most talked about, most sought after
young writer in London. Negotiations began immediately for
the publication of the play, and managers begged to be allowed
to read anything else he had written, talking as if the pieces
were already in production. He was elected to the Dramatic
Authors' Society, a rare honour for a man of twenty, and was,
he wrote to his mother, 'looked upon as the great rising dramatic poet of the age. Lord Normanby and Mr Fitzroy Stanhope
were introduced to me on the first performance and said those
very words'.[1] He was invited to smart literary dinners where
his lilting brogue, easy manner and ready wit made him a
popular catch, and he may, as he later claimed, have been
invited to Gore House to attend the fashionable soirées held by
Lady Blessington and Count D'Orsay.[2]

For the first time since he had set out for Cheltenham three years earlier, he felt no need to hide behind the pseudonym Lee Moreton, a name, he was later to say (conveniently forgetting his time in Brighton, Hull and London), he had once used for amateur theatricals. He was proud to acknowledge that he was Dionysius Lardner Boucicault.[3] The week after the opening of *London Assurance*, he wrote excitedly to his mother in Dublin.[4]

I dare say, before this has reached you, you will have heard of the triumph I have achieved. On Thursday last March 4, a comedy in 5 Acts written by me was played at Covent Garden Theatre, and has made an unparalleled hit, indeed so much so that it is played *every night* to crammed houses and it is expected to run the whole season . . . I have now 5 pieces in Covent Garden, all accepted . . . Believe me, I am not exaggerating. If you doubt me, look in any of last Sunday's papers . . . The Queen went to see it on Saturday night (third time of playing it) and after praising it in the highest terms as the best production that had seen the stage for the last 50 years, her Majesty sent me a most gracious message by Lord Alfred Paget expressing her pleasure at seeing so young and promising an author, and hoping so early a success would not destroy my emulation and understanding.

In her journal for Saturday, 6 March, Queen Victoria simply noted that she went 'to Covent Garden where Mr Lee Morton's 5 Act Comedy called *London Assurance* was given. There were some good bits in it, but if it were not for the excellent actors, I hardly think it would do well.'

Boucicault may be forgiven for his exuberant exaggeration, for the success of the play was indeed astonishing and not even a few adverse reviews could dampen his high spirits. George Henry Lewes, writing in the *Athenaeum*, damned the play but noted that the author 'is young enough to do much better things'; Thackeray did not think much of it either, and later wrote a scathing parody;[5] and when the play was produced in New York that October, Edgar Allan Poe was not impressed, referring to it as 'that despicable mass of inanity'.

More important, however, than the fame and the attention, in which he revelled, was the fact that the success of *London Assurance* gave Boucicault an introduction on an equal footing to the group of men he most wanted to know and be associated with – men like Albert Smith, Robert Bell, editor of the *Atlas,* Tom Taylor, Gilbert à Beckett, Douglas Jerrold, Thackeray, Tom Hood, Richard Doyle and Mark Lemon, editor of *Punch.* Most of them are now forgotten, but at the time they constituted an influential, semi-bohemian circle of writers who used to meet regularly in Mark Lemon's public house behind the Olympic Theatre, or in the Percy Street rooms of Albert Smith, to spend their days and nights discussing literature, the theatre and the world. Boucicault was the only member of the group without a private income or a permanent job. Albert Smith was a dentist, Jerrold and Charles Lamb Kenney (Boucicault's school-friend who was also part of the circle) were journalists, and Mark Lemon, before his job with *Punch*, ran the pub. In the spring of 1841, Boucicault, talented, acclaimed and ambitious, had no wish to be tied to the drudgery of an office. Not that he was ever afraid of hard work; he worked longer hours on his writing than most men did in permanent employment, but he wanted the freedom to do as he wished. The success of *London Assurance* was not only personally gratifying, it showed him where he could find that freedom. The play had been written in thirty days and produced an income of £300. At a rate of £10 a day, there was no other work he could find to match it.

The £300 didn't last long, however. On the insistence of Madame Vestris, he had had to pay part of the money to John Brougham for Brougham's help with the play, and he had immediately embarked on a round of heavy spending. He moved from his lodgings in Leicester Square to a fashionable address in Pembroke Square, Kensington, purchased expensive clothes to keep up his image as the young man about town, bought two horses and a carriage, sent £15 to his mother so that she and his elder brother William could join him in London, and entertained his new-found friends, and the women who suddenly found the successful young author irresistible, to lavish dinners. Very soon he was broke. Not that he was unduly worried. His name, particularly if he told tradesmen he was the heir of Arthur Lee Guinness or in receipt of a generous allowance from Dr Lardner, was always good for credit; and he was confident that his other plays, written before *London Assurance*, for which he had received offers, would soon be put into production. He also had other schemes for making money. He sold poems to *Bentley's Miscellany* and the *Musical Examiner*; became for a time the unsuccessful editor of the music magazine *Maestro*; and wrote to the editors of the leading journals offering his services as a contributor. When they declined to use him, except for the occasional article, he decided to bring out his own magazine, a feminist tract entitled *West End*, on which he, as editor, would be the only male involved. Subscriptions to it would cost two guineas a year, and it would contain the best writing by leading women writers of Britain, France and the United States. He approached potential contributors, who agreed to provide him with articles and stories, set up a distribution deal in the States and was all set to go, but the magazine was never published. Another project, a three-volume novel called *The Adventures of Hugh Darley*, was also abandoned.

By the end of 1841, Boucicault was in serious financial trouble. In spite of all the promises, not one of his other plays had been produced, and his journalistic efforts had failed to produce any significant income. He owed money everywhere and was forced to resort to money-lenders to keep his creditors at bay. In September, Charles Gould had taken him to court over a debt of £12 13s. 6d. In February 1842, another creditor, John Hart, a Regent Street tailor to whom Boucicault owed nearly £300, also decided to sue. According to Hart, Boucicault had first obtained credit from him, and clothes on approval, two years earlier by telling him he was in receipt of £60 a month from Dr Lardner and hinting very strongly that he was the heir to a fortune. The clothes, complained Hart, had never been returned, and when Boucicault's bills of exchange had become due for payment, he had refused to honour them. As soon as *London Assurance* became a smash hit, Hart had again tried to get his money, but the glib-talking

Boucicault had not only avoided paying up, he actually managed to persuade Hart to increase his credit. When it became obvious that Boucicault had no intention of ever paying, Hart went to court and judgement was given in his favour. Boucicault, who didn't even bother to attend the hearing, immediately entered his plea of *coram nobis*, claiming that he was under age and not liable for his debts. He also had another line of defence which he expressed in a letter to the *Era*.

> This bill [he wrote] was paid with other accounts, but from ignorance of the dangerous nature of the document, I neglected to get it out of his hands . . . I must, however, confess that rather than have called my name in question at all, I would have paid the thing off, and so suffered for my negligence; but my family took the affair out of my hands, and entered a plea of minority as the only available defence against an unjust claim. Finally, allow me to add, that I never disputed a debt in my life, independently of which my public character is too dear to me to permit myself to be publicly arraigned of an act so atrocious as this would be.

The jury didn't believe him either, but with the evidence of his mother that he was indeed under age, they had no alternative but to return a verdict in his favour.

That same month Boucicault's first play to be written since *London Assurance* opened at Covent Garden. *The Irish Heiress* was eagerly awaited by both press and public, not least by those people from whom Boucicault had obtained money on the strength of it. The play was announced for the beginning of February and then withdrawn, ostensibly for Boucicault to make some alterations but in reality to sort out exactly who owned the rights. Charles Mathews, who had already cast the play, rehearsed it and completed the sets, found he had to pay considerably more than he had anticipated for it to open, only a week late, on Monday, 7 February. The play was again based on the Restoration comedy formula, but this time it didn't work. 'This theatre,' wrote one critic, 'eminent for its failures in these managerial days, added another to its already cumbrous list, and in the person of an author from whom we had looked for better things.'[6] Although most critics acknowledged that the play contained some smart and clever dialogue, they all agreed that it did not come up to the standard of *London Assurance*. 'Mr Bourcicault's new comedy . . . ,' wrote the critic of the *Theatre Journal*, 'has not equalled our expectations . . . it falls off in point, in humour, in tact, and in interest.' The first night was a disaster in which the cast did little to try to save the play. Farren forgot his lines and had to have them read to him by the prompter; Madame Vestris played an Irishwoman without an accent; and Mathews merely went through his well-known comedian's routine. Boucicault was furious. He straightaway withdrew the play and tried to repair the damage by rewriting, but even though it reappeared on the bills a few days later, it still failed to excite any enthusiasm, and after three further performances was taken off, to the delight of those who thought Boucicault conceited and in need of a put-down.

Boucicault's youth (he was still only twenty-one), his disrespect towards his elders when he disagreed with their views, his intolerance of others' shortcomings and high opinion of himself, had clearly aroused considerable animosity among both his colleagues in the theatre and the dramatic critics of the press. Blaming Mathews entirely for the failure of *The Irish Heiress*, he decided to wash his hands of Covent Garden and went to the Haymarket, where Benjamin Webster, the man who had put on his play *Lodgings To Let*, was manager. Webster had been running the Haymarket since 1837, a tenure that had been moderately successful though undistinguished. At forty-five, he was one of the most senior and respected of London managers as well as being an extremely competent character actor. Boucicault was delighted to renew their acquaintance, for Webster, unlike Mathews, who waited until after a first night before handing over money, gave him an immediate advance on his rewritten version of the one-act *A Lover by Proxy*, the play he claimed he had first offered to Mathews in 1840. Knowing that many influential people on the press were gunning for him, Boucicault asked Webster to keep his name off the bills when the play was produced on 21 April. The ploy worked. Although it was common knowledge that the piece was by Boucicault, the critics decided not to go for the man but to review the work. And they liked what they saw. The play was well written, humorous and of a far higher standard than most supporting pieces, and Webster, who starred in it, was highly praised for his portrayal of Harry Lawless.

If Boucicault needed to have his confidence restored after the débâcle of *The Irish Heiress*, *A Lover by Proxy* did just that. Its warm reception from the press, and popularity with the public, reassured him that he was not simply a one-play author and that he could turn out solid, effective work as good as, if not better than, most of the plays then being performed. Two days before the opening of *A Lover by Proxy*, he had gone with Sheridan Knowles, the distinguished dramatist with whom he had struck up a friendship, to a special dress rehearsal at Drury Lane, given for members of the profession, of *Plighted Troth*, the five-act verse drama of his uncle, Charles Darley. Leading figures of the literary establishment had been singing the play's praises in the fashionable clubs for some time and extracts had been published in the papers. Against the run of informed opinion, Boucicault didn't like it. He found the plot stupid and the dialogue weak and inflated. The following evening the public were admitted to give their verdict – and pronounced the play a total failure. Macready, who had produced it, acknowledged their wisdom and withdrew it 'for the present'. 'For his own sake, we trust, for ever!' remarked one critic.[7] People who had earlier been hailing the play as the dramatic masterpiece of the century, either kept very quiet or changed their tune; all except Sheridan Knowles, who was convinced that public opinion was wrong.[8] If, by holding to his view, he was hoping to soften his young friend's disappointment at seeing his uncle's play fail so disastrously, he was mistaken. Far from being upset, Boucicault was delighted. Both his uncles regarded his own work in the theatre as that of an errant schoolboy who ought to have been whipped back to his lessons, and he had not forgiven either of them for their hostile attitude towards his mother. Nothing could have pleased him more than to have been challenged on

46

the ground he considered to be his own, and for him to have won so convincingly.

He could not afford to be too smug, however. He had had one massive hit, one disaster and one moderate success. What he needed was another play that would consolidate his position at the same time as bringing in some much-needed money. He was to find the answer to his immediate financial problems in Benjamin Webster. Webster saw in him a talent worth nurturing and was prepared to put up with Boucicault's posturing, disrespect and frivolity to get the plays he wanted. More importantly, from Boucicault's point of view, Webster was also prepared to advance money on unwritten plays. For the next eight years Boucicault used him as a banker, drawing advances on future projects as and when he needed them. Most of the time he kept his side of the bargain, turning in a play which, if it wasn't another *London Assurance,* was always serviceable and frequently successful. Occasionally, however, he sold Webster no more than a title-page and never wrote another word.

The first play he wrote for Webster under this arrangement was *Alma Mater; or, A Cure for Coquettes*, which was produced at the Haymarket on 19 September 1842. Webster spared no expense on the production, but public reaction was lukewarm and the critics, with one or two exceptions, were decidedly hostile. The *Athenaeum* quite enjoyed it, and the *Illustrated London News* praised it in parts, but the general view was that held by the critic of the *Era*: 'It is called a comedy; but, if a prescribed plan, elevated dialogue, brilliant repartee, nice development of character, manners, and humours, be necessary for the successful accomplishment of such a work, the author has most signally failed in reaching his aim.' Not content with savaging the play, the reviewers also accused Boucicault of having stolen his plot from both an earlier play and a novel. For the first time Boucicault felt constrained to answer them.

Gentlemen [he wrote in the dedication of his next play], 'when you are unanimous – your unanimity is wonderful; to its magic influence I owe the popularity already attending my Comedy, (beg pardon) farce, of *Alma Mater*. Your

47

abuse of it was hearty, I could only have wished it to have been a little more personal – may I hope you will extend a like favour to this little extravaganza? You know I am a very young author, who have been unhappily successful more than once. Now I feel confident you will never lose sight of these palliating facts, but, with the gentle feeling for which critics have ever been proverbial, will damn me freely in your several journals, and save me in public opinion. But be it unanimous. Though *I* may destroy every unity of the Drama, I beseech of *you* all, to sup together after my piece, and preserve the unity of criticism. You remark that my conceptions are full of heartlessness – hollow – vapid – and vulgar. How very odd – that you should have found me out – *entre nous* then – once, soured by a failure, I thought of turning newspaper critic, and studied your tone so minutely, that never since could I rid my style of those very shallow essentials which I see you have detected with such a fine sympathetic and masonic touch. Again you say my wit, 'if such can be so called, is old – coarse and mediocre.' Now I like that, because it is just. I measured my Comedy expressly for your own capacities and 'Io triumphe' – It fits. With feelings, therefore, deeper than gratitude can reach, I dedicate to you as much of this little Farce as you can understand. P.S. A friend advised me to invite you all to a champagne supper – for security – but I say, No! let well alone – in a moment of inebriety you might praise me!! Oh Lord! the thought! I should be lost irretrievably in the esteem of all your readers.

The farce he proposed dedicating to the gentlemen of the press, in a manner which cannot have won him any friends and which was typical of the contempt he had for critics, was a one-act play, written with Webster, that had its première on 24 September, one week after *Alma Mater* was first produced. Called *Curiosities of Literature*, it was a worse piece than *Alma Mater* and the critics could barely conceal their delight.

His next play, *The Bastille*, which was produced at the Haymarket on 19 December, was also a joint effort with Webster. Adapted from a popular French drama, it was a competent though uninspired piece of craftsmanship with a tale of intrigue at the court of Louis XIV that the audiences found appealing. Boucicault didn't put his name to it, so the critics refrained from attacking him. Most found the play quite agreeable. It was the fifth Boucicault play to be produced in the West End that year. None of them had come anywhere near approaching the success or popularity of *London Assurance*, but this, in itself, didn't matter to him. A playwright was paid a flat fee for his work, which might be increased if the play ran above a specified number of nights, negotiated when the piece was bought. Very few plays ever reached the required number. The advantage of a box-office hit was that the writer's power was increased for his next round of negotiations. Adapting *The Bastille* for Webster offered Boucicault a convenient solution to his twin problem of making money and thinking up new ideas: he could use the French he had learnt at school to adapt and translate.

I was a beginner in 1841 [he later explained the position which he found himself in[9]], and received for my comedy *London Assurance* £300. For that amount the manager bought the privilege of playing the work for his season. Three years later I offered a new play to a principal London theatre. The manager (Webster) offered me £100 for it. In reply to my objection to the smallness of the sum he remarked, 'I can go to Paris and select a first-class comedy; having seen it performed, I feel certain of its effect. To get this comedy translated will cost me £25. Why should I give you £300 or £500 for your comedy of the success of which I cannot feel so assured?' The argument was unanswerable and the result inevitable. I sold a work for £100 that took me six months' hard work to compose and accepted a commission to translate three French plays at £50 apiece. This work afforded me child's play for a fortnight. Thus the English dramatist was obliged to relinquish the stage altogether or to become a French copyist.

At the close of 1842, Boucicault was not ready to sell out to commercialism by doing straight translations. He still had several unproduced plays he was hoping to sell and was trying as best he could to write high-quality, original drama. That he was eventually forced to accept Webster's offer was not entirely his fault. The age in which he lived did not want original, quality drama. Audiences did not want subtle writing or to be made to think; they went to the theatre to be entertained, and the more magnificent the spectacle the more they enjoyed it. The stage in the mid nineteenth century was no place from which to express social commitment or challenge values, as the great writers of the time, men like Dickens and Thackeray, realized. The few playwrights who did try to produce a drama worthy of a country that had produced Shakespeare, Sheridan, Congreve and Restoration comedy, vanished quickly or else, like Tom Robertson, died in penury, neglected and forgotten. Boucicault was not a great social writer. He had the stage in his blood and his life was so inextricably bound up in the theatre that he could not, even if he had wanted to, have broken from it. When the moment came and he had to choose between Webster's offer of a pittance for an original work on which he had sweated love and care, or an easy, regular income from translating and adapting, he had no real choice. 'Drama,' he was later to write,[10] 'is the necessary product of the age in which it lives, and of which it is the moral, social and physical expression!' The mind of the dramatist, he said, had

to be practical, utilitarian, to be in sympathetic accord with the minds of the people. He must not consider anything too deeply; his audience cannot follow him. He must not soar; their prosaic minds, heavy with facts, cannot rise. He cannot roam; their exact information turns him back at every step . . . There is always a Homer, a Virgil, a Dante, and a Shakespeare in existence, but mankind is pleased not to call them forth . . . If we have no such poets, painters, sculptors, or philosophers now, it is simply because the mind of the nineteenth century has other aspirations. So our Milton has been directed to dismount Pegasus and bestride the lightning which science has bridled, Shakespeare is occupied in editing a morning newspaper, Dante in exploring the Isthmus of Panama to locate an interoceanic canal, Bacon is trying to reach the North Pole, while Michael Angelo is inventing a sewing machine.

Boucicault had not quite come to that cynical, bitter, but accurate, assessment of the drama of his time, at the start of 1843, for, at twenty-two, he still had hopes of making a name for himself as a writer to follow in the footsteps of the dramatists he admired from the past. He did, however, have a living to make, and he spent the first few months of the year working in various provincial theatres as a jobbing writer, turning out translations and adaptations to order from French plays without putting his name to them.[11] There were two reasons for his anonymity: he was still too proud to put his name to what he considered to be only hack-work, and, perhaps more important, he did not want his many creditors in London to know how much he was making.

His next West End play was *Woman*, the play that had been at the centre of the Green Room row between Mathews and Macready two years earlier. Although Boucicault had written to his mother in 1841 that Mathews had offered him £500 for it, and that it had been announced for production, the play was never performed so he offered it instead to Webster. Webster liked it and agreed to put it on, but when Charles Kean refused to play the leading role, Webster abandoned it. Boucicault then gave it to Henry Wallack, uncle of Lester, for the opening of his tenancy at Covent Garden. The house was packed for the first night on 2 October, but it was a poor play which suffered from a poor cast, poor production and some abominable acting. James Anderson, Walter Lacy and Edmund Phelps all received atrocious notices. The exception was Louisa Nisbett, but her part had so little to do with the main plot that she was unable to save the night. 'The piece was tolerated . . . ,' wrote a critic, 'and must soon be retired.' Boucicault hastily withdrew it, rewrote one of the acts and tried again, but it met with no greater success and soon disappeared.

A week later, on 9 October, *The Old Guard*,[12] a revision of the very first play he had written when at school in Brentford, appeared as an afterpiece for the opening night of the new Princess's Theatre in Oxford Street. Although it was a short piece, in one act, *The Old Guard* took all the notices. 'Let the triumphant success of this little drama,' opined the *Era*, 'teach M. Bourcicault to depend on the stories of his own fancy, and leave the conventionalities of the drama to such authors as have neither the genius to conceive nor the power to create character.'

If Boucicault was encouraged by this reaction to think he could still make his living by writing original dramas, he was sadly disillusioned by the success of his next play, a two-act drama of the French Revolution. *Victor and Hortense* was produced by Webster at the Haymarket on 1 November, starring himself and Madame Celeste. 'The drama, with not a little of the melodrama, and an infinity of improbabilities, was received throughout with applause, and was announced for repetition "every evening until further notice," amidst a tumultuous and unanimous consent.'[13] A play he had only adapted from the French, that he had knocked off in a short time, was more warmly received than those on which he laboured diligently. Two weeks later this impression was confirmed when another adaptation, the one-act *Laying a Ghost*, joined *Victor and Hortense* at the Haymarket and proved to be just as popular.

The whole question of adapting French plays was the subject of earnest discussion at the meetings of Boucicault and his literary friends, most of whom dabbled in the theatre, held in various pubs or in Albert Smith's rooms. At that time there was no copyright to protect dramas, and nothing could be done to prevent writers taking other people's plots, ideas and characters. It was a practice encouraged by the managers, and no sooner did a play become popular than half a dozen versions of the same story would be rushed out at rival theatres. The success of translations and adaptations at the box office only served to strengthen a manager's hand against the dramatist who was trying to be original. When Boucicault complained to his friends that Webster had refused him £500 for a new, original comedy because he could pick up a French translation for £50, the idea was suggested that there should be a free trade in thoughts and, just as Shakespeare had borrowed from the Italians, so contemporary dramatists should borrow from the French. 'Go to Paris,' suggested Charles Lamb Kenney, 'take their stuff and put it to better use.' 'The Dramatic Authors' Society will become a den of thieves,' complained a member of the group. 'Why not?' retorted Douglas Jerrold. 'So long as the thief takes enough, he remains respectable.' The rights and wrongs of plundering the French stage for ideas were discussed in animated conversation until a policeman arrived to complain about the noise. It took only a glance for the company to see that it was their host, Albert Smith, in disguise. 'Gentlemen,' he said gravely, 'I am sorry to interrupt, but there is an invalid neighbour, whose rest you are disturbing. The lady is on the hall door-step outside, very drunk, and she complains of your noise.' The genteel, elderly woman who lived above Smith had come down to have a private word with him. Hearing her complaint so delivered, she fled back upstairs.[14]

These evenings may have been jocular, boozy affairs, at which each speaker tried to outwit the other, but the points discussed were very serious, particularly for Boucicault, for they raised issues of morality that were to reverberate throughout his long career. He had tried, and was still trying, to write plays worthy of the name drama, to follow in the footsteps of Wycherley, Congreve, Sheridan and Goldsmith, but the public demanded French melodrama. His dilemma was increased by the fact that he always lived well above his income and to make money he had to give the public what it wanted. When he finally decided to give up trying to be original, he found he could complete a translation or adaptation in a matter of days and the pattern was set for the remainder of his career. Although only a handful of the 200 or more plays he wrote or adapted are worthy of attention today, at the time they were the finest and best examples of melodrama on the English-speaking stage.

Another of his early adaptations, *Used Up*, appeared at the Haymarket on 6 February 1844. This was written in collaboration with Charles Mathews, though the extent of Mathews's contributions does not seem to have gone beyond

ROYAL ENTERTAINMENT.

◆◆◆

By Command.

◆◆◆

Her Majesty's Servants will Perform, at Windsor Castle,

ON THURSDAY, JANUARY 4th, 1849,

A Comic Drama, in Two Acts, adapted from the French by DION BOURCICAULT, entitled

USED UP.

Sir Charles Coldstream, Bart.,	· ·	Mr. CHARLES MATHEWS,
Sir Adonis Leech,	· · · ·	Mr. GRANBY,
Honorable Tom Saville,	· · ·	Mr. BELLINGHAM,
Wurzel, *(a Farmer)*	· ·	Mr. F. COOKE,
John Ironbrace, *(a Blacksmith)*	·	Mr. HOWE.
Mr. Fennell, *(a Lawyer)*	· ·	Mr. HONNER,
James,	· · · · ·	Mr. CLARKE,
Mary,	· · · · ·	Mrs. JACOB BARROW,
		(Late Miss Julia Bennett,)
Lady Clutterbuck,	· · · · ·	Mrs. HUMBY.

After which, a Farce, in One Act, by JOHN MADDISON MORTON, entitled

BOX AND COX,

A ROMANCE OF REAL LIFE.

John Box, *(a Journeyman Printer)*	·	Mr. BUCKSTONE,
James Cox, *(a Journeyman Hatter)*	·	Mr. HARLEY,
Mrs. Bouncer, *(a Lodging-house Keeper)*	·	Mrs. STANLEY.

Director,	· · · · · ·	MR. CHARLES KEAN,
Assistant Director,	· · · ·	MR. GEORGE ELLIS.

A Command Performance at Windsor Castle, given under the
direction of Charles Kean. It is interesting to note that Charles
Mathews, who is sometimes credited with having written *Used Up*,
made no such claim on this occasion.

the suggestion of a few pieces of business, and the title. Boucicault wanted to call it *Bored to Death*, but Mathews held out for *Used Up*. The play opened two days before Mathews was due to be examined by the bankruptcy commissioners, and the public, which had been following the details of his financial difficulties avidly, flocked to see him in the leading role of Sir Charles Coldstream. They were quick to detect similarities between the actor and the character he played, a world-weary nobleman who longs to return to Nature. In the play, one of the very best of his comedies, Boucicault showed that he was much more than a hack translator. Although some lines are a direct rendering of the French, he adapted, refined and revised the original to make it wholly English, and gave Mathews a part he was able to play for the rest of his career. Mathews scored an outstanding triumph. Even George Henry Lewes was moved to praise him, though he doubted Mathews's disguise as a ploughboy in the second act: 'a jewel-led hand', he observed, 'is not usually seen directing a plough'.[15]

More adaptations followed in quick succession. In March 1844, *Lolah; or, The Wreck-light* was seen at the Haymarket; in April, *Love in a Sack*, also at the Haymarket; in September, *Mother and Son* at the Adelphi, another theatre under Webster's management; in October, *The Fox and the Goose* and *Don Caesar de Bazan*, both at the Adelphi; and in the same month the Haymarket's new season opened with Boucicault's revision of Vanbrugh's *The Confederacy*. Seven plays in eight months. It was a fantastic amount of work and typical of the industry Boucicault always showed in his writing. Fortunately for him, he was able to work quickly and his manuscripts needed very little revision before they were put into production. It was no wonder that he used to joke that his epitaph should be – 'Dion Boucicault – his first holiday'.

Charles Rosenberg, author of *The Life of Jenny Lind*, was living with Boucicault and his mother at this time, following a nervous breakdown. Rosenberg recalled seeing Boucicault one day, while writing, take a small piece of something from his waistcoat pocket, break off a lump and start to chew it.

I became interested enough and summoned sufficient energy to ask him, what it was? 'Oh! That! Why, it is opium.' 'And do you actually eat opium?' I asked in my intense astonishment. 'Yes! Sometimes. When I have work to do, as I have at present, which must go on – day and night – until it is finished.' For the first time, during many months, was my curiosity excited. 'Is De Quincey's picture of its effects a true one?' I asked. 'Not with me, most certainly,' he emphatically replied. 'It makes me more capable of mental labour, whilst I eat it. That is all. But as for visions of beauty, palaces of gold, rivers of wine, lakes of honey, mountains of amethyst, et cetera – Pshaw! I suppose my skull must be too thick and my brain too commonplace to entertain them.'[16]

When Rosenberg had sufficiently recovered from his breakdown to start work, he began to help Boucicault with his translations. In one year, according to him, they collaborated on seven plays other than those that were performed in the West End, and Boucicault unaided wrote a further twenty-one for various provincial theatres. Small wonder he didn't want his name attached to anything produced outside the major London houses, and sometimes not even then. It also makes his claim of having written approximately 250 plays look much more realistic.

Boucicault may have entered boldly on to the treadmill of adapting, but he had not given up all hope of writing a really fine, original drama, and on 18 November 1844 *Old Heads and Young Hearts* opened at the Haymarket. A five-act comedy, it had taken him six months to write and he pinned a lot of hope on it. The production, however, did not go smoothly. The Haymarket season had opened in early October with Boucicault's version of Vanbrugh's *The Confederacy*, for which Webster had engaged Charles Mathews and Madame Vestris. In spite of the success of *Used Up* nine months earlier, there was still little love lost between Boucicault and the two stars. They had not forgiven him for the Macready affair, and he was convinced that they had deliberately sabotaged *The Irish Heiress*. Although only twenty-three, Boucicault had become an experienced man of the theatre. At least eighteen of his plays had been seen in the West End, and when, that autumn, Webster offered a prize of £500 for a new five-act comedy (won by Mrs Gore with *Quid Pro Quo*), he had refused to enter, even though he could have used the money, on the grounds that he was already an established playwright and the competition was to discover new talent. He felt he knew as much, if not more, about the theatre and stagecraft as Mathews. It was not long before the rows began. 'What am I to do about the Confederacy?' he complained in a letter to Webster. 'The Mathews's want Everything altered, their own and other people's parts — "Oh! that mine enemy would write a play." '[17]

By the time the rehearsals started for *Old Heads and Young Hearts* he had had enough; it was his play and he knew exactly how it should be played. Mathews and Vestris had been cast in the leading roles of Littleton Coke and Lady Alice Hawthorn, and when Mathews followed his customary practice of altering the dialogue to suit himself, the young writer stepped in. During rehearsals for *London Assurance*, Boucicault had been only too willing and eager to accept any alteration or suggestion that would improve his play; on this occasion he was determined to have the final word. He told Mathews he could not alter the part and that he didn't know what he was talking about. Mathews was furious and immediately sent his and Madame Vestris's scripts back to Webster.

> After the gross impertinence of Mr Bourcicault this morn-
> ing in your presence you cannot be surprised . . . [he wrote
> in his accompanying note]. His last words were these : 'I
> want no one's opinions but my own as to the *consistency* of
> the characters I draw — *your* business is to utter what *I*
> create.' As I differ in toto from this inflated view of the
> relative positions of actor and dramatist I at once decline
> subscribing to it. I can only regret our not being in the
> comedy on account of any inconvenience it may cause you.
> It is of course a relief to escape from parts which, though
> they might be rendered consistent by dint of alteration,
> could never be rendered palatable to us.[18]

Webster was too experienced and wily a manager to let a mere disagreement between his leading artists and his author stand in the way of production, and he managed to reunite the warring parties in time for the play to open as scheduled, with Mathews and Vestris in their allotted roles. News of the row had leaked out and the publicity did no harm at the box office. The house was packed and the play, which had been produced with great attention to scenery and properties (giving rise to what one critic referred to as 'the upholstery school of comedy'), was warmly received. Boucicault had frequently been condemned for his often cynical, sardonic view of mankind, and the dubious morality of his characters. This time there were no complaints. 'May our hearts ever be young enough, and our heads never too old, to relish the fruit of good writing and good acting conjoined in the new comedy at the Haymarket,' enthused the critic of the *Era*.

Old Heads and Young Hearts, drawing its inspiration, like *London Assurance*, from the comedies of the Restoration, is in almost every respect a better play than its predecessor. It is a minor masterpiece of nineteenth-century dramatic comedy writing, and yet, at the end of 1844, it barely survived, appearing on the bills only intermittently until the middle of February 1845, when it was withdrawn. It was, remarked Boucicault, a play that added more to his literary than his pecuniary credit, and it was to be his last original drama for many years. The need to make money and be successful took precedence over any thoughts of becoming a distinguished literary figure living in poverty. At the beginning of his career, he later recalled, 'a distinguished literary man advised me to keep to one object – the Drama. The only impression that can be made on the skull of the public he said, must be done by a tenpenny nail, always struck on the head. The public is like a woman, quick to appreciate, slow to reason. The dramatist, to succeed, must amuse . . .'[19] After *Old Heads*, Boucicault was to devote himself entirely to giving audiences just what they wanted.

4

THE FRENCH YEARS

ONCE HE had seen *Old Heads and Young Hearts* on to the stage of the Haymarket, Boucicault packed his bags and travelled to France. Having come to the reluctant conclusion that to survive as a dramatist he had to accept Webster's offer to translate and adapt French plays, he had become Webster's house author in all but name, and, in December 1844, Webster sent him to Paris for the first time to see which of the current crop of plays were worth considering for London. He immediately felt at home. With his fluent command of the language and his French-sounding name, he was, he believed, French in everything except the land of his birth. Remembering stories he'd been told by his father, which he was certain were true, of ancestors who had fought gloriously at Agincourt, he spent much of his time on what were to become regular visits during the next five years trying to trace the Boucicault line. As soon as he discovered that the French spelt his name without an 'r', he decided to drop the 'r' from his, and he convinced himself, and was later to swear in court, that his father had been French, not fourth-generation Irish.[1]

On his first trip that December, he moved into rooms in the rue de la Paix and began work immediately on preparing English versions of the plays he had seen. 'You shall receive a piece this week . . .,' he wrote to Webster on the 16th. 'I keep a sharp look out for novelty.' Only a short distance from where he was staying was the house where Dr Lardner, his guardian, was living with Mary Heaviside. Whether they ever met is not known, but one person whom Boucicault did meet, and who was to have a profound effect upon him, was the American showman, Phineas T. Barnum. Barnum, having spent the summer and autumn of 1844 exhibiting his protégé General Tom Thumb to the British public, had struck up an acquaintance with Boucicault's old friend, the writer Albert Smith, and when he announced his intention of taking the general to Paris, it was natural that Smith should put him in touch with Boucicault. Barnum couldn't speak a word of French.

> I was very fortunate [he wrote in his autobiography], in making the acquaintance of Mr Dion Boucicault, who was then sojourning in that city, and who at once kindly volunteered to advise and assist me in regard to numerous matters of importance relating to the approaching visit of the General. He spent a day with me in the search for suitable accommodation for my company; and by giving me the benefit of his experience, he saved me much trouble and expense. I have never forgotten the courtesy extended to me by this gentleman.

If Barnum never forgot Boucicault, Boucicault certainly never forgot Barnum, for in the few hours they were in each other's company, the young playwright was given a lesson he was to remember all his life. During his days as a provincial actor and struggling writer, Boucicault had begun to realize the value of the press. He had seen how the rows with Mathews and Macready, and his disagreements with Mathews and Vestris, far from being damaging to him had resulted in increased interest at the box office. From Barnum he was to have confirmed that no publicity is bad publicity (the philosophy by which Barnum lived), to hear how the press could be manipulated and how adverse comment could always be turned to advantage; in short, how a skilled and clever showman operates. And that was what Boucicault had decided he was going to become.

His letters from Paris indicate that, as well as trying to decide where his future lay, Boucicault was kept busy attending theatres and turning out plays for Webster, but there are no records of any of the titles he mentions being produced. After a month or so in Paris, he returned to London for the production of *A Soldier of Fortune*, a two-act adaptation made with Webster, at the Adelphi on 6 February 1845. On 23 June his version of *Peg Woffington*, Charles Reade's novel about the famous eighteenth-century actress, was produced at the same theatre.

Money was still Boucicault's greatest problem, for no matter how much he received from Webster, his expenses were always higher than his income, and he was being plagued constantly by tradesmen demanding that he settle his accounts. A letter from his mother, probably to Webster, explains his predicament:

> Upon reconsideration I do not object to my son's translating or adapting pieces provided he does not put his own name to them. Any piece produced with his name his creditors will in future require the proceeds of and it is just and fair and what I feel most anxious they should have . . . It seems before the present comedy was produced, dreading being left without money he informed his creditors that you had advanced him during the last three years money on it from time to time so that only that sum was due on it, that is seventy pounds. Consequently should any of them call on you will you be so good as not to say he has received three times since. Pray frighten him about being absent and tell him for his sake you will refuse sending him any more money to Paris. If he wishes to tell you how much work he is doing for you do not believe him – he is talking soft nonsense and dancing the Polka and spending his money.[2]

In the summer of 1845, Boucicault discovered a new way of solving his problems. On 9 July, at St Mary's Parish Church,

Lambeth, he was married to Anne Guiot. Very little is known about her. She was French, the daughter of Étienne St Pierre, and a widow considerably older than her twenty-four-year-old second husband. Her greatest attraction seems to have been that she had money. In all probability she was a member of the *Petite noblesse* (Charles, Vicomte de Secqueville, was her witness at the wedding),[3] and she certainly possessed some property in France which produced a regular income. Gossip always supposed that Boucicault had met her during his stay in Paris, while his enemies claimed that he had been introduced to her through a matrimonial agency. Genio Scott, an American journalist hostile to Boucicault, was clearly repeating such gossip in his 1862 article for *The Spirit of the Times*, 'the American Gentleman's Newspaper', when he wrote that 'he not only discovered a Quaker lady who possessed a fair fortune, which he knew where to place his hand upon, but he soon fell as deeply in love with her as the circumstances of the case and the obduracy of his own affections would permit him to. He adopted a hat of wider brim and more square set, and was seen, in unexceptionable quaker guise, to be quietly waiting upon his adored one.' They were, of course, married in an Anglican church. Their relationship and their life together is shrouded in mystery. Anne does not feature in any of Boucicault's recollections of this time or contemporary accounts of his movements; she is rarely mentioned in his letters, except in passing. It does seem possible that he married her just for her money.

Enquire Within, a one-act farce based on a French source, was produced at the Lyceum on 25 August, and only then did the Boucicaults set off on honeymoon, making a short Continental tour before ending up in Paris where they moved into Meurice's, the very fashionable hotel. With a French wife, Boucicault was more than ever convinced of his own French aristocratic connections and took to calling himself the Vicomte de Boucicault,[4] a title that not even he had the gall to use when they returned to London. He had, however, discovered that the aristocratic line came from Poitiers and, for a while, signed himself Dion de P. Boucicault.

Even on honeymoon he did not stop working, visiting

theatres with his wife and keeping a sharp look-out for new stories and ideas. In 1846 he had five plays produced in the West End. In February, *The Old School*, a two-act adaptation, was seen at the Haymarket. In May, *Up the Flue*, a one-act farce on which he collaborated with Charles Lamb Kenney, was hissed on its first night at the Haymarket, and *Mr Peter Piper*, a three-act comedy taken from a French source and produced at the same theatre, was attacked for its immorality and coarse language. In July, *The Wonderful Water Cure*, a one-act operetta written with Webster, appeared at the Haymarket, and at some time during the year *Shakespeare in Love* (of which no record survives) was also produced. This high output continued into the following year. In February 1847, *The School for Scheming*, a five-act comedy of manners which attempted to recapture the mood of *London Assurance*, was hissed on its first night at the Haymarket but still managed a respectable run, and, in May, *La Salamandrine*, a ballet for which he had written the story, was produced at Covent Garden. Boucicault, at twenty-six, with nearly thirty known plays to his credit in the West End alone, had established himself as a prolific and competent craftsman who could turn out a play ready for rehearsal in less than two weeks if pushed. He began work on the outline of *The Wonderful Water Cure*, sent to him by Webster, on Sunday, and had the piece finished by Tuesday.[5] But he didn't always find it so easy. His correspondence of this period is full of ideas and titles on which he was working which never saw completion (though some of them may have been performed outside London without his name on them), and in one letter to Webster he wrote: 'I have been trying to make a silk purse out of your sow's ear – but I fear I shall not be able to complete the task by tomorrow. I never undertook anything so much against the grain. I have begun its form several times and thrown aside enough manuscripts for two pieces already.'

Although he was reticent about putting his name to many of the pieces he wrote, to try to outwit his creditors, and had kept very quiet about his marriage, he decided to put into practice the lessons he had learnt from Barnum in Paris. On 7 June he was one of many literary and theatrical figures who went on a publicity flight with veteran balloonist Charles Green in the famous Great Balloon of Nassau, the balloon in which he had made his historic flight, from Vauxhall Gardens, London, to Nassau, Germany, a distance of 480 miles, eleven years earlier. It was a fine summer evening when Boucicault, in company with Albert Smith, Shirley Brooks, John Lee and others, climbed aboard the gondola in Cremorne Pleasure Gardens. The balloon drifted slowly over Chelsea, South-wark and Rotherhithe, eventually coming to land in the marshes of Essex, from where the passengers had to walk three miles to the nearest village to celebrate the ascent in the inn and arrange transport to get them and the balloon back to London. The flight was widely reported in the papers, as Boucicault had hoped.

He had no further plays produced in London that year. In September it was announced that he had been engaged to write a new piece for the opening of the Lyceum under the management of Mathews and Vestris, but the play never materialized, and in November it was announced that he had a comedy in preparation for the Haymarket. This was probably *A Confidence*, an adaptation from the French which the *Athenaeum* described as 'scarcely worth a mention', which was not produced until May 1848, by which time Boucicault was back in Paris. He was living there during the two-day revolution in February which established the Second Republic. Forced to stay indoors while the mobs rampaged through the streets, Boucicault taught himself to cook. He was very proud of his culinary expertise and claimed to have invented, while on a Scottish hunting expedition, a method of cooking steak in a minute – tenderloin steak cut into strips, rolled in mustard, salt and pepper, covered with fresh butter, and cooked over a fire on a toasting fork.[6]

Why, one wonders, was Boucicault having to cook for himself? Where was his wife? According to Agnes Robertson, Boucicault's second wife, Anne Guiot had died at Aix-la-Chapelle in March 1848, after a long illness during which she had been nursed by Boucicault. If this was true, it would certainly explain Boucicault's long absence from the London theatrical scene during the second half of 1847, but not how he

performances. John Mitchell, lessee of the St James's, stepped in and offered them sanctuary at his theatre, which they gratefully accepted, Having been driven from Drury Lane, their last two appearances in London were made without interruption.

Boucicault was again without a job. During the previous few years he had been earning steadily, though not spectacularly, from his writing. Few of his plays had brought him any great financial return, and even though *London Assurance* was still being performed regularly in London and the provinces, it did not bring him anything extra. He was so short of money, and sinking further and further into debt, that he had had to sell the rights to Webster. By the time his engagement with the Théâtre Historique had ended, he could no longer escape the fact that he couldn't pay his bills. The £1,200 left him by his wife had been quickly dissipated in a bout of profligate spending, entertaining his friends and women, frequenting the gambling dens of Soho. He owed money to his hairdresser, to the coachbuilders, to the livery stables where he kept his horses, to tailors, to stationers, to printers, to shopkeepers and to moneylenders. Even if he did write another play, the fee would do no more than cover the cost of his day-to-day living.

In June 1848, he applied to be declared bankrupt but his petition was dismissed. In November he tried again, and this time, with admitted liabilities of almost £800, his petition was accepted. When the day in December came for his debts to be proved, one of the first to try and get his money was John Hart, the tailor to whom Boucicault still owed money from eight years previously, but poor Hart's application was refused because it exceeded the time laid down by the Statute of Limitations. At the end of the hearing, Boucicault was declared insolvent and his immediate financial difficulties had passed.[10]

While the hearing was in progress, *The Knight of Arva*, a two-act comedy set in Spain (which Boucicault once claimed to have visited on a yacht), had been produced at the Haymarket on 22 November. In the character of Connor the Rash, an Irish soldier of fortune who marries a Spanish princess, Boucicault created a real, living person with whom the audience could identify, and the play enjoyed a moderately successful run. Continuing to demonstrate his ability to write quickly, Boucicault had completed *The Knight of Arva* in a week, and Webster paid him £350 for it. With money very much in his thoughts at the time, Boucicault was determined to try and do something about the financial position of the dramatist. It annoyed him that an author received only a flat fee for his work while the actors engaged to play it received large sums. As he explained his position twenty-five years later:

> When I entered the world of letters as a dramatist . . . I found my fellow-authors in the condition described in Gil Blas, living on the pittance doled out to them by the managers of theatres, who drank their wine like the warriors of Odin out of the skulls of the victims – the dramatic authors. I received just £300 sterling for my comedy *London Assurance*. Mr Farren, an actor, received £3,000 a year for playing in it. Douglas Jerrold received £100 for *Black-Eyed Susan*. Mr T. P. Cooke, who played in it, made £60,000 out of his performances. Sheridan Knowles received, I believe, £400 for *William Tell* and Bulwer received £500 for his comedy *Money*. Mr Macready was paid £120 a week for playing in these plays. It appeared to me that the literary element ought to be placed on a equal footing with the artistic, and I set myself the task of raising my profession to the only standard which the English mind applies to everything – the standard of money.[11]

Boucicault's love of making money had nothing to do with greed and everything to do with the age in which he lived. He desperately wanted to be successful, to be recognized, and to be acceptable in society – and the way to all of those was through money, the acquisition of which was considered a virtue by the Victorians. If he had a failing in contemporary eyes, it was that he did not stop at making fortunes, he spent generously.

His frequent trips to Paris, as well as giving him ideas for plays, had also given him the idea of how he could raise the financial status of the playwright. French dramatists, unlike their English counterparts, did not accept a straight fee for their work, collecting instead a 10 per cent royalty on box-office takings. This was the system Boucicault, on his return to London, tried hard to get his fellow writers in the Dramatic Authors' Society to accept, for he knew that without a concerted effort by all writers, his chances of success were nil. His proposals immediately angered managers and actors, and drew little support from other dramatists. A few were sympathetic, but doubted whether such a move could ever be successfully accomplished; the majority, who had never written a play that ran and who preferred cash in hand, no matter how bad their work, to taking their chances on earning large sums if they were successful, were totally opposed. Boucicault's persistence brought him many fresh enemies, but he was eventually forced to abandon his idea and wait for the right moment, a moment that was not to come for another twelve years. When it did, it was to have a profound effect upon the English stage.

On 26 November 1849, his first new play for a year opened at the Adelphi, and enjoyed a successful run. This was *The Willow Copse*, a five-act melodrama written in collaboration with Kenney. On 9 January 1850, his version of a French farce, *La Garde Nationale,* was produced at the Queen's Theatre, and on 12 September, *Giralda*, an adaptation of Scribe's opera, was produced at the Haymarket with Boucicault supervising rehearsals. The years 1849 and 1850 were lean ones for him. The lessons of his insolvency had done nothing to make him cut down on his spending, and with only three plays produced, he was again finding it hard 'to make ends meet. His salvation this time came in the shape of Charles Kean.

Kean, son of the great actor Edmund Kean, was only a moderately accomplished actor himself but a highly influential manager. A keen antiquarian (he was a Fellow of the Society of Antiquaries), his plays were carefully chosen, well rehearsed and costumed lavishly with great attention to detail. He did his research in the British Museum and took great pains to ensure the accuracy of his settings, props and lengthy programme notes. In August 1850, he embarked upon the most important period of his managerial career when, in partnership with actor Robert Keeley, he took over the Princess's Theatre in Oxford Street for an initial lease of two years. He planned to produce the entire canon of Shakespeare in the most sumptuous, authentically detailed productions ever mounted, and the season opened on 28 September with *Twelfth Night*. But Kean knew that his theatre could not survive on a diet of nothing but Shakespeare and he wanted good, popular, contemporary drama to build up audiences and keep them coming. So he turned to Dion Boucicault, at twenty-nine the most competent, successful writer in London, and offered him a reputed £700 a year to become his house dramatist,[12] searching out new French dramas, writing plays and adapting old ones. It was a move that was to prove crucial to Boucicault in both his career as an artist and as a person.

While he began work on his first play for Kean, Boucicault had completed and sold two others to Webster. *Belphegor*, written with Webster, was produced at the Adelphi in January 1851, and in April, *O'Flannigan and the Fairies*, a possible revision of an earlier play by Tyrone Power, appeared at the same theatre. Two more of his pieces were also performed outside Kean's management: *Sixtus V*, written with John Bridgeman, enjoyed great success at the Olympic in February, and *The Queen of Spades*, a translation of a play by Scribe, failed at Drury Lane in March.

On 6 March, Charles Kean was able to present the first play written expressly for the Princess's by his new author. *Love in a Maze* was a five-act comedy, based loosely on a French source, set in Norfolk. The play was carried by the production and pronounced a success, but Boucicault was not entirely happy with it, rewriting it and reducing it in length. Among the many people who enjoyed the play was Queen Victoria, who found it 'full of wit – with an excellent moral, particularly for young ladies'.[13] Kean's acting, she thought, was quiet and gentlemanlike. She returned to see the play a second time on 31 March, five days later, after which we saw a most intensely interesting Drama, in 3 acts, called *Pauline*. I never saw anything more exciting. The Keans acted beautifully and she acted really wonderfully in the most crucial and alarming moments, literally keeping one in a state of terror and suspense, so that one quite held one's breath, and was quite trembling when the play came to an end.

Although Boucicault's name never appeared on the bills for *Pauline*, he later claimed to have adapted the play for Kean. It was certainly the sort of play that Kean had engaged him to write.

Kean's first season at the Princess's closed in October, as it had opened, with *Twelfth Night*, having made a profit of £7,000. Throughout the season Boucicault had been hard at work on new pieces, some of which he was paid for, not all of which he saw produced. The second season opened on 22 November with Kean in sole charge of the company. Keeley and his wife had given up their interest backstage, but stayed with Kean as performers. On 24 February 1852, Boucicault's third major play for Kean was given its première. This was *The Corsican Brothers*, and it was again just the sort of play which Kean had looked for. Based on a French play, itself a dramatization of a story by Alexandre Dumas, *The Corsican Brothers* became the sensation of the season, running for sixty-six nights. Before the year was out there were seven other versions of the story to be seen on the London stage alone, but none of them came anywhere near to matching the Boucicault version in popularity. It was, declared George Henry Lewes, 'the most daring, ingenious and exciting melodrama I remember to have seen'.[14] Kean, playing the twin brothers, excelled himself.

> You must see him before you will believe how well and how *quietly* he plays them [continued Lewes]; preserving a gentlemanly demeanour, a drawing-room manner very difficult to assume on the stage, if one may judge from its rarity, which intensifies the passion of the part, and gives it a terrible reality. Nothing can be better than the way he steps

forward to defend the insulted woman at that supper; nothing can be more impressive than his appearance in the third act as the avenger of his brother. The duel between him and Wigan was a masterpiece on both sides: the Bois de Boulogne itself has scarcely seen a duel more real or more exciting. Kean's dogged, quiet, terrible walk after Wigan, with a fragment of broken sword in his relentless grasp, I shall not forget.

The duel scene also made a deep impression on another member of the audience, Queen Victoria, who went to see the play five times during the season and sketched the scene in her Journal, the only sketch she ever made of a professional performance.

I have never seen Kean act better or more naturally, than in the 1st scene, where he comes on in the Corsican mountaineer's dress [she recorded]. The effect of the ghost in the first act, with its wonderful management and entire noiselessness, was quite alarming. The tableau of the Duel, which Fabien witnesses, almost immediately after the vanishing of the ghost, was beautifully grouped and quite touching. The whole, lit by blue light and dimmed with gauze, had an unearthly effect, and was most impressive and creepy . . . We both, and indeed everyone was in admiration at the whole performance and much struck by it. We told Kean so, when he accompanied us downstairs.[15]

Boucicault's careful adaptation showed the originality that was the hallmark of most of his work, a feature of his adaptations that was often not recognized by those of his detractors who dismissed him as a mere copyist and plagiarist. It is significant that his version of the story was to hold the stage for more than fifty years as a vehicle for star performers, the last great exponent of the dual roles being Henry Irving. Boucicault also concerned himself with the play's presentation. The long, interleaved trap he devised for the first appearance on stage of the twins together became known as the Corsican Trap, and most theatres in Britain installed one.

Just how effective it was can be judged from Lewes's review in the *Leader*:

> Fabien is now restless and uneasy, convinced that something has happened to his brother Louis; and, while he writes to him, to learn the truth, the spectre of his brother, with blood on his breast, appears to him. Nothing can exceed the art with which this is managed; with ghostly terror, heightened by the low tremolos of the violins, and the dim light upon the stage, the audience, breath-suspended, watches the slow apparition, and the vision of the duel which succeeds; a scenic effect more real and terrible than anything I remember.

'The Ghost Melody', which had been composed especially for this scene, became one of the most popular pieces of music in town, selling, in sheet form, in its thousands. A preoccupation with staging and stagecraft was to remain with Boucicault for the rest of his life and was to lead to him producing some of the most important theatrical innovations of the century.

The Corsican Brothers marked an important stage in the history of English drama. Although melodrama had been popular for several years, the blend of chivalry and adventure to be found in Boucicault's play was far removed from the atmosphere of earlier melodramas or even the plays Boucicault had himself adapted. The era of 'gentlemanly melodrama' had begun.

It was the custom at that time for actors and actresses to take benefits; a night during the season when, after the theatre had covered its costs, they received everything taken at the box office. Many minor players, particularly in the provinces, relied upon a benefit to turn their paltry wage into something respectable, though some, in the more remote areas, as often as not failed to make anything on the night. Boucicault himself had missed out on a take of about £50 when his Hull benefit of 1840 had been cancelled. Charles Kean and his wife, Ellen Tree, decided to take their benefit on 14 June, not, surprisingly, in the hit of the season, *The Corsican Brothers*, but in Lovell's *Trial of Love*. As an added attraction to the evening, which the Queen and Prince Albert had agreed to attend, Boucicault was asked to write an afterpiece. Turning again to French sources, he came up with *The Vampire*, a tale spread, in three acts, over a hundred years. Since Kean was playing in *Trial of Love*, it is most unlikely he ever considered the leading role of the Phantom and the part was given, not to a member of the company, but to the author. As Kean had anticipated, the announcement that Boucicault was to appear in his own play provoked widespread interest. Boucicault was a well-known figure, a colourful character who featured in the gossip columns, and it was common knowledge that he had once taken part in 'amateur theatricals'. The public, with encouragement from the press, couldn't wait to see him on stage. For Boucicault, the venture was more than a calculated move to increase the box-office take for the Keans' benefit night. If he had had his way two years previously, and had succeeded in introducing a royalty system for playwrights, he would have been coining it from *The Corsican Brothers*. As it was, he had had to accept a flat fee, and a three-act afterpiece would not add much to his account; as an actor, however, he would be able to more than double his earnings.[16]

The house was packed for the benefit, and although *The Vampire* was a critical failure – 'a mistake about which the less said the better', remarked Kean's secretary; 'the extreme point of inanity', commented Henry Morley – Boucicault's acting drew unbridled praise and kept the public coming for many nights after. He 'looked the Vampire to perfection, and spoke and acted it exceedingly well', reported the *Era*. 'His deathy hue and rigid cast of countenance, his high and bald forehead and spare figure, his measured accents and grave demeanour, were all in keeping, and his "make up" was in each act quite a study.' 'Mr Boucicault,' wrote the Queen, who commissioned a watercolour of him in the role for her collection at Windsor Castle, 'who is very handsome and has a fine voice, acted very impressively. I can never forget his livid face and fixed look, in the first two Dramas. It quite haunts me.' When she returned a week later to see the piece for a second time, she only stayed for the first two acts. 'It does not bear seeing a second time, and is, in fact, very trashy,' she commented.

One other reason Boucicault had been pleased to accept the role was that it kept him in the close proximity of Agnes Robertson, a young member of the company who was appearing in the play. She was barely mentioned in the reviews, and when she was it was not complimentary. Agnes Robertson, wrote the critic of the *Era*, was 'not exactly suited to her character'; she was 'convulsive and spasmodic, and unintelligible in her efforts to be forceful'. She was nineteen, twelve years younger than Boucicault. Born in Edinburgh, where her father Thomas Robertson was an art publisher, she had first appeared on stage as a child singer, when she was ten, at the Theatre Royal, Aberdeen. She was a last-minute replacement for a girl who had fallen ill, and was so well liked that the management offered her a two-week contract to complete the run of the play, *The Spoiled Child*. From then on she never had any career but the stage in mind. During the late 1840s, she appeared with various provincial companies in Manchester, Hull, Liverpool and Glasgow, and while in Liverpool had acted on the same bill as the Keans for five nights. When Kean assumed responsibility for the Princess's, he had invited her to join his company. Since she was then only seventeen, she had moved in to live with the Keans and became temporarily their ward. She made her London début on 16 October 1850, playing a page in *A Wife's Secret*. 'It was at the Princess's,' she later told a journalist, 'I met my fate. Dion Boucicault was then writing plays for the Keans and was, indeed, the regular author of the house.'[17]

Boucicault, who enjoyed the company of women, was immediately taken by her charms and good looks, and became her constant companion, taking her for long rides in his carriage. In the summer of 1852, unknown to the Keans, they became lovers, and Agnes spent more time with Boucicault in his Soho apartments than she did with the Keans. Boucicault showered her with gifts and gave her money to supplement the paltry wage of £3 a week she was receiving from Kean. She was playing mostly very small, supporting roles, and Boucicault was determined to do all he could to further her career. He wrote, for her, a two-act sentimental piece, *The*

Prima Donna, designed to show off her delicate talents. Although Boucicault was taken to task for his pessimistic view of the relationship between men and women – 'his experience gives him an advantage we do not enjoy', commented one reviewer, hinting that there were other liaisons which were public knowledge[18] – when the play opened the Princess's autumn season on 18 September 1852, Agnes proved that she was a more than competent actress and it was played for thirty-four consecutive nights. Kean immediately increased her salary by £1 a week.

Fond though he was of her, and surprised by her success in *The Prima Donna*, Kean could never see Agnes becoming a great actress, and, since she was his ward, he advised her to use her looks and position to catch herself a noble, wealthy husband. The man both he and Mrs Kean favoured was the twenty-one-year-old Earl of Hopetoun, son of the Marquess of Linlithgow. To their surprise and astonishment, Agnes turned his lordship down flat. Then they discovered the reason. They had both been worrying because Agnes was taking a long time to get home from the theatre. One evening, when it was getting late and she still hadn't shown up, Kean went in search of her and was horrified to find her at Boucicault's, sitting at the head of his table, entertaining his friends. The discovery led to a blazing row; Agnes packed her bags, left the Keans' house to move in with Boucicault, and quit the company to join Madame Vestris at the Lyceum. Boucicault, whose proposal to Agnes had been refused on Kean's advice, promptly resigned from the Princess's before Kean could fire him, leaving behind several completed plays, including *Faust and Margaret* and *Louis XI*. It was almost two years before Kean allowed his judgement to get the better of his anger and he produced them. *Faust and Margaret* proved a popular hit when it was performed on 19 April 1854, and in the title role of *Louis XI*, produced on 13 January 1855, Kean enjoyed a success comparable to that of *The Corsican Brothers*. But he never forgave Boucicault for what he considered to be his treachery. Ten years later he wrote to a friend:

As to Boucicault, my dear friend, he is a gentleman to

whom I can never speak again, and indeed any man would lose cast here by being seen in his company. His character is so bad that there is not a crime under the Sun of which he is not accused. The most dreadful stories are told of him.[19]

For some time prior to his sudden departure from the Princess's, Boucicault had been thinking of visiting the United States. Almost all his plays had been produced there and his reputation was as high in New York as it was in London. He had spent hours backstage and in alehouses, 'talking American' with American actors visiting England and English artists who had played in the States, until he had convinced himself that the New World was the new world for which he strove. Life in London was turning stale. In the twelve years since he had burst on the scene with *London Assurance,* he had established himself as a writer with few equals and as an actor of some competence. He was thirty-two; he needed new horizons, fresh fields to conquer. In April, his father had died in Athlone. His mother was in good health and living with his elder brother William in London; there was nothing to keep him in England any longer. The break with Kean, and the failure of Vestris's season at the Lyceum, which put Agnes out of work, decided him: they would go to the States together. Through a friend in London he managed to arrange for Agnes to play a season at Burton's Theatre, New York, that autumn, and turning to his old friend Webster for help (he had debts of £1,500), raised the money for their passages by selling him plays both written and promised. On 17 August, aboard the *SS Hermann,* Agnes sailed from Southampton bound for New York. Three weeks later, on 7 September, Boucicault embarked on the *SS Arctic* in Liverpool and followed her to their new world.

5

THE NEW WORLD

Boucicault landed in New York on 18 September 1853.

> It was not a city [he was later to recall]. It was a theatre. It was a huge fair. Bunting of all nationalities and of no nationality was flaunting over the streets. Poles of liberty accentuated the 'Rights of Man.' Bands of music preceded processions of a dozen boys bearing flags and tattered targets. Irish was spoken in the wharves, German in the saloons, French in the restaurants. But the chiefest feature in this polyglot city was its boyhood. A boy in heart, but a man, and a very shrewd one, in head![1]

New York in the 1850s was a city of a quarter of a million people. Most eminent visitors from Britain tended to treat the inhabitants as country bumpkins they had come to imbue with a little culture, and were naturally resented. That was not Boucicault's attitude at all; he loved the city, he loved the people, he loved the opportunities and the pioneering spirit he found; he was immediately at home.

His most pressing need, however, was to make money. He had managed to scrape up enough to pay for his and Agnes's boat tickets, but he had no capital and no income, and

78

although he had a big reputation as a dramatist, he was relying on Agnes's engagement at Burton's to keep them while he looked around and established himself. Agnes, however, was not even in New York. She had arrived on 1 September and gone straightway to Montreal in Canada where she opened at the Theatre Royal on Monday, 19 September (the day after Boucicault had reached New York), in *The Young Actress*, Boucicault's version of Edward Lancaster's play, *The Manager's Daughter*. Agnes later recalled that there had been an epidemic in New York at the time of her arrival and that she had been forced to go to Montreal instead of making her début at Burton's.[2] Although there was an epidemic in some parts of the States, and some boats in New York harbour had been placed in quarantine at the beginning of September, there is no evidence that Burton had to change any of his programmes because Agnes hadn't appeared. And since Boucicault was on the high seas, there would have been no opportunity for him to have altered Agnes's routing. In all probability the Montreal début was part of Boucicault's carefully worked out plan to get Agnes some favourable publicity before her New York opening. If that was the case, the plan worked perfectly. Montreal, which was normally omitted from the itinerary of visiting European artists, turned out to welcome her in force. 'The playgoers of Montreal have never, within our recollection, been gratified with the sight of such a charming actress as Miss Robertson,' declared the *Gazette*.[3] 'She possesses all the requisites of success, beauty, grace, a fine voice, and an intellect to appreciate what she plays. We have never seen anything more exquisite than her rendering of the Scotch part in the *Young Actress*.' The play was designed expressly to display Agnes's talents as an actress, singer and dancer, in five different roles. It was 'the most successful piece ever produced in Montreal'. The following night Agnes appeared in *The Prima Donna* and confirmed the *Gazette*'s high opinion of her. 'This lady,' wrote its critic, 'is certainly one of the most talented artists it has ever been our good fortune to see.' The Montreal public agreed with him and nightly Agnes played to packed houses. On 27 September she was given a benefit which was so over-subscribed that she was given another, on

79

10 October, to mark her farewell performance. Once more there was not enough room in the theatre to hold all those wanting to see her, and there had to be a repeat farewell the following night.

News of Agnes's triumphant appearance in Montreal travelled south, as Boucicault had hoped it would, and offers to present her poured in from every major city in the States. But first she had her engagement to fulfil at Burton's. As soon as the curtain had come down in Montreal, she travelled to New York. She and Boucicault had been corresponding regularly while she'd been in Canada, but for the sake of propriety, and because she wanted to be as sure of his feelings for her as she was of her own for him after a separation of almost two months, she booked into a different hotel. That evening they met for dinner. When the time came for her to leave, Boucicault begged her to stay; if, he said, she would consent to become his wife, he would agree to become her husband, and that, according to the laws of New York State, would constitute a valid marriage. Without hestitation, Agnes accepted his proposal and moved in with him.[4] She also agreed that he should become her manager.

Boucicault was right. At that time in New York a formal declaration between two people was sufficient for them to become husband and wife. There was, however, an ulterior motive for his decision not to have a church wedding – he did not want the American public to know that they were married. He had already publicly denied the rumour that they had been married in London[5] following the dramatic break with Kean (the details of which had preceded them to New York), and he reasoned that Agnes, who was twenty, good-looking and attracted a strong following among young gentlemen, would prove to be a much bigger draw at the box office if she appeared as a Miss rather than Mrs. When four months later from the stage of the Boston Museum he admitted they were married, it came as no surprise to those who knew him to find out he had denied his wife for a few extra dollars. It was the start of a long, hard life for Agnes, of years of struggle during which, although she bore him six children, she was rarely off the stage, of endless travel and living out of suitcases in a succession of seedy boarding houses, of loyalty to a highly sexed husband who took every opportunity he could to be unfaithful (though he always tried to make sure she never found out).

In the autumn of 1853, their future looked bright. Agnes opened at Burton's, under Boucicault's personal managership, on 22 October in *The Young Actress*, and New York fell at her feet. For a week she played to packed houses before the bills changed and she appeared as Master Bob Nettles in *To Parents and Guardians*, a piece Boucicault claimed was his but which may only have been his reworking of the play by Tom Taylor. Agnes could have continued in these two pieces for many weeks, but in New York plays changed regularly, no matter how successful they might be, and her next role was as Cleopatra in Placide's burlesque *Antony and Cleopatra*. Playing Antony opposite her was an American actor, George Jordan, who was to feature prominently in their lives ten years later.

While his wife was enjoying her spectacular success at Burton's, Boucicault did not remain idle. He rewrote his 1847 play *The School for Scheming* as a three-acter, which was produced at Wallack's Theatre, the senior house on Broadway, on 7 November under the title *Love and Money*, and for Agnes wrote a new comedy, *The Fox Hunt*. Her appearance as Laura St Leger, when the play opened at Burton's on 23 November, guaranteed good houses, and although it was a poor work, it enjoyed a respectable run. Most of the critics were disappointed that the first Boucicault play to be written on American soil was not better, and the *New York Times* even accused him of stealing it in its entirety from a French play, *Sullivan*. Even though this may have been true (and that is by no means certain), Boucicault denied the allegation, maintaining that he had neither read nor seen the French play. The accusation of plagiarism was one that was to haunt him throughout his career.

Playmaking [he said, contemptuously dismissing his critics] is a trade like carpentering. Originality, speaking by the card, is a quality that never existed. An author cannot exist without progenitors any more than a child can. We are born of each other . . . I am an emperor and take what I think best for Art, whether it be a story from a book, a play from the French, an actor from a rival company . . . I despoil genius to make the mob worship it.[6]

The *New York Times* was not prepared to let Boucicault get away with a straight denial and set out, by comparing the two plays, to prove its case. Boucicault had admitted using the same basic idea in one of his scenes (an incident from the life of David Garrick), and the *New York Times* was on shaky ground, proving to its satisfaction, if no one else's, that it was right. Boucicault was furious and wrote an indignant letter to the editor, which ended with a challenge to take the two plays before an independent jury, the loser to pay 1,000 dollars to a charity. The *New York Times* huffily declined the challenge, remarking that a bet is 'the last argument of a baffled man'. Furthermore, the article declared, Boucicault was not a gentleman: 'Vituperation will only place Mr Boucicault on a lower level than the one he now occupies.' To be accused of not being a gentleman must have stung the playwright, but whatever his feelings may have been, he apologized for his language and the matter ended, in time for the *New York Times* to run an advertisement announcing Boucicault's forthcoming series of lectures at the Hope Chapel.

Many English literary figures, including his guardian, Dr Lardner, who was said to have made £40,000 from a tour of Cuba and the United States, had given rewarding and successful lecture tours in America, and Boucicault was convinced he could do the same, cashing in on his popularity as a playwright. In December, he booked the Hope Chapel on Broadway, a former church which had been converted into a lecture hall, in which Oliver Wendell Holmes had just given a series on English poets of the nineteenth century, and announced four 'literary soirées' in which he proposed to illuminate New Yorkers about literary life in Europe (illustrated by paintings of London and Paris), discourse on Woman, her rights and wrongs, recount the story of the stage, and conclude with an account of his own career entitled 'My Life'. The first lecture was moderately well attended (he had to compete with the tenth performance of his own play *The Fox Hunt*, starring his wife, as well as other attractions inside the Hope Chapel), and was quite successful. His other lectures were no better patronized, and he started to switch around subjects and dates in the hope of picking up bigger audiences. For his lecture on his life, the December snows kept New Yorkers at home and he found himself addressing his smallest audience of all. Boucicault, however, was on top form and was given a warm reception and hearty applause. These lectures may not have been the great success Boucicault was hoping, but they were certainly not a financial disaster and he tried again with his talk on 'European Society' at the Athenaeum Club on 30 December, and his lecture on 'Woman' at the Odeon the following night. It was clear, however, that he was not going to make a living from giving lectures, and he was thrown back on the talents of his wife as his only immediate source of income.

Agnes had been appearing in New York for three months with phenomenal success, and offers to present her elsewhere were mounting up. On her behalf, Boucicault accepted a two-week engagement in Boston, starting in January 1854. Some idea of the impact she made can be gathered from an account of her Boston appearance written three years later.[7]

The excitement caused by her performances spread throughout the city and environs; it gained the neighbouring villages, towns and cities, and special trains were run to bring thousands to witness this exquisite actress. The engagement was prolonged from two to four weeks, then to six, and subsequently to eight weeks. By this time the furore had become beyond all precedent. The tickets of admission were sold at a premium of five and six dollars each, and at her benefit, the last night of her engagement, the applicants for seats blocked up the access to the theatre and the street in front. The manager, Mr Moses Kimball, induced Miss Robertson to prolong her performances for the ninth week, and within four hours, such was the crowd that every seat in the theatre was bought up for the ensuing week. Such was the enthusiasm created by Miss Robertson amongst the ladies of Boston, that her promenades through the streets were beset with crowds who followed her from place to place. The corridors of the Tremont House, where she resided, were blocked up with fair admirers who fairly invaded her apartments.

'Except Jenny Lind,' Agnes was to recall later, 'no woman was ever received in America as I was. The papers called me the "Fairy Star"; managers looked upon me as the mascot of their enterprises.'[8] As well they might. Her nine-week season at the Boston Museum netted Moses Kimball in the region of $20,000.

For her appearance in Boston, Boucicault had turned out another new play designed to show her off to advantage, *Andy Blake*. Adapted from the French, it opened on 1 March with Agnes in the title role, a part that was very similar to her successful and still popular Bob Nettles in *To Parents and Guardians*. Again her acting was a delight. 'Her performance of the Irish boy was a beautiful creation, and drew from her audience tears and smiles of sympathy.'

In Boston, Boucicault again gave his series of lectures, but with little more success than in New York. Those who heard him were of the opinion that they had listened to an entertaining though not profound speaker. Most of his time, however, was spent in preparing new pieces to add to his wife's repertoire and arranging a tour for her, from which he hoped to make between $400 and $1,000 a week. From Boston, they travelled to Washington, where Agnes played to capacity houses for two weeks, and then to Philadelphia, where she appeared at the Chestnut Street Theatre in a new Boucicault pot-boiler, *The Devil's In It*, a comic drama in two acts. After a month in Philadelphia, it was off on the road again to Baltimore, to Chicago, to Rochester, to Buffalo (where another new piece, *Janet Pride*, was added to the repertoire), and back to Chicago. By September they had returned to Boston. Perhaps slightly peeved that his wife's success was eclipsing his as a dramatist (for he was astute enough to know that audiences were packing the houses to see Agnes, not his plays), Boucicault decided to return to the stage himself and made his American début as an actor in Boston on 22 September 1854, playing Sir Patrick O'Plenipo in a farce (not by him) called *The Irish Artist*. He continued to appear throughout the remainder of the Boston engagement, and when he and Agnes finally returned to New York for a short season at the Broadway Theatre, he made his New York début on 10 November. The role he chose was Sir Charles Coldstream in his play *Used Up* (the part Mathews had scored such a success with at the Haymarket), the play he had intended to make his Boston début in but, for some reason, probably illness, hadn't done so. His acting produced

> a favourable impression on the audience, who cheered him repeatedly. At the conclusion of the play, Mr Boucicault, in obedience to a very general call, stepped before the curtain and addressed the audience. He apologized for ill health; thanked them for their kind reception; disclaimed any idea of being an actor; thought they would have a natural curiosity to see an author in his own work, (*Used Up*) and so made his appearance before them. The evening passed off with much congeniality.[9]

He may have told the audience he had no thoughts of being an actor, but he had been bitten by the acting bug again, and from then on, he and Agnes were constantly to appear together, his popularity, especially as a light comedian, coming close to rivalling hers.

For the Broadway engagement, Boucicault had prepared another new piece, and on 6 November Agnes had appeared in the comic sketch which was to give her her popular soubriquet, *The Fairy Star*. In it she sang, danced and interpreted five characters, again delighting audiences with her ability. The engagement finished on 18 November, and they entrained for Philadelphia where, two days later, they opened at the Walnut Street Theatre, with Agnes playing in *The Young Actress*. On 27 November, Philadelphians were able to see the try-out of the latest Boucicault play starring his wife, *Apollo in New York*. 'A good humoured but sharp piece of local satire,' commented a critic when the play (without Agnes) opened in New York in December. 'The localization . . . is clever, and considering the short time Mr Boucicault has been in the country, displays much observation.'[10]

The year 1855 found the Boucicaults still on the road, visiting Mobile, Alabama, at the start of January, and then New Orleans for a short engagement at the Pelican Theatre, where Agnes appeared in another offering designed to cash in on her popularity, *Agnes Robertson At Home*. For some time, Agnes had known that she was pregnant but she could not afford to give up work until the last moment. On 10 May, in New Orleans, the Boucicaults' first child was born. A son, he was named Dion, after his father, and William, after Boucicault's brother. There was to be little respite for Agnes, for within a month of young Dion's birth they had all moved to Philadelphia and she was back on stage, acting in her husband's plays and a new piece, *There's Nothing In It*. After a short rest in New York, they journeyed to Cincinnati for the première of *Grimaldi; or, Scenes in the Life of an Actress*, in which Boucicault played Grimaldi and Agnes, Violet. Supposedly founded upon incidents in the life of Rachel, the famous French actress Boucicault had seen in Paris, it was, in fact, an adaptation. It was to remain a popular piece in their repertoire for many years. They took it with them when they moved on to the National Theatre, Washington, where Agnes appeared in yet another Boucicault adaptation, *The Cat Changed into a Woman*. The new play for the St Louis engagement which followed was *Rachel is Coming*, with Agnes again playing a number of roles.

For nearly two years, the Boucicaults had been on the road, playing to packed, enthusiastic houses everywhere and making small fortunes for theatre managers. Neither of them had stopped working. Now that they had a small son, the time had come, Boucicault decided, to put down some roots, to give up the constant travel and living out of suitcases, and, more important, to put more of the money they had been making at the box office into their own hands by becoming their own management. Boucicault planned to use their savings to hire a theatre and put on their extensive repertoire (which was almost entirely written by him) with themselves as the stars supported by an inexpensive company of unknowns (who would not cost as much as famous names), so putting into their pockets the receipts that had been going to line other people's. The town he selected for this venture was New Orleans, and he and his family moved there in November. New Orleans was a popular winter resort, busier during the Christmas period than at any other time of year, and Boucicault was hoping for big things. He procured the lease of the Varieties Theatre, renamed it the Gaiety, and announced that it would open on 28 November.

Boucicault wanted the Gaiety to become the talk of the theatrical world, and he was determined that its standards should be the highest. He personally supervised the productions being prepared for the opening. This was a task usually left to the stage manager, a senior member of the company, whose job was rather to make sure the actors got on and off the stage at the right moment than give them any clues as to interpretation or the overall approach to a play. A character's motivation was left entirely to the artist. Some stars gave performances which did not vary by so much as the inflection of a single line throughout their careers, and supporting players were always expected to adjust their performances to the star's demands. With the constant changes of bill demanded by theatregoers, this system had its advantages, for it meant that once an actor had learnt a role he could walk into any theatre anywhere and go on with the minimum of rehearsal. One of Boucicault's major contributions to the theatre was that he was instrumental in putting an end to this custom. He was the first writer to insist on being consulted about the staging of his plays, and because of his dominating personality and determination to see everything was done the way he wanted, it was not long before he was directing plays in all but name. And once one man was imposing his ideas on the play, the nature of that play began to change, and broad farce and spectacular melodrama gave way to a drama that concentrated on human beings and their interaction. Unwittingly, the man who was the greatest of all melodramatists paved the way for his own downfall by opening up the way for men like Ibsen, Strindberg and Synge.

Boucicault was a strict disciplinarian when taking rehearsals, working hard to get the results he wanted. J. B. Howe, a member of one of his companies, recalled how stern he was with Agnes when she wouldn't do a bit of business correctly.

On the morning of the rehearsal of *The Life of an Actress*, Miss Agnes Robertson failed to do a little bit of business of kneeling and falling at the feet of the gentleman who played the heavy part, and Dion asked her to do it again. Agnes did it again, but in the same manner as before. 'No, no; that won't do,' said Dion. 'Can't you rise slowly from your chair, giving the audience the idea that you are still under the influence of the narcotic? Grasp the corner of the table so, and, as if fearing to fall you still retain your hold on the table until your left knee touches the ground; then is the time to seize Mr Ralston's right hand with your left, so, and you turn gently round and fall in the centre at his feet.'

'I know that, Dion dear, but is there any necessity for me to do all that now? I've played the part before.'

'I know that, but not with the present members. I want *them* to see what you are going to do; go back, please. Please, Mr Ralston, once more, to oblige Mrs Boucicault. Now, if you please.' But the sweet little creature did not please. She burst into tears, and Dion exclaimed, 'Never mind, ladies and gentlemen; dismiss the rehearsal.' That was all; we dispersed, and need I say, in the most elegant confusion.[11]

The Gaiety Theatre, New Orleans, opened its doors to the public on 1 December, four days later than advertised, possibly because Boucicault had been ill; there were some newspaper reports that he was seriously ill, which became so exaggerated that his death was actually announced, giving Boucicault a rare opportunity to read his own obituaries. These spoke very highly of him and regretted his untimely demise.[12] It was a very surprised public that learned that the supposedly dead dramatist had not only written and produced a new play, *The Chameleon* (a musical interlude in one act), but had starred in it with his wife on 20 December!

The season was not nearly as well patronized as Boucicault had hoped it would be, and when he heard of the success the Keller Troupe was enjoying in Havana, he immediately signed them up to appear at the Gaiety. The twenty-strong troupe, under M. Louis Keller, were not actors: their forte was the posing of living pictures, and while they presented their spectacular tableaux – 'The Birth of the Flowers', 'The Battle of the Amazons', and a living representation of Rubens' paintings of 'The Crucifixion' – to packed and incredulous houses, Boucicault rehearsed his next production, *Azael; or, The Prodigal Son*, a play written previously for Charles Kean but never produced.[13] Being a biblical drama, set in Egypt and Israel, there was no part in it for John Owens, the comedian of the company. Boucicault had no wish to write one in especially, but neither did he wish to have the highest-paid member of his company (after himself and Agnes) drawing a salary for doing nothing. He solved his problem, in a most untypical lapse of taste, by having Owens go out after the final curtain and sing 'Villikins and his Dinah'.[14]

In spite of the care and attention which Boucicault had given to its staging, with clever groupings and superb tableaux arranged by Louis Keller, and the high standard of the acting, *Azael* was not a success. The out-of-town visitors on whom he was relying for his audiences didn't understand the play. After the curtain fell on one of the most impressive scenes, the Temple of Memphis, a visiting group were heard discussing it. It was, they all agreed, quite inaccurate: people in Memphis just didn't dress like the characters on stage and Memphis didn't possess a temple; they knew, they'd been there – to Memphis, Tennessee. *Azael* had to be withdrawn and Boucicault reverted to their standard, familiar repertoire to try and save the season. He tried one more new piece, *Una*, on 10 February 1856, but audiences had had enough of spectacle (it was another biblical drama) and stayed away.

His three months in New Orleans had failed to establish the Gaiety as either a gold mine or one of America's leading theatres, so Boucicault decided to pull out. He wasn't a man to sit around and wait for results. If a play was a failure, he wrote another; if a venture failed, he moved on to the next. The Gaiety had used up most of the money he and Agnes had saved during their two years of touring and it was time to look for something else. He sold the theatre and, on 8 March, the Boucicault family started to make their way back to New York, stopping off to make appearances (and make some money) in Charleston, Richmond, Washington and Philadelphia, where they began a short season at the National on 1 May. As a new offering to the citizens of Philadelphia, Boucicault gave them *Violet* and *The Phantom*. *Violet* was none other than *Grimaldi*, which had first been seen in Cincinnati the year before, and *The Phantom* was his London success of 1852, *The Vampire*, shortened to two acts. Retitling and revising was a common Boucicault trick. By skilfully ringing the changes and perhaps doing a small amount of rewriting, he could more than double the life of a play. Each new town thought it was seeing a new piece, and even a failure, with a new name and a few alterations, could be given another try out and a second lease of life. Only much later did the critics wake up to what he was doing and, to the charges of plagiarism from the French, add the charge of plagiarism from himself.

The Philadelphia engagement closed on the 17th, and two days later they were back in New York to open a short season of their most popular repertoire, giving *The Chameleon* and *Violet* their first New York performances. New York was pleased to see them, and for the summer season, beginning on 1 July, they were signed up to appear at Wallack's, performing almost exclusively in Boucicault's pieces. While they were there a significant event, upon which Boucicault had had some bearing, took place in Washington: on 18 August, Congress passed an amendment to the 1831 Copyright Act.

Boucicault's experiences in dealing with managers, his observation of the French system of royalties (which he had tried unsuccessfully to persuade English dramatists to adopt in the late 1840s), and his discovery when he reached America that playwrights did not print their plays for fear of having them pirated, had convinced him that something must be done as a matter of extreme urgency. Although he had become a manager, he had been producing almost entirely his own plays; it was when it came to negotiating with other managers, who were still producing his plays regularly, that he wanted a stronger hand. 'While managers and star actors were reaping a golden harvest by means of the dramatic works furnished by the phalanx of dramatists,' he wrote, 'the authors received a miserable pittance of thirty dollars a week for the use of such plays as *Richelieu*, *The Rent Day* and *London*

Assurance.'[15] And that was if they were lucky. Many managers simply refused to pay the writer anything if they were putting on a play that had been around for some time. It was this exploitation that Boucicault wanted to end. If he was to achieve his desired aim of raising the status, and financial position, of the playwright, he first had to obtain adequate safeguards for his work.

Boucicault was not the first writer to become involved with trying to change the law. Others before him had objected to the system and expressed dissatisfaction with the 1831 Act, and two, Robert Montgomery Bird and George Henry Boker, had been actively campaigning for a new Act. Bird, who had abandoned drama for novel writing after failing to get money owed him by actor Edwin Forrest, started, in a small way, to try and interest Congress in doing something about the plight of dramatists, but his efforts came to nothing. In 1853, Boker, who had also suffered from the injustices of the system and been forced to give up writing for the stage, tried again. On Bird's advice, he went to Washington to enlist support for a Dramatic Authors' Bill he had drafted, but he made little headway until he was joined by Boucicault in 1855.[16] Between them, they mounted such a campaign that in 1856 the amendment to the 1831 Act was carried. It gave to the author of a dramatic composition, for the first time, 'the sole right to print and publish the said composition, the sole right also to act, perform, or represent the same, or cause it to be acted, performed, or represented, on any stage or public place'. Any manager who pirated a play in future 'shall be liable for damages . . . such damages in all cases to be rated and assessed at such sum not less than one hundred dollars for the first, and fifty dollars for every subsequent performance'.

It was, in many ways, an imperfect amendment, for the title-page of a work had to be registered before publication or performance, and the script deposited within three months for the copyright to be effective. Since most pirated versions of a play were brought out within a few days of the original being performed, it was very difficult to prove infringement. Furthermore, the remedy for infringement provided by the Act was costly and unwieldy, and many playwrights simply couldn't be bothered to use it. Not so Boucicault. In November 1856, three months after Congress had passed the amendment, he became the first playwright to avail himself of it when he brought about the arrest of the manager of a Boston theatre, accused of stealing his play *Violet*. Throughout his career, Boucicault fought hard and long to establish the rights of the dramatist and was involved in frequent litigation. Looking back, it may seem that he was cruel and relentless, hounding even managers who had gone bankrupt and were in jail, for the sake of a few pounds and a principle. But it was a principle in which he believed passionately, for which someone had to fight, no matter how unpopular it might make him, before the theatrical conditions were established that would allow writers such as Ibsen, Pinero, Wilde and Shaw to flourish. Boucicault was that man.

The Boucicaults' summer season at Wallack's had been so successful that, when the autumn season opened, they had been retained with Boucicault as general manager. To their usual repertoire they added *Old Heads and Young Hearts* and *London Assurance*, in which Agnes played Grace and Boucicault played Dazzle, both for the first time, and so popular was it that it was retained on the bills for two weeks. Towards the end of October, they went to Boston for three weeks and then back to New York to appear at Burton's Theatre on 17 November in the first New York production of *Genevieve*, a play Webster had presented at the Adelphi in 1853. Ten days later, Agnes starred in another new play, a two-act fairy spectacle adapted from the French, *Blue Belle*. This was, according to one critic, 'displeasing, vulgar trash', and Boucicault was again accused of stealing a French play without acknowledgement. A French farce had, it was claimed, been 'Bourcicaulted', thereby coining an expression which was to be repeated frequently as a synonym for plagiarized.[17] Boucicault showed that, although he may have been instrumental in getting the copyright act through Congress, he was not averse to stealing someone else's work if he pleased, but it hardly seemed worth it: *Blue Belle,* in spite of some charming playing by Agnes, failed to please the audiences and had to be withdrawn.

New York was only a temporary resting place, for no sooner had they closed at Burton's than they were on their way to open in New Orleans at Christmas, and engagements in Charleston, Boston, St Louis, Chicago and Buffalo before, in early August 1857, returning to New York, where Boucicault had accepted to become the general director of the promenade concerts at the Academy of Music. An orchestra and chorus of 120 musicians took part under the direction of Robert Stoepel, Agnes sang solos, and according to a report in the *Era*, Boucicault himself took his turn on the podium with the baton. The public stayed away. By the beginning of September, the Choral Opera, as it was called, had been abandoned, and legitimate opera, with which Boucicault had nothing to do, was again the academy's main attraction. What may well have been the first matinée performances in America took place while Boucicault was at the academy, when on 15 August he announced an afternoon concert for three o'clock.[18]

Not for the first time in his life, Boucicault found himself desperately short of money. Although he had been turning out new pieces regularly, none had made any appreciable impact at the box office, and without Agnes starring in them, it is doubtful if any of them would have done as well as they did do. He had had enough of the endless round of packing and unpacking, living in hotels and waiting at railway stations. He wanted to be in New York. Agnes was again pregnant, and since they had lost all their capital in the New Orleans venture, they had to keep working. On 3 September, they opened at Wallack's, playing Dazzle and Grace in *London Assurance*, the one play Boucicault knew would guarantee a full house, and he also accepted a commission to rewrite a play especially for Matilda Heron, wife of Robert Stoepel. When his critics heard the news they laughingly remarked that there were the plays of one Mr Shakespeare he could turn to next, 'that very bad piece *Othello*, for instance. What a fine thing he might make of it, writing up worthy Montano for himself.'[19]

After only three nights in *London Assurance*, Agnes withdrew from the cast, and on 10 October, at the Boucicaults' apartment on East 15th Street, their second child, Eve, was born. With two children to support, in addition to his other expenses, what Boucicault needed was a smash hit. On 28 October, *The Invisible Husband* (a revision of *Giralda*) opened at Wallack's, but played to only moderate business, and although *Wanted A Widow*, a one-act farce written with journalist Charles Seymour, was greeted on 9 November as a 'good, jolly, funny farce, capitally acted, and completely successful', it failed to last more than a week. His financial situation was becoming embarrassing, and on 16 November an unusual benefit for him took place at the theatre.

> In consideration of the fact that for sixteen years *London Assurance*, *Old Heads and Young Hearts*, *The Irish Heiress*, and many other comedies, written by Mr Dion Boucicault, have been played without returning any remuneration whatever to the author, whose new comedy *The Invisible Husband*, is now drawing crowded houses, in a moment of depression elsewhere, the management beg to announce the performance on Monday, Nov. 16 for his benefit, when will be performed the first three acts of *London Assurance* . . . [20]

It would seem that the benefit was the idea of Wallack's manager, William Stuart. No other New York managers felt moved to follow his example.

The money raised by the evening helped Boucicault out of an immediate crisis but did nothing to alter the fact that he needed a real success. One evening he was discussing subjects for a play with his collaborator on *Wanted A Widow*, Charles Seymour (editor of the *Daily Times*), and two other journalists, Goodrich and Warden. They proffered the idea of something based on a financial panic that had recently hit New York. Boucicault knew the ideal French play on which to base such a story, and they began to write it together, Boucicault doing the bulk of the work, Seymour, Goodrich and Warden chipping in with advice. Within seventeen days *The Poor of New York* was finished, in the theatre and ready to open on 8 December. It was advertised as being 'by the *** Club', and it was not until the thirty-seventh performance that it was discovered who the collaborators were. And then the accusations of plagiarism were hurled at Boucicault. He was described as 'the author of *London Assurance* and 3,647 other original and successful pieces'.[21] But much as the critics might rail at him, the public did not share their contemptuous attitude. They judged his work on its appeal; and *The Poor of New York* was voted a unanimous hit.

The story was a simple, melodramatic tale of love, unhappiness and treachery, with the obligatory happy ending, which was used in countless imitations and less dramatic versions taken from the same French source Boucicault had used. What made his play so different and such a success was the scene in the last act when the house where Badger, the repentant villain, lived, was set on fire, a real fire engine arrived on stage, the fire was extinguished and Badger emerged from the smoking ruins clutching the document that will convict the guilty banker. The scene created the sensation it was supposed to, providing a spectacle that was considered to be well worth the price of admission. Although the play is a very good example of effective melodrama, it was to see that scene as much as the rest of the play that the crowds flocked to Wallack's.

Boucicault had worked out how the effects of the sensation scene were to be achieved very carefully.

The house is painted on three separate pieces, the top one of which is swung from the flies; this constitutes the roof. Upon the second is painted half the wall, and it is joined to the bottom piece in an irregular zig-zag line. The simple dropping in succession of these pieces to the stage produces the falling of the roof and wall. The fire itself is represented by chemical red fire and powdered lycopodium used separately, the former to give a red glow and the latter to represent flames. The shutters, which are to fall, are fastened to the scene with a preparation called 'quick-match'. This is made of powder (possibly gunpowder,) alcohol, and a lamp wick. The window frame and sashes are made of sheet iron. They are covered in oakum soaked in alcohol or naphtha. These sashes and frames are not fastened to the scene at all, but are placed a short distance behind it upon platforms. The quickest possible touch of flame ignites the oakum, and, in a moment, the fire runs round the sash, and nothing is

95

apparently left but the blackened and charred wood. Steam is used to represent the smoke that issues from crannies in the walls of the burning building; and an occasional crash, followed by the ignition of a little powder to produce a sudden puff of smoke, gives the spectator an idea of a falling rafter. Behind the entire scene is placed a very large endless towel upon which is painted a mass of flames. This is kept in constant upward motion; and, when viewed through an open window of the house, gives a good idea of the raging furnace within. Add to these things a real fire engine on the stage, a host of yelling supernumeries in discarded firemen's uniforms, and the spectator is easily filled with a sense of tremendous danger. Nevertheless the only flames upon the stage are those arising from the burning lycopodium in a 'flash torch,' and they are only allowed to blaze up for a second or two at a time.[22]

The Poor of New York was to be an important work for its author, and there can be no doubt that in spite of the help given by Seymour, Goodrich and Warden, the lion's share of the writing was Boucicault's. The play was copyrighted under his name alone, and whenever it was produced after its initial run, Boucicault was the only writer to be given a credit, a situation the others would not have allowed had it not been true. For some time prior to The Poor, he had been churning out slight pieces designed basically to show off his wife's talents. He needed a challenge, a stimulus, to provoke him into writing something better. The Poor of New York showed him the direction in which he had to go. For the first time he had written a play based on contemporary events, and it had caught a mood he had not previously suspected to exist. He was never a profound or very original thinker, but he did have a journalist's ability to catch the mood and manners of his time with a deftness and wit few of his contemporaries could match. The play also contained the one magnificent sensation scene. From the response of the public it was clear to him that contemporary events and sensation were the two ingredients he must, in future, exploit.

6

CREATING A
SENSATION

BOUCICAULT WAS still convinced that the only way he would ever make the sort of money, and have the artistic freedom, he wanted was to be his own master. Undeterred by his failure with the Gaiety in New Orleans, he had entered into negotiations for the lease of Carusi's, a converted dance hall, in Washington, in partnership with William Stuart, the man who had been responsible for organizing the November benefit of *London Assurance* for him at Wallack's. Stuart was to have charge of the administration while Boucicault took care of artistic policy and stage direction.

Boucicault and Agnes were to be the stars of the new season but when the theatre, renamed the Washington, opened on 6 January 1858, it was with vaudeville and ballet. There had been many delays in getting the theatre ready on time, and even after the opening there were still alterations and finishing touches being made to the interior, Boucicault himself helping with putting up the lace curtains in the private boxes. There were also problems with the company. Boucicault had engaged artists from New York and Boston, and some of them failed to arrive on time, while on top of that, Agnes was ill. She did not make her first appearance until the 18th. According to J. B. Howe, a member of the company, the appearance of the two stars had guaranteed a sell-out, but the venture didn't last beyond the end of the month because of disagreement between Boucicault and Stuart. As Frederick Chatterton, another manager with whom Boucicault had violent rows, once remarked, everyone rowed with the playright if only they knew him long enough. The cause was money. According to some reports, the first four weeks of the Washington season took $11,000, of which Stuart was entitled to half. He received only $2,000. Boucicault, of course, claimed that it was Stuart who was withholding money from him, not the other way round. Four weeks after the Washington Theatre had opened its doors, the Boucicaults had packed their bags and were on their way to Baltimore for Agnes to make an appearance on Monday, 8 February, and New York, ready to begin rehearsals at Wallack's for Boucicault's new play, *Jessie Brown; or, The Relief of Lucknow*.

Following the success of *The Poor of New York* (which had only just finished at Wallack's), Boucicault had decided to look for other contemporary events to dramatize, and he found what he wanted in newspaper reports of the Sepoy rebellion that had occurred in India the previous September. The horror of the massacre at Cawnpore and stories of the heroism displayed at Lucknow were still fresh in the public's mind, and in the courageous figure of Jessie Brown, the young Scots girl who kept up the spirits of the besieged Europeans by claiming she could hear the pipes of a Scottish regiment coming to rescue them, he knew he had found the character and the drama to excite and move audiences.

Jessie Brown opened at Wallack's Theatre on 22 February with Agnes playing Jessie and Boucicault taking the part of Nana Sahib, to become the hit of the season. Like *The Poor of New York*, it had no pretensions to being a literary composition, but it achieved exactly what it set out to do — entertain. The fighting, the shooting, the flag-waving patriotism and the stirring last-act rescue of the besieged garrison by the Campbell Highlanders, pipes skirling, put together in the most skilful way, all produced the desired effect: a rapturous, delighted audience. The great puzzle for the critics was where Boucicault had found his source play, for they knew of no

French work like it. Some said it was based on a similar play then running in London (but omitted to note that Boucicault could not possibly have read or seen it), others contented themselves with insulting the author and dismissing his work. 'Of true poetic heart, soul and feelings, he does not, to our thinking – nor are we alone – possess a single grain; but what of that – the public are none the wiser, for whilst true genius starves, bunkum feasts in purple and fine linen.'[1] Advertisements for the play claimed it to be 'by the only author now living, of the English drama, whose works have withstood that truest and greatest of all critics – Time'. Since those words were written by that author himself, it was small wonder that mere mortal critics should seek to wound such vanity. Their harsh opinions and contemptuous comments made no difference at the box office, however, and *Jessie Brown* ran for six weeks.

The part of the villainous Sepoy Nana Sahib had caused some difficulties during casting for none of the resident company at Wallack's would accept it. News had reached New York that the actor playing a similar role in the version then on in London (the play Boucicault was falsely accused of stealing) was showered with missiles every time he set foot on stage, and not just orange peel and rotten fruit; bottles, sticks, hats and even umbrellas were being thrown. Boucicault, who enjoyed a good fight, was the only person who would take the part, and he delighted in walking to the footlights and, by his very presence, defying the audience to throw something. They never did.

The New York run finished only because the Boucicaults had an engagement in Boston which they couldn't put off any longer. They opened on 6 April at the Boston Theater in, naturally enough, their latest success *Jessie Brown*, but failed to take the city by storm. Boucicault was ill for much of the time and unable to appear, and after only two weeks *Jessie* had to be withdrawn, to be replaced by plays in which Agnes could star on her own. At the end of the month, when Boucicault had recovered, they moved on to Philadelphia where *Jessie Brown* was much more favourably received and played for four weeks.

On 25 May, Boucicault's latest play, again based on contemporary incidents, opened at Wallack's. *Brigham Young; or, The Revolt of the Harem,* was a pot-boiler about the founder of the Mormon Church, written with the assistance of his newspaper friends. It's highly unlikely that Boucicault had then travelled as far west as Salt Lake City, but the story of Brigham Young was well known and seemed a good subject for drama. The idea and probably the storyline were Boucicault's, but most of the dialogue and the characterization were not, and it is surprising that Boucicault, who had always been so careful to keep his name off hack work, should have allowed himself to be publicly associated with the project. The play had been beaten on to the New York stage by another account of Young's life (which had been written, rehearsed and produced at Burton's after the first announcement that Boucicault was working on his play), and since his version offered no insights into the man or his beliefs, and was in every respect an inferior work, it quickly disappeared.

The success of *Jessie Brown* did not stop Boucicault writing, and two more of his melodramas appeared in New York during 1858. On 7 September, at Niblo's Garden, Boucicault and Agnes began an autumn season with *Jessie*, which was still drawing large crowds. On 2 October the theatre closed for the dress rehearsal of his latest play, *Pauvrette*, which opened two days later with him and his wife in the leading roles. It was a spectacular drama, adapted from the French with all Boucicault's skill and cunning as a playwright. It is not a translation but a much cleverer rewrite, with some well-written dialogue, some well-maintained suspense and some stunning sensations. An idea of the effectiveness of the staging can be gained from the directions for one of the scenes:

Large blocks of hardened snow and masses of rock fall, rolling into the abyss . . . The avalanche begins to fall – the bridge is broken and hurled into the abyss – the paths have been filled with snow and now an immense sheet, rushing down from the Right entirely buries the whole scene to the height of twelve or fifteen feet, swallowing up the cabin and leaving a clear level of snow – the storm passes away

– silence and peace return – the figure of the Virgin is unharmed – the light before it still burns.

In spite of a trite plot and its sentimentality, *Pauvrette* proved to be very popular, much to the annoyance of those critics who found it hard to accept that four of his plays – *London Assurance*, *The Poor of New York*, *Jessie Brown*, and now *Pauvrette* – had all been successfully produced within the space of a few short months, with his name as large on the playbills as the title of the play. 'Of these four pieces he is not the bona fide author of one,' whined a critic. 'He, probably, had as much as any one else to do with the manufacture of *London Assurance*, but it is well known that, in the process of its construction, other brains were liberally mixed in with his . . . But to the paternity of the other three he has about an equal title as your bootblack to call himself your shoemaker.'[2] Criticism such as this misses the essential nature of Boucicault's craft. Certainly he took, stole, adapted or translated the majority (though by no means all) of the works that appeared on the stage under his name, but in so doing he invariably improved the original. He possessed such a high degree of understanding of stagecraft that he was able to alter everything he took to make it better. 'Like Shakespeare and Molière,' said Charles Reade, the author with whom Boucicault was to collaborate on a novel, 'the beggar steals everything he can lay his hands on; but he does so so deftly, so cleverly, that I can't help condoning the theft. He picks up a pebble by the shore, and polishes it into a jewel. Occasionally too he writes divine lines and knows more about the grammar of the stage than all the rest of them put together.'[3] 'If he steals satin,' observed the actor Joseph Jefferson, 'he embroiders it with silk.'[4]

Three weeks after the opening of *Pauvrette*, Boucicault and Agnes appeared in yet another new play, *The Pope of Rome*. This was not simply taken from a French source but was an adaptation of an earlier Boucicault adaptation, *Sixtus V*, which had first been seen at the Olympic in London seven years earlier. The critics were not too put out, however, for the play lasted only five nights and had to be replaced by the ever-popular *Jessie Brown,* which proved to be such a successful substitution that their engagement, due to end on 19 September, was extended for another month, proving once again that the Boucicaults were among the most popular performers on the American stage.

His financial difficulties of the previous year forgotten in the success of both his acting and his most recent dramas, Boucicault's thoughts turned again towards management. Whatever problems there may have been between him and William Stuart in Washington, the two men were sufficiently reconciled by the beginning of 1859 for them to enter partnership again to run a theatre in New York. Boucicault announced that he had started negotiations for the site of the old Union Square Theatre, on which he proposed building a magnificent new iron theatre (to reduce the risk of fire) that would incorporate many novel features of his own design. The plan was soon abandoned when he realized how long it would take to build the place and get it working, so instead he took out a lease on the Metropolitan, a vast mausoleum of a building which had never been successful, and set about rebuilding it. During the four months it took to get the theatre ready for the public, the Boucicaults gave up touring. Boucicault wanted to be on hand to supervise the alterations personally and also to spend the summer preparing his new stock of plays ready for the autumn opening. And in May there had been another addition to the family. Darley George, their third child and second son, had been born in New York on the 23rd. Dot, as he was always known, was to follow his parents on to the stage and later became an important and influential director in both Australia and England, being the first man in Britain ever to be employed on a production in the sole capacity of director.

Boucicault's new theatre opened on 14 September. Renamed the Winter Garden (after the Paris theatre where amusements were presented in a kind of conservatory filled with tropical plants), it was supposed to provide patrons with a place where they could go for a complete evening out, with restaurants, bars, covered walks and a play – a forerunner of the present-day civic theatre. Boucicault, however, did not have sufficient money to carry out all his plans, as Joseph Jefferson, a member of the company for the opening season, recalled:

> If I remember rightly [he wrote in his autobiography], the treasury of the management was not in what could be called an over-flowing condition; and although the actors whom they engaged were quite strong, the horticultural display was comparatively weak. Some sharp pointed tropical plants of an inhospitable and sticky character exuded their 'medicinal gums' in the vestibule, and the dress circle was festooned with artificial flowers so rare that they must have been unknown to the science of botany. To give these delicate exotics a sweet and natural odour they were plentifully sprinkled with some perfume resembling closely the sweet scent of hair-oil, so that the audience as they were entering could 'nose' them in the lobby. Take it altogether, the theatre was a failure; for, added to the meagre decorations, the acoustics were inferior, and the views of the stage from the auditorium unpardonably bad.[5]

Boucicault had managed to overcome the vastness of the building by decreasing the seating capacity, but this meant that even if every seat was sold for every performance, the receipts at the box office could never be enough to cover running expenses. However irritated the perfectionist playwright may have been by such drawbacks, he was too deeply committed to the venture to back out. There were, of course, the usual delays caused by builders.

> It is impossible for you to open as you desire on the first of September [Boucicault wrote in exasperation on 29 August]. The work has been pressed forward with all the despatch we could use but the roof of the Theatre has been in an unfinished State and is so still. Last Saturday the rain entering through the openings left unprotected spoiled two sets of new scenery all of which have to be repainted. It has drenched our decoration in part but this latter is not so great an impediment . . . I cannot accept any blame in the postponement.[6]

The Winter Garden, the 'Conservatory of the Arts
. . . Dedicated to the Culture of Comedy, Music and Ballet',
duly opened in mid September with *Dot*, Boucicault's dramatization of Charles Dickens's novel, *The Cricket on the Hearth*.
The story had been dramatized many times before
(Boucicault said he had based his version on a play, not on the
novel, which he claimed never to have read), but that did not
deter New Yorkers from thronging to the theatre to see a very
strong company led by Agnes as Dot and Joseph Jefferson as
Caleb Plummer, his first straight role. Jefferson had first met
the Boucicaults in 1854 when he was stage manager of the
theatre in Richmond, Virginia, and they were the visiting
stars. In the intervening five years, he had established himself
as one of America's leading light comedians, and was appearing in New York, at Laura Keene's Theatre, when William
Stuart approached him to join the Winter Garden company at
a greatly increased salary. He was disturbed to find that the
first role they wanted him to play was Caleb Plummer, and
went to see Boucicault.

> I told him I was rather apprehensive of my hitting the
> part . . . as I had never acted a character requiring pathos,
> and, with the exception of the love scene in *Our American
> Cousin,* as yet had not spoken a serious line upon the stage.
> He seemed to have more confidence in my powers than I
> had, and insisted that I could act the part with success. I
> agreed therefore to open in Caleb, with the understanding
> that I should finish the performance with a farce, so that in
> the event of my failing in the first piece, I might save my
> reputation in the last. He assented to the arrangement, but
> warned me, however, that I would regret it; and he was
> right, for when the curtain fell upon *Dot*, I should have
> much preferred not to have acted in the farce. So the little
> piece was taken off after the first night, and I was quite
> satisfied with Caleb alone.[7]

Part of the genius of Boucicault as a man of the theatre was
his ability to spot and nurture talent, and among the many
distinguished players who acknowledged a debt to him in

their early careers were Jefferson, Henry Irving, Maurice Barrymore, Squire Bancroft, Harry Montague and Helena Modjeska. Much of Jefferson's success as Caleb Plummer was due, the actor admitted, to the dramatist.

Mr Boucicault, I think, understood me and felt from what I had said to him on previous occasions that I was not averse to suggestions in the dramatic art, and was in the habit of listening to advice, though I always reserved to myself the right of acting on my own judgement as to whether the profered counsel was good or bad. During my rehearsal of the first scene, which I went through just as I intended acting it on the night, I saw by his manner that he was disappointed with my rendering of the part, and I asked him what was the matter. He replied, 'If that is the way you intend to act the part I do not wonder you were afraid to undertake it.' This was a crushing blow to a young man from one older in years and experience; but feeling that there was something to learn, I asked him to explain what he meant. 'Why, you have acted your last scene first; if you begin in that solemn strain you have nothing left for the end of the play.' This was his remark, or words to the same effect; and I am certainly indebted to him, through his advice, for whatever success I achieved in the part.[8]

As well as being able to spot talent, Boucicault had the ability to be able to put his finger immediately on what was wrong with a scene or why it wasn't working as it should, and he was no respecter of person or sensibilities in getting what he wanted. He reduced one actress, who had walked through the spot where a table would be standing on the night, to tears for being so stupid, and then admonished her with a cutting, 'don't run about like a hen with its head cut off!'[9] But he was always prepared to listen to advice, a trait he often carried to excess by changing his mind overnight. When Maurice Barrymore acted some business exactly the way Boucicault had directed him, the playwright accused him of being little better than a schoolboy. Barrymore pointed out that the interpretation was Boucicault's own. 'Yesterday, certainly my boy, I told you to do it that way,' Boucicault replied, 'but the world is just twenty-four hours older, and we have advanced that much, so do it this way today.'[10]

Thanks to Jefferson as Caleb, Agnes as Dot (a performance 'distinguished by . . . delicate artistic perception and polished execution') and some good supporting playing, *Dot* played to good business for four weeks and set the standard for the rest of the season. On 19 October it was replaced by a triple bill that included a new Boucicault piece, *Chamooni III*, a musical, fantastic, historical piece of extravagance, which starred Agnes as Jamaica Gravesend, a sewing-machine operator from New York, and Jefferson as Yonkers. 'All mortals make mistakes,' wrote one critic. 'The managers of theatres are mortals, hence the managers of theatres sometimes make mistakes. This lamentable syllogism has a present application to the directors of the Winter Garden, who, on Wednesday night produced for the first time an extravagance called *Chamooni III*.'[11] Although Boucicault wrote his usual press releases, claiming the play to be an outstanding success, he was obliged to withdraw it after a week and substitute it with *Dot* while the company rehearsed his third new piece, *Smike*. Turning once more to Dickens for inspiration, Boucicault picked out scenes from *Nicholas Nickleby* (a version of which he had played in in Bristol during 1839), cast Agnes as Smike, Jefferson as Newman Noggs, and himself as Mantilini, and again produced a hit. *Smike* opened on 1 November and ran for four weeks.

For his next new play, *The Octoroon*, Boucicault returned to the vein he had started to mine so profitably with *The Poor of New York* and *Jessie Brown*: contemporary drama. In America at that time there was no topic more discussed or more likely to arouse passions than the issue of slavery. *The Octoroon*, set in Louisiana and dealing with current attitudes towards blacks and slavery, opened on 6 December and created a sensation. The portrayal of slavery on stage was not original – *Uncle Tom's Cabin* had been successfully dramatized – neither was much of the story, which Boucicault took from Mayne Reid's novel *The Quadroon*, but the setting and the mood were, and Boucicault again demonstrated his skill as an adaptor by producing a stunning entertainment that was, to all intents, an original play. Judged by modern standards, the attitudes of the play are superficial and little more than a good peg on which to hang a story of murder, treachery, love and sentiment, with two remarkable scenes of sensation and suspense: the firing of a Mississippi river boat, and the unmasking of the villain by means of a camera, the first time this device was used on stage. At the time, however, it was strong stuff, and, as one of the very first 'American' plays, it gives considerable insight into how the problems that produced the Civil War were being viewed.

Boucicault knew exactly what he was doing when he wrote the play, and he managed to keep a fine balance between antagonizing the South and alienating the North. He was also able to indulge in his penchant for publicity. The day before the play opened (four days after John Brown had been hanged, and not the same day as Boucicault later claimed), Agnes, who was playing Zoe, the girl with one eighth Negro blood (the octoroon of the title), received an anonymous letter saying that if she went ahead with the performance she would be shot.[12] In all probability the letter was written by her husband, but its mere existence enabled Boucicault to gain column inches of free publicity.

Rehearsals for *The Octoroon* were not without their incidents either. Jefferson, who was to play Salem Scudder, the loyal Yankee overseer, found out that his name did not feature in advertisements for the play and in a fit of pique sent his part back to the theatre, claiming the omission had cancelled his contract. Since this was on the Saturday before the Monday when the play was due to open, both Stuart and Boucicault hurried round to the actor's rooms straight away and were horrified to find him, stripped to the waist, sparring with an ex-fighter. Jefferson, having been knocked under the piano by his enthusiastic partner, had just delivered a stunning blow to the man's head when they appeared at the door. Boucicault, to whom the idea of physical violence was abhorrent, was relieved to find that Jefferson was not warming up in readiness for their arrival, but took boxing lessons to keep fit.[13] Their differences were soon sorted out and *The Octoroon* opened on schedule with Jefferson in his allotted role, a part for which he received unstinted praise.

The play, dealing as it did with slavery, was, wrote Jefferson,

produced at a dangerous time. The slightest allusion to this now-banished institution only served to inflame the country which was at a white heat. A drama told so well had a great effect on the audience, for there was at this time a divided feeling in New York with regard to the coming struggle. Some were in favour of war, others thought it best to delay, and, if possible, avert it; and it was deemed unwise, if not culpable, by many for us to act *The Octoroon* at such a time. Then there were various opinions as to which way the play leaned – whether it was Northern or Southern in its sympathy. The truth of the matter is, it was non-commital. The dialogue and characters of the play made one feel for the South, but the action proclaimed against slavery, and called loudly for its abolition. When the old negro, just before the slave sale, calls his coloured 'bredrin' around him and tells them they must look their best so as to bring a good price for the 'missis,' and then falling on his knees asks a blessing on the family who had been so kind to them, the language drew further sympathy for the loving hearts of the South; but when they felt by the action of the play that the old darky who had made them weep was a slave, they became abolitionists to a man. When Zoe, the loving octoroon, is offered to the highest bidder, and a warm-hearted Southern girl offers all her fortune to buy Zoe and release her from the threatened bondage awaiting her, the audience cheered for the South; but when again the action revealed that she could be bartered for, and was bought and sold, they cheered for the North as plainly as though they had said, 'Down with slavery.'[14]

Boucicault's own attitude towards slavery was that he was against it. He and Agnes employed a black nanny to look after their three children, and on their tours to the South, they had met many slave-owners and slaves. In a letter to *The Times*, written after the first London performance of *The Octoroon*, he explained his feelings.

A long residence in the Southern States of America had convinced me that the delineations in *Uncle Tom's Cabin* of the condition of the slaves, their lives, and feelings were not faithful. I found the slaves, as a race, a happy, gentle, kindly treated population, and the restraints upon their liberty so slight as to be rarely perceptible. A visitor to Louisiana who might expect to find his vulgar sympathies aroused by the exhibition of corporal punishment and physical torture, would be much disappointed. For my part, with every facility for observation, I never witnessed any ill-treatment whatever of the servile class; on the contrary, the slaves are in general warmly attached to their masters and to their homes, and this condition of things I have faithfully depicted. But behind all this there are features in slavery far more objectionable than any hitherto held up to human execration, by the side of which physical suffering appears as a vulgar detail.

As an Irishman, a member of a subjugated nation, Boucicault felt keenly the indignity of slavery, of one race being beholden to another. He was neither a political animal nor a reformer – he reacted to situations with his emotions and feelings – but he did try to do what little he could, as a writer of popular drama, to make his audiences aware of the true plight of the slave as he saw it, and there can be little doubt that in *The Octoroon* he tried his best, within the accepted dramatic conventions of his time, to portray the lot of the slave as being inhuman. It was, he felt, an honest picture, even if, to get the play on at all, he had had to show slavery in its best light. That he succeeded far better than he is often given credit for can be seen from the hostile reviews the play received from certain sections of the press.

The Winter Garden [wrote the critic of *The Spirit of the Times*], a very appropriate name for this dreary theatre, for there has never been a really green spot in its history – has been struggling, under the management of Dion Boucicault, all the season to sustain itself by the representation of Cockney plays. The legitimate attractions of the house, it seems, finally proved abortive, and as a last resource, Boucicault has taken advantage of the existing anti-Southern excitement, for it is no longer aimed at the slave, but at the citizens of the South, to bring out a play, which, for all practical purposes, is more pernicious than anything which has heretofore been conceived in the spirit of sectional hate . . . As false as the incidents of the play are in fact and sentiment, as a literary composition it is wretchedly bad, judged even by the low standard applied to all the modern trash of the Boucicault school.

Boucicault, the critic accused, was trying 'by false sympathy, to break down caste, and elevate the negro to the same level with the whites'. The auction scene, in which families were broken up by the bidding, was denounced as an outrage, as offensive and disgusting. As for Zoe herself,

the ignorant and degraded beings who are trafficked in by the South have none of the sentiments and feelings accorded to Zoe; in that country, if such a being as Zoe ever existed in person, her mind and the taint of her blood would create a gulf between her and the whites that would be wider than the poles assunder, and all the sympathy and sentiment the incendiary author of this piece creates is founded upon the false idea that there is an equality in the races, an idea that is preposterous, unnatural, and profane . . . We have no disposition to pursue this disgusting subject further; the fact is patent that the play is nightly greeted by a crowded audience, and the basest attack that has yet been made upon the South is likely not only to do its damaging work in poisoning the minds of our people, but will possess the additional sin of putting money in the pockets of the base creatures who have clubbed together their mercenary brains to produce this outrage.

It was clear from this, and similar reviews, that Boucicault had touched a raw nerve in a confused and undecided society. He may have been the inspiration, if not the architect, of much of the hostility that was directed towards him and the play (for he knew a good row in the press would be reflected at the box office and he wanted audiences more than he wanted critical acclaim), but he can hardly have been prepared for such vituperation.

The Octoroon might have made him the small fortune predicted by *The Spirit of the Times*, but it didn't. At the end of the first week, he and Agnes left the cast and walked out of the Winter Garden. For the second time he and Stuart had fallen out over money. It had become increasingly clear, ever since the theatre opened, that, although every play had been doing capacity business (with the exception of *Chamooni III*), they would never break even and Boucicault wanted to get out. For the first week of *The Octoroon*, Boucicault and Agnes had received a share of the receipts amounting to $1,363, and they wanted more. A row between Agnes and another actress in the company, Josephine Shaw, coupled with Stuart's refusal to increase their salaries, gave Boucicault the excuse he wanted to end the partnership. Much to his annoyance, *The Octoroon* continued at the Winter Garden without them. Stuart, having learnt from his previous dealings with the hot-tempered playwright, was not prepared to be bullied and, despite Boucicault's threats, refused to take it off. Boucicault straightway applied for an injunction to prevent Stuart continuing to present his play, but the court, reflecting public sympathy which was wholly on the side of Stuart (especially since it was widely rumoured that Boucicault had already signed to appear with Agnes at Laura Keene's rival theatre a few blocks away), turned him down, and *The Octoroon*, with Mrs John Allen playing Zoe and Harry Pearson playing Boucicault's role as the grunting Indian, ran at the Winter Garden until 12 February 1860.

7

THE COLLEEN BAWN

THE RUMOURS turned out to be true: while he and Agnes were appearing at the Winter Garden, Boucicault had been setting up a deal with Laura Keene for them to move to her theatre. It was quite a *coup* for the gifted young actress who had, in November 1856, become the first woman in America ever to manage a theatre. In 1858 she had enjoyed considerable success with Tom Taylor's *Our American Cousin*, but nothing she had presented in the current season had come anywhere near approaching it in popularity and she was looking to Boucicault to save her artistically and financially.

On 9 January 1860, one month after they had parted company with Stuart, Boucicault and Agnes made their first appearance at Laura Keene's in *Jeanie Deans*, Boucicault's adaptation of Scott's novel, *The Heart of Midlothian*. Whatever the public may have thought of the playwright's treatment of his former partner, it did not stop them going to see him as the Counsel for the Defence and Agnes as Jeanie. 'Long before the rising of the curtain, the theatre was crowded to excess'; and as the curtain fell Laura Keene knew her season had been saved. *Jeanie Deans* drew capacity houses for fifty-four nights, and was then replaced by *Vanity Fair*, a three-act comedy Boucicault had adapted from a French source 'to ridicule the weakness of many young men of the present day, who think it fine to affect vices they do not really possess, and who profess tastes for things which really disgust them, or exhibit coarse manners foreign to their feelings'.[1] In spite of its title, the play had nothing at all to do with Thackeray's novel. With Boucicault, Agnes and Laura Keene in the cast, the play was given a marvellous reception on opening night and looked good to end what, for Laura Keene, had suddenly become a triumphant season. After the first night, however, business began to drop off, and showed no sign of picking up, and within a few days it was obvious the play would have to come off if Laura Keene was not to lose everything she had made on the season and a lot more besides. The crisis was made worse by being so unexpected. Boucicault hadn't had a total failure for a long while, and so confident was Laura Keene of the play's success that she had prepared nothing to follow it. In desperation she turned to Boucicault for another play to put on in its place, but he had nothing except the outlines for dramatizations of *Little Dorrit* and *Bleak House*, neither of which were in a fit state to be useful. What happened then was recalled many years later by Agnes.

My husband and I were walking down Broadway one afternoon and we stopped to turn over some second-hand books. Turning over the pile, my husband picked out a little green volume, read the title: *The Collegians, or the Colleen Bawn*, and said to me: 'Would you care for this?' I said, 'No: I have read it before,' and he was tossing it back into the box when I said: 'Stay! buy it for me, I think I would like to read it again.' As I read it that evening, I said to my husband: 'Dion, I think you could get some good ideas for an Irish play from this. We have had a Scotch play, why not have an Irish play to follow it? I am sure you could write one if any man could.' He took the book from me, read it that night, and by noon the next day he had the *Colleen Bawn* as it now stands, mapped out in his head, and the opening scenes on paper. He wrote it in nine days, and we rehearsed it in bits, as the manuscript was ready.[2]

Boucicault's own recollection of the play's genesis is very similar, though it differs from Agnes's in some details.

It was a bitter night [he remembered], and the sleet driven by a northerly blast lashed the author's face as he turned up Broadway. A few doors from the theatre a dim light in a cellar showed that a thrifty little Italian, who sold cheap publications and small stationery, invited the belated pedestrian to buy a home-made cigar. His name was Brentano. Descending into the den, where he knew he should find the usual display of ten-cent literature, Boucicault asked for two novels, over which he intended to spend the hours of the night. Brentano pointed to a shelf where a scanty row of cheap novels represented his stock in trade; from these the visitor selected a dozen at hazard, and with the pockets of his overcoat stuffed he pushed his way through the sleet and the darkness to Union Square, near which he resided. The following morning Miss Keene received this letter: 'My dear Laura: I have it! I send you seven steel engravings of scenes around Killarney. Get your scene-painter to work on them at once. I also send a book of Irish melodies, with those marked I desire Baker to score for the orchestra. I shall read act one of my new Irish play on Friday; we rehearse that while I am writing the second, which will be got ready on Monday; and we rehearse the second while I am doing the third. We can get the play out within a fortnight.'[3]

There is little doubt that Boucicault completed *The Colleen Bawn*, one of his most successful and significant works, in a few days, or that the play was rehearsed piecemeal while the ink on the manuscript was barely dry, for it was produced at Laura Keene's only seventeen days after the first night of *Vanity Fair*. What is definitely romanticized in both Agnes's version and Boucicault's own account, is the time at which Boucicault read the novel, for he had been working on the idea of dramatizing it for some weeks before the failure of *Vanity Fair*. In the autumn of 1859, while he was busy at the Winter Garden, he had been approached by actor-manager Barney Williams for an Irish play to be ready for the autumn of 1860. Williams, an American of Irish extraction, and his wife, Maria Pray, had been touring the States for many years playing in Irish comedies. In 1855 they had gone to London, and when they returned to New York four years later, they wanted a new play to add to their repertoire. Who better to ask than the leading Irish dramatist of the age? While it is far less romantic than Boucicault's, Maria Pray's account of the writing of *The Colleen Bawn* is much more likely to be the true one.

The Boucicault trademark meant a great deal in those days and carried a star a long way [she told Townsend Walsh, Boucicault's first biographer]. Well, in January or February, we met Mr Boucicault who read us the first two acts. The play was *The Colleen Bawn* and we were both very much pleased with it . . . Imagine our indignation and surprise to find that *The Colleen Bawn*, which had been written for us according to contract, had been brought out at Laura Keene's! He was profuse in his apologies. He had been caught in a corner, so he said, and having nothing else up his sleeve had to give them the *Colleen Bawn*. He would write us another piece. But my husband said no. Mr Boucicault had broken faith with us and we didn't propose to give him another chance. There was a little bitter feeling, but when we came to think it over we agreed that we might have done the same thing if we had had the same temptation. We are all of us human, and Dion Boucicault was very human.[4]

Any obligation Boucicault might have felt towards Barney and Maria Williams was soon forgotten in the success of the play when it opened on 29 March with Agnes playing Eily O'Connor (the Colleen Bawn, or fair-haired girl), Laura Keene playing Anne Chute, and Boucicault playing Myles-na-Coppaleen, a role in which he was to become world famous. *The Colleen Bawn* was Boucicault's seventh play in as many months, and for six weeks until the end of the season on 12 May, it played to capacity houses.

The Collegians, the novel by the Limerick-born writer Gerald Griffin on which Boucicault's play was based, was itself founded on a true incident. In 1819 the bound body of Ellen Hanley, a sixteen-year-old peasant girl, was discovered on the banks of the River Shannon. Ellen, orphaned at six and brought up by her bootmaker uncle, was strikingly beautiful,

and when she was fifteen caught the eye of the rakish Lieuten-
ant John Scanlan, from near-by Ballycahane Castle. Scanlan
was completely infatuated. He persuaded her to steal her
uncle's savings and run away with him. With his boatman
Stephen Sullivan masquerading as a priest, they went through
a bogus marriage ceremony, but it was not long before Scanlan began to tire of his peasant wife, and he decided to get rid
of her. She was last seen, with Scanlan and Sullivan, at a
remote farmhouse on Carrig Island in the river estuary. Seven
weeks later her body was washed ashore. Soldiers were sent to
look for Scanlan and Sullivan, but they had vanished and their
arrest became a matter of considerable importance, for the
murder began to assume overtones of the greater national
struggle then going on within Ireland: with the people identifying with Ellen and demanding justice from the ruling class
represented by Scanlan. He was eventually caught when a
soldier, searching Ballycahane Castle, plunged his lance into a
pile of straw and Scanlan leapt out. The trial took place in
Limerick, and for a time it seemed as though Scanlan, with
friends in high places and defended by the great Daniel
O'Connell, might get off, but he was found guilty and, still
protesting his innocence, led to the scaffold. The boatman
Sullivan was eventually discovered in Tralee Gaol where he
was being held, under an assumed name, on a charge of
uttering forged banknotes, and he too was sentenced to death.
Throughout his trial he had protested his innocence, but on
the gallows he made a last-minute confession. He told how, at
the behest of Scanlan, he had taken Ellen out into the middle of
the river and there bludgeoned her to death. His final cry from
the gallows was, 'May the Lord have mercy on me!'[5]

As a young reporter, Gerald Griffin had attended the trials
of Scanlan and Sullivan, and ten years later used their story as
the basis for a serious, and rather tedious, attack on the current
social conditions in rural Ireland. He altered the setting to
Killarney, changed the names of the protagonists, and introduced the love interest of the aristocratic Anne Chute. Taking
only the climax of Griffin's interminable plot, Boucicault
omitted the moral preaching and social criticism, and instead
concentrated on action and character. He altered the ending so

that the murder of Eily (the Ellen Hanley character) became a failed attempt and was unknown to Hardress Cregan, the Scanlan figure; he introduced a new twist to the secondary love interest; and, above all, turned the one-dimensional characters of Griffin's novel into living, breathing people. It's in his handling of the complexities of the plot and his skilful characterization that he demonstrates just what a fine playwright he is, and his genius is nowhere better seen than in the role of Myles-na-Coppaleen. In the book, Myles appears fleetingly and soon disappears from the story to which he is irrelevant. In the play, he becomes the comic hero and a leading figure in the working out of the plot: it is Myles who sees the attempted murder, rescues Eily (with whom he is in love) and brings about the obligatory happy ending. He is a lazy, lying rogue, a horse-thief, a poacher and an operator of an illicit whiskey still – everything that was an anathema to respectable Victorians. And yet it was Myles who proved irresistible to Victorian audiences. Fifty years after he first stepped on stage, the Abbey playwrights were to condemn Boucicault for writing such characters which, they claimed, had perpetuated the myth of the stage Irishman being a blarney-loving buffoon. It was ironic that Boucicault, in creating his stage Irishmen, had also attacked their predecessors as 'low down, good for nothing blatherers'. Certainly Myles is a sentimental character, full of charm, wit and cunning, and in creating him, Boucicault was concerned primarily to entertain his audience, but he is much more than a caricature: he is a rounded character and, in the history of the stage, his appearance marked a major step forward towards a truly indigenous Irish drama.

It was to see Myles (and Boucicault playing him) as much as to see the play that audiences flocked to Laura Keene's Theatre. It was a part in which few actors could go wrong, and although many attempted it, few surpassed Boucicault's interpretation. He continued to appear in the role until well into his sixties, his bald head covered with a wig, and still making the spectacular 'dive'. In the sensation scene of the play, Myles, in his cave by the lake, tending his illicit still, sees Danny Mann, the villainous boatman, push Eily O'Connor

into the lake because she will not yield up her marriage certificate; he shoots Danny and dives into the lake (created by
twenty small boys shaking yards of blue gauze) to rescue her.
His running header (the idea for which was suggested to him
by Laura Keene's stage carpenter, who thought a dive would
look more impressive than a jump) became the sensation of
the day. 'Sensation,' he told critic William Winter, 'is what the
public wants and you cannot give them too much of it.'[6] After
The Octoroon, the term 'contemporary drama' had been
coined; after *The Colleen Bawn*, it was to be 'sensation drama'.
It was a phrase that was to haunt him, and later he bitterly
regretted having used it. Sensation became the order of the
day, and each new play had to outdo its predecessor if it was to
have any chance of success. But, for the time being, in\March
1860, he could not have been happier.

I have written an Irish drama for the first time in my life.
The field of Irish history and romance is so rich in dramatic
suggestions that I am surprised that the mine has never been
regularly opened before. I had long thought of writing a
play from material gathered from my native country but
this is the first time I ever tried it. I hope that the play will
lead other greater men, of finer genius and talents than I
possess, to give you plenty of Irish plays.[7]

It was to be another forty years before the founding of the
Abbey Theatre in Dublin and the plays of Lady Gregory,
Synge and O'Casey, among others, were to realize his hope.
The Colleen Bawn was the play for which Boucicault had
been searching, artistically and financially. The ill-fated ventures in New Orleans and Washington, his hasty exit from the
Winter Garden, were all forgotten as the money poured in
and, for the first time in many years, he could sit back and
enjoy his wealth and family. He bought two houses, one in
Astor Place as an investment, the other at 39 East 15th Street as
a residence.

His tact at arranging the scenery of a theatre was observ-
able in his domestic menage [wrote a journalist, Genio

Scott, in a specially commissioned article about the play-wright]. He transformed the inside of the house: took down all partitions, and took out all closets from the basement, throwing it into one capacious room, on the walls of which, all the kitchen utensils appeared like so many mirrors. The storey above the parlour was also thrown into one room, divided only by a bed, to be approached from each side by cushioned steps. Having seen, in the castle at Versailles, the famous bed-chamber of Louis XVI, I am prepared to say that the dormitory of Boucicault's was decidedly the most comfortable.[8]

His bathroom was tiled with tiles manufactured especially for him by Minton, and all the fittings were silver. He entertained lavishly and was seen in the politest company without a tie, wearing an open-necked shirt of his own design, a custom that quickly became as fashionable as the red Connemara cloak Agnes wore on stage as Eily.

Boucicault was nearly forty. Although he had vowed in 1853 that he would never set foot in London again, his thoughts had been turning increasingly towards the city in which he'd been brought up and where his mother was living. News of the death of his guardian, Dr Lardner, in Naples the year before had made him anxious to see her, and he desperately wanted to show off the three grandchildren she'd never seen. He was also keen to get away from New York and the constant carping of the critics. Even though he had acknowledged Griffin's novel on the playbills and dedicated the play to Griffin, extolling the virtues of the novelist in his curtain speech on the first night, his enemies accused him of stealing his subject and not saying where he had found it. During the previous two years he'd received many offers from London managers (which he'd always turned down) to present him and Agnes in the plays about which they had heard so much. The success of *The Colleen Bawn* decided him that the time had come for him to make a triumphant return to England. Accepting an invitation to go to Paris to produce the French version of *The Octoroon*, he planned a short trip to London as well, during which he would present *The Colleen Bawn*, the play, he was certain, in which he and Agnes would make the sort of impression on London audiences he wanted.

At the close of Laura Keene's season on 12 May, they took the play to Philadelphia for a short engagement and then returned to the Winter Garden to play a brief farewell season. Their appearance at the theatre which they had left under a cloud came as a surprise to the public and the acting profession.

About three months since [complained the puzzled comedian George Holland, who was still trying to get money he was owed by the playwright], the respected Mr Boucicault ('another honest man') published in the newspaper that Mr Stuart was insolvent and his engagements worthless and the man himself anything but a gentleman. And now the Public is respectfully informed that Mr Boucicault and Mr Stuart have again shook hands – a circumstance devoutly to be wished – and that Mr Stuart has kindly consented in conjunction with Mr Boucicault to display his peculiar abilities again in the swindling line – and these men are patronized and make fortunes.[9]

Agnes was given a benefit on 16 July, their last performance, and received a tumultous reception. The critics, while not regretting Boucicault's departure, were sad to be losing Agnes, 'who is on the point of leaving us to follow the fortunes of her lord overseas, whilst Mrs Wood (another actress who had taken a benefit at Laura Keene's the same evening), being her own mistress, has the wit and good taste to stay at home'.[10] On 18 July, the Boucicault family sailed from New York to Liverpool, having promised Stuart that their stay abroad would be brief and they would be back in time to open at the Winter Garden that autumn, and from there made their way to London. Madame Celeste, an old friend from his days at the Haymarket and the Adelphi, was then lessee of the Lyceum, but she was unable to fit him in with her own plans, and so on 6 August Boucicault signed a contract with his former mentor, Benjamin Webster, to open in *The Colleen Bawn* at the Adelphi the following month.

Although Boucicault owed Webster an immense debt for the number of times the manager had bailed him out in the 1840s and given him advances on often fictitious plays, he did not allow gratitude to stand in the way of making as much as he could from his play. The agreement he reached with Webster (made without solicitors) was that, in addition to a straight fee for himself and Agnes as the stars, he would, after Webster's expenses had been deducted, receive £50 a week for the play, or share, at his option, any takings over £80 a night. This arrangement would last as long as the weekly returns exceeded £600 and would run, in the first instance, for a year with an option to renew after six months. For his part, Boucicault agreed that neither he nor Agnes would play in any other London theatre.[11] It was a tough agreement, heavily loaded in Boucicault's favour, but Webster had little choice other than to accept it for the Adelphi had not been doing good business and he desperately wanted a success to revive his flagging fortunes. London was anxious to see the two stars who'd been away for seven years and eager to see their Broadway success; if Webster hadn't agreed to Boucicault's terms, they would have gone elsewhere.

The Colleen Bawn opened at the Adelphi on 10 September 1860, to become the biggest success seen in London for decades. Even the ever-confident Boucicault was astonished by its popularity. For ten months, with only a short break in April when the theatre closed between seasons, it was performed every night in what was to become the first long run in the history of the English stage, a record that was to have beneficial effects upon the acting profession. With the introduction of 'the long run', the basis of an actor's engagement became the run of the piece rather than a season of anything up to ten months, which might have its successes but would also include a number of failures, and so an element of financial stability was introduced that permitted actors to be paid reasonable salaries.

Altogether *The Colleen Bawn* was given 230 performances at the Adelphi. It was the first 'sensation drama' the West End had seen, and no sooner had it opened than the burlesques, imitations and straight thefts began to appear and Boucicault entered upon the litigation, trying to protect his property, that was to occupy him for the rest of his life. Among the many other versions was the opera *The Lily of Killarney,* on which Boucicault himself collaborated with John Oxenford and composer Julius Benedict. It was produced at Covent Garden on 10 February 1862. He had tried once before to write an opera, in 1843 with the Irish composer Michael Balfe, but the project came to nothing because of his ignorance of the musical shape of an opera. When Benedict asked to turn *The Colleen Bawn* into one, Boucicault was not keen.

> I related my experience with Balfe, over which we laughed together very heartily, but Benedict clung to his affection for the Irish play, and we took John Oxenford into our counsels. Our names are coupled on the title page of the libretto, but all my share in the business consisted of witnessing how my lamb was butchered into a marketable shape . . . All the sentiment, all the tenderness, all the simple poetry was swept away. We attended the first performance and I could have cried over it, but it was so drolly burlesque that as I sat and witnessed the attempted murder of Eily, laughter got the best of us both. 'Yes,' said John, 'but listen to that!' The house was on its feet, and amid enthusiastic shouts the singers were called out to receive an ovation.[12]

Boucicault may not have enjoyed what *The Colleen Bawn* became as an opera, but *The Lily of Killarney* became one of the most popular of all British operas, and is still performed by amateur societies.

Among the thousands of people who went to the Adelphi to see the sensational new play was Queen Victoria. In her journal for 4 February 1861 she noted:

> Went with Albert and the two girls to the Adelphi to see the celebrated melodrama in 3 acts by Dion Boucicault, called 'Colleen Bawn', taken from 'The Collegians.' D. Boucicault and his wife (former Miss Robertson whom I remember some years ago at the Princess's) acted admir-

ably as the ragged Irish peasant and the Colleen Bawn. The scenery was very pretty and the whole piece very characteristic and thrilling.

Two weeks later she went again and commented, 'One could appreciate it even more the 2nd time, but my enjoyment was damaged by seeing dear Albert so uncomfortable, though he managed to laugh a good deal. Four weeks later, on 14 March, she and Prince Albert paid the Adelphi a third visit, and 'enjoyed seeing *The Colleen Bawn* again and all the cleverness of it'. It was to be her final visit to a public place of entertainment. On 16 March, the Duchess of Kent, her mother, died and the court entered mourning. Before the official period of mourning was over, Prince Albert, the Prince Consort, was also dead, and Queen Victoria never again set foot inside a theatre.

Boucicault had always maintained, in spite of his experience managing Agnes during their early days in America, that the play was more important than the star, and to cash in on the enormous popularity of *The Colleen Bawn*, he decided to mount his own authentic touring productions. As soon as the play had opened, he followed the usual procedure of granting licences to provincial managers to put on local productions, but gradually he stopped giving his permission and started to insist that they took his production instead. A licence to present a play could cost anything from £5 to £30 a week, and the cachet of presenting a production of *The Colleen Bawn* mounted under the author's personal supervision did not outweigh the disadvantage of having to pay Boucicault half the receipts, which would almost certainly be in three figures. The managers were understandably reluctant to fall in with Boucicault's plans, but his refusal to issue licences and his pursuit of any manager who dared to put on an unauthorized performance into the courts, forced them, since they wanted the box-office success the play would bring, to accept his terms. On 4 February 1861, the first of Boucicault's touring companies opened in *The Colleen Bawn* at the Theatre Royal, Sunderland, followed a week later by a second company in Brighton. Before long, he was drawing £500 a week from them, and during their first year of operation he personally made £10,000. It was the first time a 'West End production' had been toured. Previously the London stars had visited provincial theatres after the West End season had finished to appear in the local production, supported by the local company. Just as the long run of *The Colleen Bawn* at the Adelphi helped to introduce security for actors, so the touring of the play by one management helped to introduce financial security for playwrights, for it guaranteed them a greater income than the old system of licences. Boucicault's avowed intention to raise the status of the dramatist was beginning to be realized.

In the first year of their return to England, Boucicault and Agnes between them had earned £23,000, with which he paid off his debts from his 1848 insolvency and bought Hereford House, an imposing mansion in the Brompton Road at Earl's Court, at which all the notable literary and theatrical figures were frequent guests and where he scandalized society by introducing late-night supper parties on Sundays. For these he employed the finest chefs in London, and after the meal it was his custom to invite the chef in to partake of a glass of wine. On one occasion the chef was unable to attend and a message was sent to Boucicault asking him to go to the kitchen.

> The corps of the man who had cooked the dinner just eaten, lay on a table, in a winding sheet. Boucicault thought it was a sell. He approached it, felt of the face, chin, and forehead, exclaiming: 'Capital! Could not be better done! Well really, I don't see that it *could* be better done!' And as he said the last word, he raised the eye-lid, and in the coolest possible way remarked, 'Why it's real; but don't for the life of you mention it so that Agnes hears of it.' The cook had died of an apoplectic fit, after getting the dinner, and Agnes first learned of it by the announcement in the papers.[13]

After three months of appearing nightly in the same play, Boucicault was beginning to feel constricted. It was the longest period he had ever spent on a single project, he had virtually given up writing (the one activity in which he could lose himself completely) and not even his involvement with the touring companies could prevent him from becoming bored. He was also beginning to chafe at acting under Webster's management, and was irked that the agreement they had signed the previous August, which had seemed to be so much in his favour, was not bringing him in as much for *The Colleen Bawn* as it would if he were his own manager. With the end of the first six months approaching (with its option to renew), he began to look for ways of breaking the agreement or of forcing Webster to give him better terms. He began to find fault with everything Webster did; nothing at the Adelphi was ever right. Then, when Webster inadvertently left Boucicault's name off the bills as author, the playwright saw his chance and took legal advice as to how he might quit the Adelphi without being sued. Before he had time to take any action, Webster had apologized and put his name back, but that did not stop Boucicault issuing threats. In January 1861 he wrote to Webster:

I adhere to the notice I have given you, and I avail myself of the notice contained in your note that you will maintain the theatre in its present inefficient state, to consider my engagement with you at an end on and after Monday, 11th Feb. . . . We part then – and wishing you well, but feeling certain that you will blindly founder in the confusion around you, to which your eyes will not open.[14]

It was a bluff. On 12 February, the curtain rose on *The Colleen Bawn* with Boucicault and Agnes in their allotted roles, and they continued to perform until the end of March, when the Adelphi closed for a short break. Webster had had no wish to end a season which was still drawing packed houses, but Boucicault had insisted. He had developed an urge to return to Dublin for the first time in nearly twenty years, and, much to Webster's disgust, nothing would prevent him going. Their agreement specified that the Boucicaults would not appear at another London theatre; it said nothing about Dublin.

On Easter Monday, 1 April, *The Colleen Bawn* opened at

the Theatre Royal, Hawkins Street, and played to packed houses for twenty-four nights. Boucicault was welcomed back by his countrymen as a prodigal son. He and Agnes were lionized by Dublin society, they were entertained by Sir William and Lady Wilde (the parents of Oscar, who was to become a friend), and whenever they left Gresham's Hotel, where they were staying, crowds of admirers followed them through the streets. For their engagement, they received almost £4,000. 'I look at all this more astounded than I can tell you,' he wrote to a friend in America. 'I feel exactly like Montecristo when he found the treasure; or Aladdin – only I find my head to be the lamp. I have only to rub it to get all I want. I could not be more prosperous, more happy.'[15]

He may have been happy with the money he was making and his reception in Dublin, but he was still far from happy with his relationship with Webster. He had consistently refused to take up the six-month option to renew their agreement, and when he and Agnes reopened at the Adelphi on 29 April to begin the second half of their contract, he was still looking for ways to renegotiate better terms or an excuse to leave. Since Webster showed no sign of meeting any of his demands, he decided to force the issue. At the start of June he told Webster that he thought it was time to withdraw *The Colleen Bawn* since both he and Agnes, who was desperately tired, were in need of a rest. He proposed taking her away on a six-week holiday. Webster, who could see no sign of interest in the play flagging and who was happily making more money than he had in a long while, was dumbfounded by the suggestion. Why couldn't Boucicault engage another actress to play Eily while Agnes had her rest? Because, said Boucicault, there wasn't another actress in London capable of playing the part as well as Agnes; there was no alternative but for the play to come off. Webster found himself in the corner Boucicault wanted him in and told Boucicault to name his terms for continuing. These were that the two men should join forces in running the Adelphi; the stage and all its departments to be under Boucicault's control, the front of house to be under Webster's. For every night that he and Agnes appeared on stage, they would be paid £5 each; for each

Dion Boucicault, 1820 – 1890. A lithograph by F. D'Avignon, once owned
by the dramatist Pinero, made in 1855 when Boucicault was thirty-four.

Samuel Smith Boursiquot

Anne Maria Darley, Boucicault's
mother and wife of Samuel Smith
Boursiquot. (Both are miniatures in
oils by an unknown artist)

Dr Dionysius Lardner. A portrait by
Alexander Craig painted in about
1840, the time when he eloped to
Paris with Mrs Heaviside and his
allowance to Boucicault ceased.

(After which will be presented (for the First Time) a Legend, entitled The

VAMPIRE
A Phantasm:
RELATED IN THREE DRAMAS.

By DION BOUCICAULT, Author of "Love in a Maze," "London Assurance," &c.
THE OVERTURE AND INCIDENTAL MUSIC COMPOSED EXPRESSLY BY Mr. R. STOPEL.

TIME OF THE FIRST DRAMA,
AUGUST 15, 1660.

Sir Alan Raby, — Mr. BOUCICAULT.
Lord Arthur Clavering, Mr. G. EVERETT.
Ralph ap Gwynne, Mr. DALY, Nevil of Greystock, Mr. ROLLESTON.
Sir Guy Musgrave, Mr. JAMES VINING.
Watkyn Rhys, Mr. J. CHESTER, Griffyths, Mr. F. COOKE.
Lucy Peveril, Miss CARLOTTA LECLERCQ.
Lady Ellen Clavering, Miss J. LOVELL.
Maud Nevil, Miss DALY, Mercy Gaveston, Miss GREGORY.

THE VILLAGE of RABY PEVERIL,
AT THE FOOT OF SNOWDON. (Gordon)

The RUINS of RABY CASTLE. (F. Lloyds)
THE PEAKS OF SNOWDON. (Gordon)

TIME OF THE SECOND DRAMA,
AUGUST 15, 1760.

Sir Alan Raby, — Mr. BOUCICAULT.
Edgar Peveril, Mr. J. F. CATHCART.
Trevanion, Mr. HERMAN VEZIN, Forsyth, Mr. BRAZIER.
Watty Rys, Mr. MEADOWS.
Lady Peveril, Mrs. PHILLIPS.
Alice Peveril, Miss ROBERTSON Augusta Nevil, Miss MARSHALL.

RABY CASTLE RESTORED FROM THE RUINS. (F. Lloyds)

TIME OF THE THIRD DRAMA,
AUGUST 15, 1860.

Sir Alan Raby, — Mr. BOUCICAULT.
Captain Peveril, Mr. C. WHEATLEIGH.
Walter Rees, (Attorney-at-Law) Mr. HARLEY.
Postman, Mr. HAINES.
Mrs. Raby, Mrs. W. DALY, Ada Raby, Miss DESBOROUGH.

THE TOWN OF RABY PEVERIL,
AT THE FOOT OF SNOWDON. (Gordon)

RABY CASTLE. (F. Lloyds)
ALAN RABY'S BEDCHAMBER. (Gordon)

THE RUINS OF THE CLOCK TOWER. (Dayes)

THE NEW PLAY OF THE

TRIAL of LOVE
WILL BE REPEATED EVERY EVENING.

THE CORSICAN BROTHERS
Will be Repeated (at Second Price) on WEDNESDAY & FRIDAY NEXT.

Shakespeare's Historical Play of KING JOHN
Will be Repeated (by Desire) on MONDAY NEXT, June 21st.

On this Evening a Portion of the Pit is divided off as Stalls.

To-Morrow (TUESDAY)—The Trial of Love, with a Drama.
WEDNESDAY—The Trial of Love, with The Corsican Brothers.   THURSDAY—The Trial of Love, with a Drama.
FRIDAY—The Trial of Love, with The Corsican Brothers.   SATURDAY—The Trial of Love, with a Drama.

Acting Manager, Mr. EMDEN.   Stage Manager, Mr. G. ELLIS.
Musical Director, Mr. ROBERT STOPEL.   Ballet Master, Mr. FLEXMORE.
Box Office Open from 11 until 5 o'Clock.   Doors Open at Half-past 6.   The Performances to Commence at 7
Half-Price will commence as near Nine o'Clock as is consistent with the Non-interruption of the Performance.
GALLERY DOOR IN CASTLE STREET.   Children in Arms cannot possibly be Admitted.
Private Boxes and Stalls may be obtained at the Libraries, and of Mr. MASSINGHAM, at the Box Office of the Theatre,
Oxford Street, where Places for the Dress Circle and Boxes may be secured.
Applications respecting the Bills to be addressed to Mr. TREMAWAY, Stage Door.

Part of the playbill for the Keans'
benefit night on 14 June 1852 at the
Princess's Theatre, Oxford Street.
Boucicault, aged thirty-one, was
making his first stage appearance for
twelve years. Also in the cast was
Agnes Robertson.

Boucicault as Sir Alan Raby in
The Vampire. The earliest known
portrait of Boucicault, it was
commissioned by Queen Victoria
from Edward Henry Corbould, R.A.,
and is now in Windsor Castle.

A sketch by Queen Victoria, made in
her Journal, of the last scene of Act
of Boucicault's *The Corsican Brothers*
The dates of her first three visits are
noted in the bottom right-hand
corner. Charles Kean, as Louis, lies
dying; Alfred Wigan, as Château-
Renaud, stands triumphant.

Boucicault in one of his greatest role
Conn the Shaughraun. He played it
successfully on three continents from
1874 until 1888, two years before his
death. This pose – held a considerabl
time for the camera – belies his
undoubted skill as an actor.

The sensation scene from *After Dark*, 1868. This was the scene that Boucicault stole from Augustin Daly – in spite of having helped to introduce the copyright law and using it remorselessly to protect his own work. *After Dark* became one of the earliest films and the scene, eventually with Pearl White tied to the rails, became synonymous with silent films.

Charles Mathews as Dazzle in the
first production of *London Assurance*.
From a series of water-colour drawings
found among Mathews's effects and
attributed to James Warren Childe by
William Beverley, the scenic artist.

Madame Vestris, lessee of Covent
Garden in 1841 and wife of Mathews.
She played Grace Harkaway in *London
Assurance* and was largely responsible
for the production.

Donald Sinden as Sir Harcourt Courtly in the Royal Shakespeare Company's highly successful 1970 production of *London Assurance*, which was seen both in London's West End and on Broadway. The part was played originally by William Farren.

Dion Boucicault and his second wife Agnes Robertson. These photographs were taken in 1861, at the height of their fame in *The Colleen Bawn*, for use in a copy of the play that was presented to Queen Victoria. She saw the production four times.

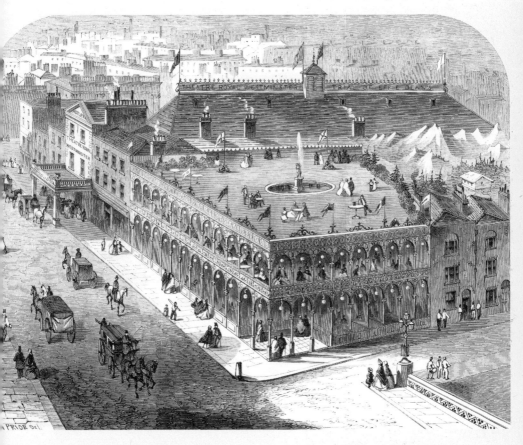

Part of the prospectus sent out by the New Theatre Company in 1863 of the proposed pleasure garden and leisure complex, facing the Houses of Parliament across the river, that Boucicault planned to incorporate on the Astley's site. He went bankrupt before work could start.

Two of the men who played an important part in Boucicault's life:
Benjamin Webster, manager of the Haymarket and the Adelphi, appearing as
Tartuffe; Charles Kean, son of Edmund, actor and manager of the Princess's.

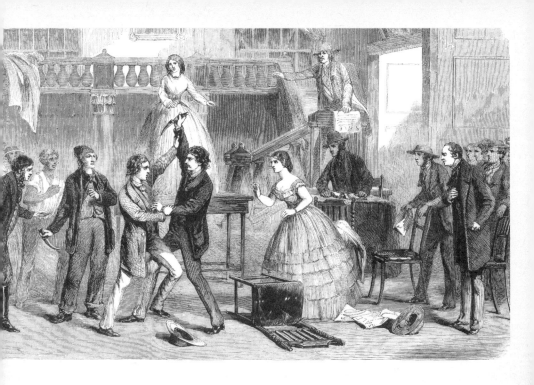

The slave auction from *The Octoroon* at the Adelphi Theatre 1861. Agnes
Robertson as Zoe stands on the table.

Scene from *Arrah-na-Pogue* at the Princess's Theatre, 1865. Both these
engravings first appeared in *The Illustrated London News*.

Scene from *Babil and Bijou* which was produced at Covent Garden on 29 August 1872. An extravagant spectacular, it ran for six months but lost £11,000, the greatest loss the West End had ever seen.

THIS WAS DONE FOR SHAKSPEARE—WHY NOT FOR BOUCICAULT?

One word for the Fenian Prisoners, and how many for the
"Shaughraun?"

Two cartoons by Alfred Bryan:
(above left) 1880, in *The Entr'acte Annual* and
(right) 1876 following his letter to Prime
Minister Benjamin Disraeli
demanding, in the name of the
audiences who had paid to see *The
Shaughraun*, the release of Fenian
prisoners in Australia.

Cartoon by Sem, following the
'shocking' success of *Formosa*, a play
about a lady of easy virtue, produced
at Drury Lane in 1869.

Boucicault's most famous children:
Nina as Peter Pan in the first
production, directed in 1904 at the
Duke of York's by her brother Dot
– still probably the best Peter Pan of
all; and Dot (Darley George), also
known as Dion Jnr, in *Her Husband's
Wife* in which he starred with his own
wife Irene Vanburgh.

VIRGINIA CARVEL

DION BOUCICAULT.

LONG CLEAR HAVANA FILLER, SUMATRA WRAPPER, HAND MADE, 5 CENT CIGAR. TRY THEM.

Boucicault advertising cigars shortly before his death in 1890 at a time when he was desperate for money.

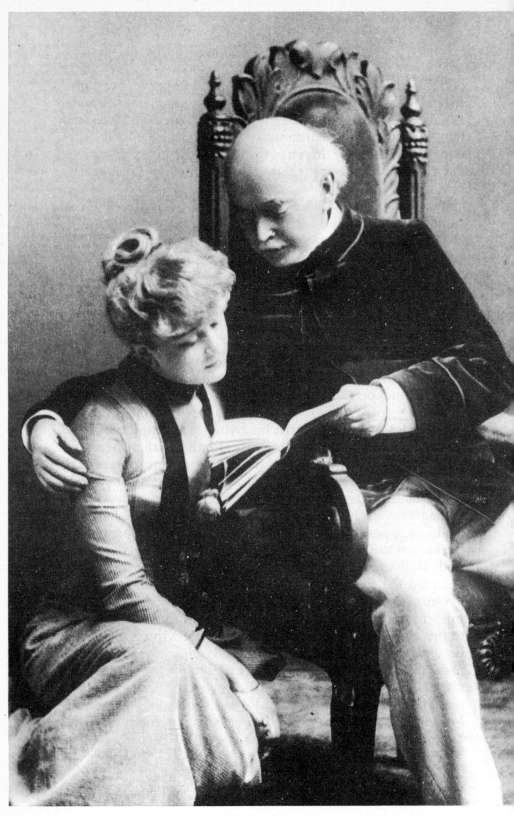

Boucicault and Louise Thorndyke, his third wife. He was sixty-four, she was
twenty-one, when they married in Australia in 1885.

of his dramas presented, he would be paid £1 per act per night. All profits would be shared equally. To sweeten his demands, Boucicault also agreed that they would share any losses and that Webster could continue to act if he wished. In other words, Webster, the doyen of theatrical managers, was to take a back seat in his own theatre and have no say in its artistic policy!

The agreement, unique in the annals of stage history, was signed in July, to run for three years from the beginning of October when their first agreement came to its end. Never before had an author stood out for and won the right to control the presentation of his plays in such a manner. Never before had a British writer been accorded a nightly royalty payable upon performance of his work. Boucicault, like other writers who had produced and presented their own work, had taken a share of box-office profits before, but only in his capacity as manager, never as the author. This was the first time a dramatist had managed to wring such an agreement from an independent management, and its effect on future generations of writers is obvious: for the first time it made it possible for a writer to earn his living by writing plays and nothing else. A little over ten years after his first unsuccessful attempt to change the status of the playwright and obtain a fair reward for his work, Boucicault had discovered the way to do it. Of course, the system did not change overnight. Other managers were appalled by Webster's action and did all they could to oppose such agreements becoming widespread. But the breach had been made and, during the next twenty years, with Boucicault continuing to lead the way, the previously accepted flat fee for a play became a thing of the past.

Once Boucicault had got his way, Agnes's tiredness miraculously disappeared and she and Boucicault again took to the stage as Eily and Myles. At first, everything seemed to be going well. Londoners, visitors and trainloads of excursion passengers filled the Adelphi night after night, and it looked as if the play could run for ever. By the end of October, however, Boucicault and Agnes really had had enough. They had been appearing in the play for over a year with hardly a break, and both wanted a change. Boucicault told Webster that he planned to replace *The Colleen Bawn* with another of his successes from New York, *The Octoroon*. Webster wasn't keen on the idea. He could still see a lot of mileage in the old play, which was showing no sign of losing its drawing power, but under the terms of their new agreement (which had just come into operation), he was powerless to prevent Boucicault doing as he wished.

The Octoroon, with Agnes repeating her role as Zoe and Boucicault playing Salem Scudder (the part created at the Winter Garden by Joseph Jefferson), opened at the Adelphi on 18 November. It was given a sumptuous production, under Boucicault's personal supervision, with an overture especially composed by Sir Julius Benedict, and was well advertised. Much to everyone's surprise, it flopped badly. The first four acts went well and were enthusiastically received by an audience which felt that the play was giving them an understanding of events then taking place in the United States (the first shot of the Civil War had been fired at Fort Sumter on 12 April 1861), but when it came to the final act, everything went wrong. The audience simply would not accept that Zoe should die. They identified the character with the actress they loved, and would not allow her to be killed, and the cheers turned to boos as they demonstrated their feelings. Boucicault was puzzled, as well as annoyed, by their attitude. How, he asked, could people who had sympathized a few years earlier with Uncle Tom when he was given the lash on stage, now resent the death of a slave who dies rather than submit to degradation? To demand a happy ending, as the audience did, was to destroy the point and moral of the drama. But as far as he was concerned it was not a principle worth fighting for; if the public wanted a happy ending, they would get one. A few days after the first night the playbills proudly announced that *The Octoroon* would again be given with a new last act 'composed by the public and edited by the author'. For once, Boucicault's play-doctoring failed to do the trick and attendance at the theatre continued to fall. Although the play was given for a total of sixty-nine nights (more than an acknowledged success like *The Corsican Brothers*), after the run of *The Colleen Bawn* it was considered a failure. 'He

THEATRE ROYAL
NEW ADELPHI.

SOLE PROPRIETOR AND MANAGER,
MR. BENJAMIN WEBSTER.

297th 298th 299th 300th 301st & 302nd
NIGHTS of the Engagement of MR. & MRS.
DION BOUCICAULT

Mr. WEBSTER begs to announce
that during the
CATTLE SHOW WEEK
FOR THAT WEEK ONLY,

In order to gratify many country visitors who have written for places to
see the "Colleen Bawn," Mr. and Mrs.
BOUCICAULT have consented to
appear in both the

OCTOROON
AND THE
COLLEEN BAWN
ON THE SAME NIGHT!

Mr. BOUCICAULT begs to acknowledge the hourly receipt
of many letters, entreating that the termination of the
"Octoroon" should be modified, and the Slave Heroine
saved from an unhappy end. He cannot resist the kind
feeling expressed throughout this correspondence, nor refuse
compliance with a request so easily granted. A New Last
Act of the Drama, composed by the Public, and edited by
the Author, will be represented on Monday night. He trusts
the Audience will accept it as a very grateful tribute to their
judgment and taste, which he should be the last to dispute.

The "Octoroon" will commence at 7 o'clock & end at 10 minutes past 9.
The "Colleen Bawn" will commence at 20 past 9 & conclude at half-past 11.

MR. BOUCICAULT
Having recovered from his late indisposition, will appear
As Salem Scudder and Myles - na - Coppaleen:
MRS. BOUCICAULT
As the Octoroon and the Colleen Bawn.

MONDAY, DECEMBER 9th. 1861, and During the Week,
A NEW & ORIGINAL DRAMA,
In FIVE ACTS, entitled The
OCTOROON!

Playbill for the Adelphi during the Boucicaults' record-breaking
run in *The Colleen Bawn*, containing Boucicault's notice advising
the public that he had rewritten the end of *The Octoroon*.
His alterations failed to make the play a smash hit.

advocated the marriage of a *white* man to a nigger! thus driving all but the abolitionists from his house,' explained a contemporary.[16]

Webster, who had been holidaying on the Continent and had visited Paris to see a French adaptation of *The Colleen Bawn*, hurried back to his theatre thoroughly alarmed. Not only could he see all the profits of the successful run of *The Colleen Bawn* being dissipated by his artistic director, but he had been receiving disturbing reports of Boucicault's behaviour backstage. Ever since the new agreement came into force, the Adelphi had been split into two factions – Webster's men and Boucicault's men – and everything done by either side was being reported back to the other. Boucicault complained about Webster interfering backstage and having scenery moved without his permission; Webster complained about the cost of rope Boucicault had ordered, scenery being repainted that didn't require it, and Boucicault being abusive about his management. On his return, Webster demanded that Boucicault withdraw *The Octoroon*, which Boucicault was convinced would become a hit if allowed to run long enough, and put back *The Colleen Bawn*. Somewhat surprisingly Boucicault agreed, but only while he was preparing other plays for production. Since he no longer had any wish to become involved in a long run, *The Colleen Bawn* played for a while and was then replaced by Agnes and himself appearing in a succession of his American plays, including *The Phantom*, *The Life of an Actress* and *Dot*. None of these had the drawing power of *The Colleen Bawn*, and Webster was constantly urging him to put on the old play and let it run, but Boucicault refused. Relations between them deteriorated quickly as Webster stalked about his theatre, disapproving of what was happening but powerless to prevent it, and Boucicault resented having his every move watched.

Matters came to a head at the beginning of June 1862, after a spring of discontent. Webster, finally deciding he could stand by no longer, posted bills outside the Adelphi announcing that the Boucicaults would appear in their famous roles in *The Colleen Bawn* on Monday, 9 June, and that a new melodrama by the dramatist was in active preparation. This was a clear breach of the agreement which gave Boucicault sole charge of all artistic matters, and he immediately instructed his solicitor to write to Webster for an explanation. Webster ignored the letter and the playwright applied to the Court of Chancery for an injunction to prevent Webster announcing *his* play. The injunction was granted; Webster cross-petitioned to prevent Boucicault bringing out the play at any other London theatre; and the case was heard in mid June.

While their lawyers produced all the letters of the previous year, and witnesses, to help chart the path of their stormy relationship, Boucicault was busy dealing Webster an underhand blow. He had already decided that, no matter what his legal obligations to Webster might be, he was going to put an end to their partnership and sever his links with the Adelphi. In May he had started secret negotiations to take over the lease of the Princess's, and discovered, to his surprise, that Webster had also been making inquiries about the same lease. Finding out about Webster's interest before Webster knew of his, he decided to use the knowledge to maximum advantage. In an act of mock humility, he made his negotiations public and declared that he would proceed no further without the blessing of his partner at the Adelphi, whom he did not wish to treat unfairly. Unwisely, it may seem, the two men agreed to continue the negotiations together. Leaving Webster talking on their behalf, Boucicault promptly went round the corner from the Adelphi and signed to take over Drury Lane on his own. He then told Webster he was no longer interested in the Princess's and Webster could have the lease without him. It was not long before Webster discovered the real reason and realized why the playwright had obtained an injunction to prevent him announcing *The Colleen Bawn* at the Adelphi – he intended to produce it at Drury Lane. In court Webster argued, with complete justification, that he had the Boucicaults under contract and that their appearance in a theatre so close to his, in a play so closely associated with the Adelphi, would do him nothing but harm. The judge agreed and, having listened to the evidence from both sides, decided in favour of neither. Legally, he ruled, their partnership was still in force and he suggested that they settle their differences and try their best to make it work for the two and a half years it still had to run.[17]

Boucicault had no intention of taking any notice of the judge's direction and announced that he would go ahead with his plan to open *The Colleen Bawn* at Drury Lane the following week. As a last defiant gesture against Webster, he exercised his right of artistic control to put on *The Octoroon* at the Adelphi on 18 June, the day after the court hearing. The following day he went to the Adelphi as usual to get ready for the performance and found his way barred. The stage-door keeper, on instructions from Webster, refused to allow him to enter. That same day Webster wrote a sad note to Agnes, begging her, to save them both embarrassment, not to go to the theatre since, with great reluctance, she too would be refused admittance.

The battle did not end there. Boucicault and Agnes duly opened at Drury Lane in *The Colleen Bawn* on 23 June, and Boucicault entered into a long legal struggle to recover the furniture, stage costumes and properties he had left at the Adelphi, none of which Webster would release without a written list. While solicitor wrote to solicitor, Boucicault racked his brains trying to remember exactly what he'd left behind.

As Webster had predicted, *The Colleen Bawn* played to packed houses, even after Agnes, who was again pregnant, had had to withdraw from the cast. On 9 August, at Hereford House, their second daughter, Patrice, was born. A little over a month later, Agnes was back on stage re-creating the title role in *Jessie Brown*. Retitled *The Relief of Lucknow*, the play opened on 15 September and continued to attract large houses for two months until 8 November, the end of the season and the expiration of Boucicault's lease.

8

'FAILURES DON'T COUNT'

THE LEGAL skirmishes with Webster, and his attempts to recover his property left at the Adelphi, were only a few of the many occasions since he'd returned to London that Boucicault had needed to resort to the aid of his solicitor. Much of his time off stage was taken up with keeping an eye on the fortunes of his touring companies and making sure that no one stole his plays. Even though managers agreed terms before his company appeared in their theatres, they were often reluctant to pay up. In August 1862, he had to take the manager of the Theatre Royal, Sheffield, to court for refusing to pay him £180 due from the July engagement of his company, and among the many managers he sued for producing pirated versions of *The Colleen Bawn* was Charles Delafield of the Theatre Royal, Preston. The action, which began in 1861, dragged on for two years and was originally dismissed on the grounds that, since he first produced the play in the United States, Boucicault was not entitled to copyright in England. Boucicault was not prepared to let it go at that, for if the judgement was upheld, it would mean he would be powerless to prevent any manager putting on those plays he had written in America. He immediately sued Delafield for £2,600 damages. Delafield, who had in the meantime gone broke, as a result, he claimed, of Boucicault's injunction restraining him from presenting his version of the play and his having nothing to put in its place, counter-sued, and won. The judge awarded him 5 guineas – the cost of printing the posters – but refused costs on the grounds that, although the law stated Boucicault was not protected by English copyright, morally the play was his. From that moment on, Boucicault either rewrote his plays to make them 'original' or, if he was producing them first in America, made sure they were given a copyright performance somewhere in England or Canada (which, for copyright purposes, was considered to be English).

The writs of this period were not all one way. Shortly after Boucicault had successfully produced *The Relief of Lucknow* at Drury Lane, an actor-dramatist, William Seaman, issued a writ for breach of copyright on his play of the same name, which had been produced in February 1858, at the Britannia Theatre, Hoxton, claiming damages of £1,000 and £2 a performance. Boucicault denied the charge vigorously, claiming that if anyone had stolen the play it must have been Seaman from him since his version had been seen throughout Britain ever since its New York production in the same month of the same year. Seaman was unable to prove his charge and the action was eventually dropped with Seaman being ordered to pay costs.

There was one other case in which Boucicault featured prominently, even though he did not appear in court: the case of Jordan *versus* Colonel Gibbon. In the summer of 1862, as was usual when Agnes became pregnant, Boucicault's attentions turned towards young actresses, on this occasion, Emily Thorne, the second wife of the American actor, George Jordan, and a member of his Drury Lane company.[1] The Boucicaults had known Jordan for a long time in America – Agnes had played Cleopatra opposite his Antony in the burlesque of *Antony and Cleopatra* at Burton's Theatre when she made her New York début in 1853, and later George became a member of one of Boucicault's companies. When the Jordans arrived in London in July 1861, it was only natural that their acquaintance should have been renewed. The two families became firm friends, and when, in June 1862, Boucicault was setting up his company to open at Drury Lane, he offered Emily an engagement which, against her husband's wishes, she accepted. Before long she had become Boucicault's mistress. Since her relationship with Jordan was not going well, Boucicault persuaded her to leave him and move into rooms in Pall Mall, just around the corner from his own *pied-à-terre* in King Street, St James's, where he was conveniently staying to be close to the theatre while Agnes was confined at Hereford House. Jordan, an extremely jealous man, was naturally suspicious and took to following his wife. One September night, shortly after midnight, he was standing on the pavement opposite her lodgings in Pall Mall when he saw Boucicault's carriage approach, his wife get out and the carriage drive away. A few minutes later Boucicault returned on foot, the front door opened without his having to knock and he went in. Angrily, Jordan rushed across the street and began to pound at the door. When his wife finally opened it, he demanded to know where Boucicault was hiding. The playwright, having heard Jordan's voice, had retreated upstairs and locked himself in the rooms of another lodger, Colonel Gibbon, who was out for the evening. Jordan's angry shouts roused the landlady, who went downstairs to find out what was happening at the same time as the unsuspecting Colonel Gibbon, of the Royal Engineers, returned from his club. The landlady appealed to the colonel to remove the noisy Jordan, a scuffle broke out and Jordan ran upstairs and into the colonel's rooms where, unknown to Gibbon, Boucicault was locked in the bedroom. Jordan, convinced Boucicault was inside, insisted on staying outside the bedroom door until his wife's lover emerged. The colonel, still not quite clear as to what was going on, sent for the police to have Jordan removed; the actor was arrested and Boucicault was able to creep from his hiding place and make his escape.

The matter did not end there. The following day Jordan sued Gibbon for wrongful arrest, and although Boucicault was not called as a witness, his name was mentioned freely in court and it was clear that Jordan had taken the action to get even with him. Boucicault was reduced to writing to the press to put his version of events.

I deny most indignantly the guilty imputations and disgraceful acts laid to my charge [he thundered to *The Times*].[2] I heard that he had expressed some suspicions respecting my relations with the lady . . . I regret to say I did not tell Mrs Boucicault of these suspicions respecting me, as I did not wish to give her anxiety or trouble at the time . . . On the night in question she had begged me to lend her some books. After dropping her at the door I returned immediately with the works. I had scarcely entered the hall when I heard a knock at the door. Presuming it was one of the other lodgers and fearing my presence in the hall even might cause some remark, I withdrew to let them pass . . . Mr Jordan brought an action against Colonel Gibbon, in order that a scandalous story might go forth to the public, as it has done, without investigation or defence. This trial was not, nor was it intended to be, against the nominal defendant: it was against me.

Boucicault, although almost totally bald and slight, seems to have been irresistible to women. He could, when he chose, be the most witty and charming companion, and his conversation was generally considered to be the finest to be heard anywhere. The cleverest lines in his plays were those he uttered while talking. He was, as William Winter wrote, in the habit of writing his dialogues. 'Dion Boucicault was, without exception, the most fascinating man I ever met,' confessed Jane, daughter of the artist William Frith. 'Even as a child he fascinated me. I don't know what it might have been had I been grown up.'[3]

Boucicault lived in an age when it was accepted that men in society had mistresses, and he was no different from other men. However, while he felt free to go in whatever direction he fancied, there was never any question of him allowing Agnes even to flirt with a man. While they were at the Adelphi in *The Colleen Bawn*, the drummer in the band had fallen madly in love with her. He took to waxing his moustache, curling his hair and wearing large buttonholes to try and attract her attention. He began to follow her home, and one day, when she was walking with the children in Kensington

Park, he plucked up the courage to face her, kissed her hand passionately and handed her a letter declaring his adoration. Agnes was so amused she passed it on to Boucicault, who promptly went to the theatre and refused to leave until the writer had been identified. The drummer was sacked from the Adelphi and fled from London to take a job in Marseilles.[4]

The Jordan affair, when it became public in May 1863, had a disastrous effect upon Boucicault's fortunes. His year and a half of working with and under Webster, and the success of his short stay at Drury Lane, had again convinced him that he had to be his own manager and that he was the only person who knew how to run a modern theatre the way it ought to be run. He had decided to use the considerable fortune he and Agnes had made from The Colleen Bawn (somewhat in excess of £23,000) to put his ideas into practice. Since he begrudged paying £4,000 a year rent to someone else, he elected to build his own theatre, and outlined his plans in a letter to The Times.[5]

I plead then for the erection of a new theatre, wherein the public shall find combined the improvements of the American and French systems. Few architects have given special attention to theatrical structures, and I have never seen or heard of any engineering ability applied to stage machinery . . . In 1859 I built in New York the Winter Garden Theatre, capable of containing 2,500 persons, being very little less than the capacity of the Theatre Royal, Drury Lane. With the same entertainments as at the Adelphi Theatre, the Winter Garden consumed 20,000 feet of gas per week; the Adelphi consumes 100,000. The number of carpenters required to work the stage in London varies from 20 to 30; in New York the same work is done by six. Here we employ five or six gasmen; there the same work is well performed by a man and a boy. While in management at the Adelphi Theatre I saw three men endeavouring to move a piece of scenery. I caused a simple contrivance to be attached to it, and a child was then able to move it readily with his forefinger. One might suppose that such an economy of labour would have been generally adopted, but our English nature is jealous of improvement and suspicious of reform.

His point was valid; theatres were clumsy to operate and running costs were high. But, of course, it would take time, more time than he was prepared to spend away from acting and active management, to find a suitable plot of land, draw up plans, raise the finance and build the kind of theatre he wanted to run. So, as a temporary measure, he began to look around for the right sort of building to convert, and found what he was looking for in Astley's Amphitheatre, an old circus ring in Lambeth, just south of the river. Astley's, which was then named Batty's after the current lessee, was the home of equestrian drama (*Richard III* had been given there on horseback, with White Surrey, Richmond's horse, being given a leading role), and the shape and size of the auditorium was quite unsuitable for staging plays. In October 1862, Boucicault took out a two-year lease on it and immediately began to pour large sums of money into having it converted. He tore out the boxes and replaced them with larger ones, added balcony stalls with comfortable seats and divided the pit area into two, introducing twenty rows of 'commodious chairs' which were numbered and could be reserved for an extra 6*d.* (a scheme that didn't work out since audiences were too used to a first-come, first-served system and refused to move for latecomers who had booked). The interior was repainted blue and white, the proscenium arch and interior of the boxes were painted crimson, and the central chandelier, which provided the most illumination, was drawn up into a ceiling recess so that the occupants of the upper boxes were no longer blinded. The light from the gas jets was increased by a series of reflectors, and during the interval, to keep the audience amused, Boucicault proposed having a series of special curtains on which riddles and conundrums would be painted, the answers to be given on a special slide machine of his own design.[6]

In addition to acquiring the lease of Astley's, Boucicault also bought the eight houses next to the theatre, overlooking the river, planning to build a vast scene dock to serve that theatre and another he proposed building in the West End, and to convert the entire site into a complex that would include restaurants, bars, pleasure gardens and attractive covered walkways. It was a much more grandiose version of the ill-fated Winter Garden scheme.

Work had started on the conversion while Boucicault and Agnes were appearing at Drury Lane, and as soon as the season there was over, Boucicault sent Agnes to Liverpool with *The Relief of Lucknow*, to keep the production going while he stayed in London to supervise the alterations – and continue his affair with Emily Jordan, whom he had moved into a private hotel, for although the incident in the Pall Mall lodgings had taken place, the case of Jordan *versus* Gibbon had not yet come to court and there was no reason for Boucicault to suppose the affair was about to become public knowledge.

Completely refurbished, and renamed the New Theatre Royal, Westminster, Astley's reopened to the public under Boucicault's management on 22 December 1862, with Boucicault and Agnes appearing for the first time in London in Tom Taylor's *To Parents and Guardians*, followed by *The Relief of Lucknow*. The plays were well received by the sparse but fashionable audience that had crossed the river for the first night, and those critics friendly towards Boucicault predicted a successful future for both the season and the theatre. Those who were antagonistic lost no time in attacking. Nothing about the theatre was new, they claimed; Boucicault was unendurably conceited in presuming to have saved London playgoers from themselves – 'If he can give us a better theatre than we have at present, let him do it without this blatant self-praise and arrogance,' wrote one.[7]

The ignorant public [opined another] have it would seem been labouring under the erroneous impression that the quondam Astley's is in the middle of Lambeth-marsh, and is much nearer the New-cut than St James's Park; but the 'model manager' knows a great deal better. He has 'edited,' 'adapted,' and 'rearranged' the map of London, and we only wonder that he does not claim copyright in his new scheme of topography.[8]

THEATRE ROYAL WESTMINSTER

(ASTLEY'S)
PLAY BILL,

AND UNIVERSAL EVENING ADVERTISER.

| No. 1. | LONDON, 1862. | GRATIS. |

Under the Management of Mr. DION BOUCICAULT.

Mr. & Mrs. DION BOUCICAULT & Mde. CELESTE

Every Night at Seven & every Saturday Afternoon at Two.

On MONDAY, December 22nd, 1862, and every Night

The Performances will commence with the COMIC DRAMA IN ONE ACT,

TO PARENTS AND GUARDIANS,

BY TOM TAYLOR Esq.

Mr. SWISS ... ... Mr. MELLON.   Doggett ... ... Mr. RYAN.   Monsieur TOURBILLON (the French Usher) ... Mr. DION BOUCICAULT.
... ... Mr. D. LEESON.   ... ... Mr. REEGAN.   Boss NETTLES ... ... Mrs. DION BOUCICAULT.
SCRASE ... ... Miss ROBERTS   S. ... ... HAYMAN.   Brown ... ... Miss ITEALBY.   Thornton ... ... Miss STANTON.
Thompson ... Miss VAUGHAN.   Jones ... ... Miss BAILEY.   Nevilla ... ... Miss LEE.   Hargrave ... ... Miss PEARCE.
Spencer ... Miss HERBERT.   Howell ... Miss MILLS.   Norton ... Miss HAZLEWOOD.   Sinclair ... ... Miss BEACHA.
Mary Swish ... Miss EDITH STUART.   Lady Nettles ... Miss WELLS.   Virginie ... Miss ROSE LECLERCQ.

To conclude with (at Half-past Eight) on MONDAY and TUESDAY. the new Scotch Drama and Military Spectacle, in Four Acts, entitled the

RELIEF OF LUCKNOW!

WRITTEN BY DION BOUCICAULT, THE AUTHOR OF COLLEEN BAWN.

The Scenery by and under the direction of Mr. W. BEVERLEY. New Dresses, Scenery, and Appointments. The Military Spectacular Effects by Mr. BOUCICAULT, under whose direction the Drama is produced.

BEFORE THE SIEGE.
ACT FIRST.
THE BUNGALOW ON THE HILLS OF THE RAPTEE.
A Scotch Home in India—The Mutterings of the Storm—The Wolves around the Sheepfold—The Scotch Watch Dogs and the Bengal Tigers.
ACT SECOND.
THE ENCAMPMENT OF THE RAJAH GHOLAN BAHADOOR
In the Ruins of the Summum
The Prayer of the Ramadan—The Hindoo Festival—The Apsara—The Surprise—The Banks of the Raptee.
THE GHOORKA PASS AND RAPTEE FALLS.
The Scotch Girl brought to bay by the Rebels—Her Last Chance.
DURING THE SIEGE.
ACT THIRD.
THE MOSQUE OF SHAH JEHAN IN LUCKNOW.
The Head Quarters of the Rajah Gholam Bahadoor—The Scotch Prisoners—The Flag of Truce—The Mine and Counter Mine—The Treachery and the Rescue.
THE 25TH SEPTEMBER, 1857.

ACT FOURTH.
THE REDAN FORT.—THE LAST RATIONS.
The Guardian Angel of the Besieged—The Resolve—The Engagement of the Relieving Forces with the Rebels.
CHARGE OF THE 78TH HIGHLANDERS
AND THE RELIEF OF LUCKNOW.

CHARACTERS.—EUROPEANS.
RANDAL McGREGOR (a Captain in the 78th Highlanders)... Mr. SWINBOURNE.
GEORDIE MACGREGOR, his younger Brother, an Ensign in the 32nd Regiment... Mr. CHARLES VANDENHOFF.
THE REV. DAVID O'GRADY (Chaplain of the 32nd Regiment)...Mr. H. MELLON.
CASSIDY (an Irish Corporal in the 32nd Regiment, in love with Je... Mr. DION BOUCICAULT.
SWEENY (A Drummer in the 32nd Regiment, in love with Jessie)...Mr. D. LEESON.
... ... Mr. DION BOUCICAULT.
JE... ... Miss N... ... ... Alice ... Miss CRAVEN.
Mary ... ... Miss N...

HINDOOS.
THE RAJAH GHOLAN BAHADOOR ... ... Mr. RYDER.
MOULVIE-DEEN ... ... (a Rajpoot Prince) ... Mr. M. SMYTHSON.
ACHMET ... ... Mr. EDWIN.
Sepoys, Apsara Girls in the Train of the Rajah.

To conclude, on CHRISTMAS-EVE, Wednesday. Dec. 24th, w... New Comic Pantomime, entitled

LADY BIRD
OR
Harlequin Lord Dundreary,

ENTIRELY NEW SCENERY, BY MR. ROBERTS AND ASSISTANTS.

| EDWARD STIRLING | - - - - | ACTING MANAGER. |

[ENTERED AT STATIONERS' HALL.]

Opening night of the New Theatre Royal, Westminster (formerly
Astley's Circus Ring, Lambeth), 22 December 1862. The programme
was given away free and was paid for by advertising – four shillings
per inch per week.

And that was the real trouble with the New Theatre Royal, Westminster – it was not situated in Westminster at all, but on the unfashionable south side of the river, the side where artisans lived, where cut-throats and garrotters stalked the streets, and where no self-respecting member of society would be seen. Boucicault was aware of the unsavoury reputation of the neighbourhood, and since his theatre was only just across the river and could be seen from the north bank, he stressed in his advertisements its closeness to the parks and the fashionable areas. The theatre, which 'inasmuch as it lies in Lambeth, he as an Irishman, of course, calls the Theatre Royal, Westminster', attracted some business, but not enough to make it a real success. It was ironic that, only a year later, the manager to whom Boucicault sold his lease, E. T. Smith, was able to draw all London there to see Adah Isaacs Menken in *Mazeppa*, an equestrian drama based on Byron's poem.

For his second presentation, opening on Boxing Day, Boucicault introduced *Lady Bird; or, Harlequin Lord Dundreary*, the first new piece he had written since *The Colleen Bawn* more than two years before. This was an attempt to revive the traditional English pantomime, which Boucicault temporarily declared to be the most important aspect of English drama. The performance was given as a dumb-show, and although certain elderly critics who remembered seeing the great Joseph Grimaldi admired and praised Boucicault's intentions, most of the audiences found it boring. After a disappointing run, it was joined on the bills, on 26 January 1863, by *The Trial of Effie Deans*, and finally came off in the middle of February. *The Trial of Effie Deans* was the play *Jeanie Deans* which had enjoyed a successful run at Laura Keene's Theatre, and saved her season, three years earlier. Boucicault was hoping it would do the same for him. Agnes again played the lead, and Boucicault took the role of Counsel for the Defence, and they were supported by a strong company that included Dan Leeson, John Ryder, Edith Stuart and Harry J. Montague, a protégé of Boucicault who was making his professional début (and was later to become a popular matinée idol in the United States). The play opened to mixed reviews. Some critics welcomed the opportunity to see a play of which they had heard much, and warmly praised both the acting and the production. Others seized the chance to get in a few more attacks on the dramatist:

> Mr Boucicault, whose genius seems to consist in rather the disinterring of old dramas than in the writing and adapting of new ones . . . after publicly protesting against the term 'Sensation Drama' and asking pardon for having invented it . . . has grown sufficiently reconciled to his error to return to it; and, judging by the very emphatic manner in which he states the fact in his bill, he must feel that the attraction of his present venture depends not a little on such an announcement. [9]

But still the public could not be persuaded to patronize the theatre in large numbers, and Boucicault introduced afternoon performances for the aged, the infirm, mothers and children, and those people who were unable or unwilling to go to the theatre in the evening, a move that was denounced as disgusting and degrading for both audiences and artists who were made to paint their faces and don their tinsel in broad daylight. [10]

Undeterred by the poor houses and lack of interest shown in Astley's, Boucicault pressed ahead with his second plan, to build a revolutionary new theatre. When he had first announced his schemes in his letter to *The Times* the previous October, he had predicted profits of at least £20,000 a year and had been inundated with offers of money from people anxious to share in his good fortune. He now decided that the time had come to take up those offers and formed the New Theatre Company. In addition to its job of raising finance for the building of a new theatre on a site Boucicault had acquired in the Haymarket, it was proposed that the company should take over responsibility for Astley's, retaining his services as artistic director for one-third of the profits, and see to completion his plan for converting the eight neighbouring houses into a leisure complex. Through his social connections Boucicault was able to persuade such men as the Duke of Wellington (son of the Iron Duke), the Duke of Leinster and the Marquis of

Normanby, to become patrons, and shares were offered to the public with a proposed first year dividend of 10 per cent.[11]

> Although a large number of shares were privately subscribed for, [recalled Edward Stirling, Boucicault's manager at Astley's], the ignorant public held aloof, slow to believe or accept this very promising undertaking. Fancy twenty per cent and a life privilege of walking in a beautiful garden theatre, ornamented by grottoes, cascades, and endless attractions (on paper)! The whole thing fell flat; City men did not believe in it; West-enders simply laughed at this flight of Dion's fancy.[12]

Out of 25,000 shares offered for sale, only 1,500, at a cost of £25 each, were taken up; a pitiful number, but enough for Boucicault, on behalf of the company, to go ahead and complete the purchase of the Haymarket site.

The New Theatre Company took over responsibility for Astley's in March 1863, and it was soon apparent that, far from buying into a successful and profitable venture, the subscribers had been sold a pup. There had been, and still was, considerable opposition to Astley's from other London managers, notably Benjamin Webster, who out of hatred for Boucicault did not want the theatre to succeed; there were growing signs of unrest among the stage crew, who were not being paid; and it was becoming clear that Boucicault, who had spent more than £14,000 on the conversion, much of which had been carried out on credit, was not going to be able to meet his commitments. Hurriedly he rushed his old standby, *The Colleen Bawn*, on to the bills, but even that failed to produce good business, and the final demands started to arrive. Having used up all the money he and Agnes had made from the successful run of *The Colleen Bawn* at the Adelphi in purchasing the lease, paying the actors and starting the New Theatre Company, Boucicault sold all his furniture from Hereford Court in a vain attempt to keep the theatre alive, but it was too late. In April and May the writs from the builders, the carpenters, the property hire companies and even his solicitor began to mount up.

143

He might have been able to weather the storm but for his affair with Emily Jordan. On 12 May, at the very time he was trying to raise the money to stay afloat, the case of George Jordan *versus* Colonel Gibbon came to court, and Boucicault's relationship with Jordan's wife became public knowledge. The wealthy noblemen who had been prepared to assist him felt they could no longer be associated with him publicly and withdrew their patronage from the New Theatre Company. As more and more of his creditors decided to sue, Boucicault had no alternative but to admit defeat, and on 3 July he was declared bankrupt with debts of £31,000.

The failure of Astley's was not entirely Boucicault's fault, nor was it due completely to the siting of the theatre, important though that was. His five-month tenancy had been accompanied by an orchestrated campaign of hate in the national press, and by other managers who were determined he should not succeed. The editor of the *Daily Telegraph* refused to carry advertisements for the theatre unless Boucicault paid double the standard rate, and attacked Boucicault in scathing editorials; protestors gathered every night outside the building with placards complaining that Boucicault was responsible for high theatre rates (protests organized by Webster's manager at the Adelphi);[13] and even the Jordan case, Boucicault claimed with some justification, had been taken to court 'as one feature in a cowardly conspiracy, maintained at the expense of, and promoted by, certain rival theatrical managers who have made no secret of their resolve to ruin me at any hazard, and with my fortunes those of the New Theatre Company, with which I am associated'.[14] Boucicault was being made to pay for having come back to London and having upset the system by demanding a royalty for his plays.

His rivals may have got what they wanted, but Boucicault, far from accepting defeat, was in fighting mood. He promptly sold Hereford House and the neighbouring property, Coleherne Court, which he'd bought as an investment during the prosperous days at the Adelphi, and moved out of London to his other house in Brighton. He sold the contents of his London properties by auction and offered the copyrights of

WEST BROMPTON.

A CATALOGUE

OF THE EXCELLENT AND PERFECTLY

NEW FURNITURE

IN THE RESIDENCE, KNOWN AS

"COLEHERNE COURT,"

COMPRISING—

ARABIAN, FRENCH, AND HALF TESTER BEDSTEADS,

In Spanish Mahogany, polished deal, and Iron; First-class Bedding, Winged and other Wardrobes, Chests of Drawers, and the appendages for thirteen Bedrooms.

Superior Turkey, Brussels, and Kidderminster Carpets,

Axminster and various Rugs, portion of the

VERY HANDSOME DRAWING ROOM SUITE,

In Italian Walnut, viz., a 6ft. 3in., elegantly designed Cheffonier, Loo, Writing, and Card Tables, and richly ornamented gilt Chimney and Pier Glasses, with Marble Top Tables; a capital SET OF MAHOGANY DINING TABLES with patent screw action, a 7ft. 3in. Spanish Mahogany Pedestal Sideboard, open Bookcases, Set of Twelve beautifully made Mahogany Chairs, with seats and backs covered in hard grained morocco, three Oak Hall Tables and Benches, and other Effects.

WHICH WILL BE SOLD BY AUCTION, BY

MESSRS. DEBENHAM & TEWSON,

Upon the Premises (in pursuance of instructions from the Assignees of Mr. Dion Boucicault),

On Thursday, the 20th of August, 1863, at 12 for 1 o'clock punctually.

N.B. The Furniture enumerated in this Catalogue has only just been supplied by a West End Upholsterer, and has never been used.

May be viewed on the Monday preceding the Sale, or previously by cards to view from the Auctioneers' Offices; and Catalogues (price 6d.) had on the Premises; of Messrs. Linklater and Hackwood, Solicitors, No. 7, Walbrook; of Messrs. Harding, Pullein, Whinney, and Gibbons, Accountants, 3, Bank Buildings, Lothbury; and of

MESSRS. DEBENHAM AND TEWSON, Auctioneers and Estate Agents, 80, Cheapside, E.C.

Boucicault bought Coleherne Court, next door to Hereford House, his Earl's Court home, as a speculation in September 1862 and spent £2,300 on furnishing it. Following his bankruptcy a year later he was forced to get rid of both houses.

eight of his most successful plays (including *The Colleen Bawn*, which was estimated to be worth £2,500, and *The Octoroon*, worth £750) to his creditors. Within six weeks of being declared bankrupt, he applied for his discharge, and during his examination was able to satisfy the Commissioner that he had no personal debts, that a large part of the responsibility for Astley's belonged to the New Theatre Company, and that he would pay off as much as he could as soon as he could. The Commissioner was impressed and, congratulating Boucicault on the way he had handled his affairs, granted the discharge.

Dismissing the Astley's failure in typical fashion – 'Successes live and you record them. Failures are still-born children that don't count'[15] – Boucicault set about restoring his fortunes. He and Agnes, who had stood by him loyally, saying nothing except to deny that she was leaving him over the affair with Emily Jordan, accepted an offer to appear at the Prince of Wales's Theatre, Liverpool, for twelve nights, followed by engagements in Manchester and Edinburgh. They opened in Liverpool on 27 July in *Pauvrette*, the adaptation that had been seen in New York five years earlier, and then appeared in *The Colleen Bawn*. It was the first time either of them had appeared outside London (apart from the visit to Dublin) since they had become famous and returned from the States, and so eager were the citizens of Liverpool to see the celebrated couple that their stay had to be extended to five weeks. The curiosity and excitement were repeated in Manchester and then in Edinburgh, where they appeared for the new manager Charles Wyndham. Not surprisingly, the events of the previous six months had taken their toll on Boucicault and he was forced to withdraw from the company in Edinburgh, suffering from nervous exhaustion. After a few days' rest, he was sufficiently recovered to resume acting, and they returned to Liverpool at the beginning of December for the opening of *How She Loves Him*, a five-act play which was given on the same bill as *The Colleen Bawn*. A slight comedy, with echoes of the Restoration plots Boucicault had favoured in his early days as a dramatist, the new play, with Agnes as Atalanta Cruiser and Boucicault as Diogenes, an Irish barrel orator, afforded an interesting contrast with the popular melodrama, and the two stars won warm acclaim for their acting.

There was never any question of Boucicault and his family starving after the bankruptcy. He and Agnes could always earn an adequate income from their acting, and he had formed another touring company, under Dan Leeson, to play The Octoroon, which was bringing in a regular income. But what he really needed to erase the memory of Astley's was another massively popular hit. He had always boasted, with justification, that he was an author from whom some managers drew blanks while others drew fortunes;[16] he now needed to work the miracle for himself. It was to happen in a way that was to surprise him.

After the astounding success of the Boucicaults' first appearance in Liverpool and the enthusiasm which greeted their subsequent re-engagement with How She Loves Him, Alexander Henderson, manager of the Prince of Wales, asked Boucicault to provide him with another new piece. Since Pauvrette had gone down well, Boucicault decided to use another play that had served him well in America and not been seen in England, The Poor of New York. Changing the title to The Poor of Liverpool, he localized the setting so that Union Square, New York, became Williamson Square, Crawley's house was in Prince's Park, scenes took place outside the Adelphi Hotel and in Ranelagh Street, and there were panoramic views of Liverpool from across the Mersey. To amuse Henderson, Boucicault included a disparaging remark about Copeland, the manager of the rival Amphitheatre. 'Enterprise of any kind,' says a character, pointing to Copeland's theatre, 'never enters that house.' Henderson turned the play down. The Boucicaults did not intend to play in it (and, as far as he was concerned, they were the attraction not the play), and he was not prepared to accept Boucicault's suggestion that, in place of a royalty fee, the playwright should share in the profits. So Boucicault took it to Copeland, who agreed to put in on. When the time came for the first read-through, Boucicault realized that the remark about Copeland was still in and rushed to cut it out, but Copeland, who found the line amusing, ordered the play to be performed without alteration. To the mystification of the cast and the public, the sarcasm remained throughout the play's run.

The Poor of Liverpool opened at the Amphitheatre on 10 February 1864, two nights after the Boucicaults had started a third engagement with Henderson at the Prince of Wales, playing again in *How She Loves Him*. If the scene of the burning house, with the arrival on stage of the fire-engine, had caused a sensation in New York, it caused a riot in Liverpool. Night after night people packed the house to witness the exciting spectacle, and Boucicault realized he had found a winning formula: all he had to do was localize the play and each city had its very own special drama.

> When the wind blows, then the mill goes; and Fortune's gale is making my mill spin round likes blazes [he wrote to Edward Stirling]. I have developed a new vein in the theatrical mine, and one in which you can have an interest beyond that you always feel in my success. I have tried the bold step of producing – originally in the provinces – a sensation drama, without aid or assistance of any kind. The experiment has succeeded. I introduced *The Poor of Liverpool*, a bob-tail piece, with local scenery, and Mr Cowper in the principal part. I share after thirty pounds a night, and I am making a hundred pounds a week on the damned thing. I localize it for each town, and hit the public between the eyes; so they see nothing but fire. Eh voila! I can spin out these rough-and-tumble dramas as a hen lays eggs. It's a degrading occupation, but more money has been made out of guano than out of poetry.[17]

So *The Poor of Liverpool* became *The Poor of Leeds*, *The Poor of Manchester*, *The Streets of Islington* (when it was played at Sadler's Wells) and *The Streets of London*, when it opened at the Princess's. During its initial run in Liverpool, it brought Boucicault just under £1,000 in nine weeks, and by localizing the script and sending it out to his touring companies, he was able to more than double that figure. Taken with the fees he and Agnes were receiving for their own tours to Manchester,

Dublin, Glasgow, Birmingham and other provincial cities, Boucicault was making more money than he could have done by playing in the West End. He was, of course, keen to return to London, but before he did so he wanted to be armed with such a certain success that not even his most vociferous critics would be able to keep the public away; and he had a score to settle with those managers who had driven him into bankruptcy. Whatever they might have said in public, he knew that most of them were delighted by the failure of Astley's and he wanted his return to be a triumph, forcing them to eat humble pie. He wanted it to be with another quality play, similar to *The Colleen Bawn*, an Irish play of which he could be proud. He did not want it to be on the back of a work of which he had such a low opinion.

However, the success of *The Poor of . . .* had not gone unnoticed in London, and among those people who were keen to stage it was George Vining of the Princess's. At first Boucicault refused all overtures. He genuinely did not think much of the play, even though reaction in the provinces told him he had found another winner, and no manager would agree to his proposal that, after the first £100 taken every evening, the rest should be divided equally between manager and author. Eventually Vining, who had been having a very disappointing season and was desperate for success, and who also saw the role of Badger as one in which he could shine, agreed to Boucicault's terms. As soon as they heard of the deal, the other London managers were horrified and tried to talk Vining out of it. It was bad enough to give a writer a royalty based on box-office returns, but what Boucicault was demanding, and had got – half the profits – was a clear case of blackmail. But Vining was in no position to listen to their entreaties, and it was as well for him that he didn't. When *The Streets of London* opened on 1 August, the Princess's became the most popular theatre in the West End.

I went the other night to see *The Streets of London* at the Princess's [wrote Charles Dickens in a letter to John Forster], a piece that is really drawing all the town, and filling the house with nightly overflows. It is the most depressing instance, without exception, of an utterly degrading and debasing theatrical taste that has ever come under my notice. For not only do the audiences – of all classes – go, but they are unquestionably delighted.[18]

Just over a year after he had crashed so spectacularly in the Astley's venture and been declared a bankrupt, Boucicault had gained his revenge. He was back in London as England's most well-paid, successful playwright.

9

'HOW DOTH THE BUSY DION B.'

IT MUST have been galling to Boucicault's enemies to see how quickly and effortlessly he had managed to shrug off his misfortunes. By the middle of 1864, only a year after his discharge from bankruptcy, he was making enough money from his touring companies, and from the production of *The Streets of London* at the Princess's, to be able to give up touring himself, buy a new London home at 326 Regent Street (on the corner with Mortimer Street), and begin serious writing again. He could even afford to pay £1,000 to become a subscriber for a Grand Tier Box, holding ten seats, at the newly projected Royal Albert Hall.[1]

The Boucicaults lived close to their work in the upper part of a house in Regent Street, nearly opposite the old Polytechnic, surrounded by a large and young family, happy themselves, and a source of happiness to many others – myself amongst the number [wrote John Hollingshead, manager of the Gaiety Theatre, in his autobiography]. Boucicault was a patient and constant worker – a temperate man, simple in his habits, who treated dramatic authorship as a trade. He worked harder than a banker's clerk, and made his brother, who acted as his secretary, work also. Early and late, he never idled, and after his pleasant little dinner parties and social gatherings he regained his lost time by increased industry.[2]

Among the many visitors to the Regent Street apartments were the young American brothers, Ira and William Davenport. The Davenports had created a sensation as young boys in Buffalo in 1848 with their claims of being able to hear 'voices', and, realizing how gullible people could be, had cashed in on their talents by holding a series of profitable séances. In 1855 they were taken to New York and were exposed as frauds, but the exposure only made them rehearse their 'act' more carefully, and for more than ten years they made a very comfortable living touring the United States as spiritualists. In 1864 they decided to visit Europe, beginning with a tour of Britain. The news aroused great interest and controversy between those who 'believed' in the brothers and those who thought they were skilful magicians and nothing else; and somehow, much to his delight, Boucicault was able to persuade them to make their first appearance at a specially organized séance in his rooms in front of twenty-two distinguished friends and colleagues, who would pronounce on whether or not the brothers were genuine. Boucicault was not a spiritualist himself, nor was he particularly religious (although he read and knew his Bible well, and often spent hours discussing obscure points of theology with his brother William, who was later converted to Catholicism). The idea of spirit manifestations fascinated him, however; it appealed to his sense of theatre.

The séance took place at four o'clock one early October afternoon.[3] The room, from which most of the furniture had been removed, had been carefully checked by the observing guests, and the Davenport brothers, with their manager William Fay, had their clothes searched to make sure they had nothing concealed about their persons. The brothers were then tied, hand and foot, and placed at either end of a long cabinet, in the middle of which had been placed several musical instruments, purchased especially for the occasion. Almost at once the bells began to ring, a violin played a snatch of a tune, a guitar was plucked and a trumpet sounded before flying from the cabinet and landing on the floor. Hands appeared at various apertures in the cabinet, and yet, when the doors were opened, both men were still securely bound to their seats. For the next part of the demonstration, one of the spectators, Sir Charles Wyke, was invited into the cabinet to sit between the brothers, his hands being tied, one to each of them. While the instruments again started to play, Sir Charles's hair was pulled, his face was touched and the instruments moved against him, hitting him. When he emerged, he said he had been unable to detect any trickery. Since he was in total darkness, this is not perhaps surprising. Other 'spiritual manifestations' took place during the two-hour séance, and at the finish the guests came to the unanimous conclusion that they had been unable to detect any trickery or assistance from either machinery or associates, and that, as far as they could all tell, the events that had taken place were not the result of legerdemain. These findings were made public.

Although they had been careful not to state that the manifestations had anything to do with spiritualism, the fact that none of Boucicault's guests had been able to find anything wrong gave immediate approval to the Davenport brothers' claims, and produced derisive comments in the press. Boucicault, of course, bore the brunt of the scorn and was moved to reply.

I have no belief in what is called spiritualism [he wrote], and nothing I have seen inclines me to believe in it; indeed, the puerility of some of the demonstrations would sufficiently alienate such a theory; but I do believe that we have not quite explored the realms of natural philosophy – that this enterprise of thought has of late years been confined to useful inventions, and we are content at last to think that the laws of nature are finite, ascertained, and limited to the scope of our knowledge . . . Some persons think that the requirement of darkness seems to infer trickery. Is not a dark chamber essential in the process of photography? And what would we reply to him who would say, 'I believe photography to be humbug – do it all in the light, and we will believe otherwise'? It is true that we know why darkness is necessary to the production of the sun-pictures; and if scientific men will subject these phenomena to analysis, we shall find out why darkness is essential to such manifestations. It is a subject which scientific men are not justified in treating with the neglect of contempt.[4]

Boucicault's logical explanation of his position hardly satisfied the journalists, and they continued to mock him. 'I notice,' he wrote angrily to the editor of *The Times* in a letter the paper refused to publish, 'that on all the journals that have attacked this matter, the writers are dramatic authors, more or less; and if I tread on their toes in the theatre it is only fair that they should feel for mine on the press. This they have done consistently for twenty years past, and I continue to exchange such little civilities with imperturbable good humour.' But, he maintained, their refusal to publish his version of the séance while printing the accounts of people who were not present, 'is not fair journalism'.[5]

One person who was not taken in by the Davenport brothers was actor Henry Irving. It is often supposed that he was present at the séance in Boucicault's rooms, but his name does not feature on any list of those who attended, and he was, at the time, acting in Manchester. Although he and Boucicault were to become good friends, their acquaintance in October 1864 was slight. They had met only once, the previous February, when Boucicault had, on one of his tours, directed Irving as Hardress Cregan in a production of *The Colleen Bawn* at the Theatre Royal, Manchester. Since the playwright hardly spoke to the actor and was not to work with him again for two years, and in March Irving had appeared in a pirated version of *The Poor of Manchester*, playing the juvenile lead, it seems unlikely that Irving would have been invited to travel to London to join such an intimate gathering. However, he must have seen the Davenport brothers performing, for on 25 February 1865, he and two friends from the Theatre Royal, Manchester, company (one of whom, Frederick Maccabe, was an amateur conjuror), staged a replica of the Davenports' act before an invited audience. Every one of the brothers' tricks was successfully reproduced, and when Irving refused to repeat the show on a regular basis, he was dismissed from the company. As for the Davenports, their reception throughout Britain, though profitable, was much less cordial than it had been at Boucicault's house; wherever they appeared there were riots.

In between social engagements, Boucicault was hard at work writing. *Omoo; or, The Sea of Ice*, a reworking of a French play which had been seen in London some years earlier in a version by another writer, was written for and produced by William Copeland at the Liverpool Amphitheatre on 24 October. No expense was spared on the production, with its spectacular scenery depicting the Northern Lights and an ice-flow adrift in the Atlantic, and Boucicault travelled to Liverpool to supervise it. If the play didn't quite match Copeland's expectations – he was hoping for another *Poor of Liverpool* – it still ran for a very profitable four weeks.

After the first night of *Omoo*, Boucicault crossed the Irish Channel to Dublin for the staging of his next new piece, *Arrah-na-Pogue*, at the Theatre Royal. When the play opened on 7 November, he appeared as Shaun the Post and Agnes played Arrah Meelish (Arrah-na-Pogue, or Arrah of the Kiss). It was received with wild enthusiasm, and Boucicault became the idol of the Dublin public, cheered in the streets and visited in his hotel by well-wishers and people who just wanted to look at him. Two other Dublin theatres mounted simultaneous productions of *The Colleen Bawn* in his honour.

In *Arrah-na-Pogue*, Boucicault had returned for the second time to his homeland for inspiration. Although there are definite affinities with Samuel Lover's novel, *Rory O'More* (a dramatization of which Boucicault had played in as a young actor in Cheltenham and Brighton), *Arrah-na-Pogue* is, in almost every respect, that rarity, an original Boucicault play. Based on historical events which took place during the Fenian rebellion of 1798, its incidents and characters are an obvious attempt to cash in on the popularity of *The Colleen Bawn*, but, popular though it was, the result is in many ways inferior. The hero, Beamish MacCoul, is a dashing but stereotype rebel;

Arrah and Fanny, the two women, possess little of the vitality of Eily O'Connor or Anne Chute; and Shaun the Post (the Myles character, again played by Boucicault) has little of Myles's interest until later in the play, when he is captured and forced to become the rogue everyone expects him to be. However, the play possesses some clever and effective dialogue, and is well constructed with some notable scenes – particularly Shaun's escape from prison (which was added after the Dublin production), and the trial, in which Shaun mocks British justice. George Bernard Shaw, who knew Boucicault's plays well, paid him the compliment of basing the trial scene in *The Devil's Disciple* on Shaun's trial, and there are many parallels between the two, even down to the dialogue. Shaw's character of the languorous British officer, General Burgoyne, has its counterpart in Boucicault's Irish gentleman, Colonel O'Grady; Major Coffin is very similar in attitude and ineptitude to Shaw's Major Swindon; and several other incidents in the Boucicault play found their way into Shaw's.

The Dublin version of the play was not the version Shaw came to know, for much of it was rewritten after the Dublin performances.

I was present at the first performance [recalled Percy Fitzgerald]. It was an altogether different piece from what it afterwards became. There was a last act, in which there was an Irish duel, in a room where the faithful Shaun is so carried away by his excitement as to stand before his master, regardless of the opponent's pistol which 'covered' him, and eagerly direct his aim. Meeting him [Boucicault] on the next day, and congratulating him, he entered gravely on a discussion of the subject. To my surprise he quietly pointed out that the last act would never do and must come out altogether. The rest must be rewritten, the interest concentrated. He was glad he had made the experiment as it gave him the opportunity of removing sad defects. This was an instructive lesson in the craft. Accordingly, when it was reproduced in London, I could scarcely recognize it.[6]

John Brougham, who played The O'Grady in both the original and London productions, could not understand, after the reception in Dublin, why Boucicault should want to alter such an obvious success. When the playwright read his revised version to the cast at the Princess's, Brougham was forced to admit that it was a much better play, demonstrating Boucicault's frequent assertion that 'plays are not written; they are rewritten'.

Apart from dropping the last-act duel and condensing the plot, the major alteration for London was the inclusion of a 'sensation' scene in which Shaun escapes from prison by climbing the ivy-covered tower wall. This was accomplished on stage by special machinery which caused the tower to sink below the stage while the actor climbed, so creating the impression that he was scaling a massive height. And here another puzzle enters Boucicault's story: to whom should the credit be given for the alterations to *Arrah-na-Pogue*? Shortly after the play's London opening (on 22 March 1865), Boucicault sued John Berger, editor of the *London Herald*, for serializing the *Arrah* story without permission. Named as co-plaintiff in the case was Edward Howard House, an American journalist, sixteen years younger than Boucicault.[7] House had refused to enter his father's business, had studied music instead, and then worked as the music and drama critic on the Boston *Courier* and the *New York Tribune* before coming to London to work in theatrical management, at which time he became acquainted with Boucicault. He returned to New York to work on the *Tribune* and the *Times*, and was appointed Professor of English Language and Literature in Tokyo, where he founded the *Tokyo Times* and organized concerts to popularize Western music. Apart from his interest in theatre, the only thing House had in common with Boucicault was a strong anti-imperialist streak, and wherever he went in the world, he always did his best to stir up anti-British feeling. It may well have been House who suggested the idea of a play based on the early struggles for Irish freedom and independence, although the first mention of his involvement came when he was named, with Boucicault as author, in the case filed against Berger, as having made certain additions and alterations to the play; and when the play was registered in the United States, his name was given as co-proprietor. Boucicault later assigned him all US rights in the play, though he was never billed as joint-author or even collaborator. By the time the case against Berger (which Boucicault and House won) came to court House had returned to the United States, and there is no further record of any relationship between the two men, although a copy of one of the songs in the play, 'The Wearing of the Green', was published in America with them named as co-authors. Beyond these few facts, the precise nature of House's contribution to *Arrah-na-Pogue* remains obscure.

'The Wearing of the Green' was based on an old Dublin street ballad that Boucicault remembered hearing from his mother. He updated the words to produce an anti-English lyric, and the song, which was one of the highlights of the play, became the unofficial anthem of the Irish freedom movement. After a revival of the play two years later, in which Agnes and Boucicault repeated their original roles, an explosion at Clerkenwell Prison, which killed twelve people and injured 120, led to its being banned throughout the British Empire, and when Boucicault returned to Dublin with the play he was asked to drop the song on grounds of expediency.

Arrah-na-Pogue, revised and tightened, opened at the Princess's in March and became the hit of the season, running for 164 nights, during which neither Agnes nor Boucicault missed a performance. He had turned again to his native land for inspiration, and it had not only repaid him handsomely, he could also be proud of his work.

Throughout the summer of 1865, while he was appearing at the Princess's, Boucicault continued to live and work at his apartments in Regent Street, and among the many visitors there was Joseph Jefferson, the American actor who had taken part in the Winter Garden season of 1859. Soon after the season had closed, while Boucicault and Agnes were acting at Laura Keene's, Jefferson's wife had died and he embarked on a lengthy tour of the States and Australia, where he stayed for four years before deciding to try his luck in England. He chose a bad time to arrive. For some while American artists with big

ROYAL
Princess's Theatre,
OXFORD STREET.

Sole Lessee and Manager, ... Mr. VINING.

Engagement of Mr. and Mrs.

DION BOUCICAULT.

THIS EVENING,

Will be performed, a New Farce, by Mr. DAVID FISHER, entitled,

HEART-STRINGS
AND
FIDDLE-STRINGS.

| John Thompson, | Twin Brothers, Per- | Mr. R. CATHCART. |
| Tom Thompson, | fumers, Oxford st. | Mr. C. SEYTON. |

| Mozart Ludwig Von | Professional Violinist, Leader of the Band, | |
| Beethoven Smith | Theatres Rural, Brighton Concerts, and elsewhere | Mr. D. FISHER. |

Shop Boy, - - - Master TAPPING.
Kate, (a Florist) Miss HETTY TRACY.
Ellen Wilkinson, (Teacher of Music) Miss EMMA BARNETT

After which (at a Quarter before Eight precisely) the New and Original
Irish Drama, in Three Acts, entitled,

ARRAH
-NA-
ROGUE;
OR,
THE WICKLOW WEDDING.

By the Author of " The Colleen Bawn," and " The Streets of London."

THE NEW SCENERY BY MR. W. TELBIN.
And by Mr. F. LLOYDS and Assistants.

The New Overture and Music by W. C. LEVEY, Composer of "Fanchette," &c.
and R. W. LEVEY, Theatre Royal, Dublin.

The Drama produced under the Stage Direction of the Author.

Arrah-na-Pogue opened in London, in a revised version of the play
that had been seen in Dublin, on 22 March 1865, with Boucicault
as Shaun the Post, and Agnes Robertson as Arrah Meelish.
It became the hit of the season.

reputations at home had been failing to make any impact in London, and since Jefferson was not then enough of a star to guarantee an audience, nor did he have a specific play with which his name was linked, no manager would take the gamble of presenting him. Only Benjamin Webster at the Adelphi expressed any interest in him, and then with the proviso that he must appear in a new play which might succeed on its own even if the actor failed. All the plays in Jefferson's repertoire had already been seen in London, and so he took his problem to his old friend and play-doctor, Boucicault. Among the pieces in which he had appeared, though never with any success, was an adaptation of Washington Irving's story *Rip van Winkle*, and it was this that he suggested to Boucicault he might like to consider revising for him. Boucicault read the story, but wasn't impressed. He found the characters unsympathetic and the story dull, and it had been dramatized many times before; he could see no point in doing another version. Jefferson felt differently, however, and when he offered Boucicault money to make the adaptation, the writer's objections evaporated. Boucicault was not very pleased with his work and handed the manuscript to Jefferson with an apology for the play being so poor. Although the Boucicault version was at variance with how Jefferson viewed the character of Rip, the actor was sufficiently satisfied to take the play to Webster, who agreed to present it. Quite why Webster should have agreed to stage a play written by Boucicault, to whom he had not spoken for more than two years since the playwright walked out on him at the Adelphi, is a puzzle, but it may have had something to do with the poor business he was doing and his knowledge that, whatever his personal opinion of the playwright, a good play from Boucicault's pen would be a godsend.

When the day arrived for the first reading of the play (which Boucicault had had printed for rehearsals, possibly the first occasion on which this had happened), Jefferson went nervously to the theatre. It was his big chance and he didn't want to botch it. To his surprise neither Boucicault nor Webster were at the Adelphi, both having sent notes to apologize for their unavoidable absences, and Jefferson was left to direct the run-through on his own. At the finish, John Billington, a senior member of the company, went over to Jefferson. 'There's a hundred nights in that play,' he said. In the event, there nearly wasn't a single night in it. Throughout the rehearsal period Boucicault had kept away from the theatre, so the week before it was due to open Jefferson invited him to attend a full dress rehearsal. Boucicault watched everything without a word until something went wrong with the setting of a piece of scenery. It was only a small mistake, but he exploded, blaming it on the theatre and its management. In Webster's theatre, in front of Webster's company, he launched into a bitter condemnation of the absent manager, accusing him in the most abusive rhetoric of being incompetent and placing him on a par with the worst managers he had ever come across. At the finish of his harangue, Boucicault stalked from the house, leaving Jefferson and the entire cast shocked by his attack.

What Boucicault hadn't known (though it would probably not have stopped him if he had) was that every word he said had been overheard by Webster, who, knowing the writer would be at the rehearsal, hid himself behind the curtains of a private box to watch what was going on. Soon after Boucicault's departure, Jefferson received a terse note from Webster denouncing the playwright and saying that under no circumstances would he allow a play written by Boucicault to be performed in his theatre. Thoroughly alarmed by this sudden turn of events, Jefferson, who could see the prospect of his London début diminishing as a result of an argument he neither understood nor cared about, hurried to the manager's office only to be told he had already left for home. Jefferson jumped in a cab and followed him, turning the final corner in Kennington just in time to see Webster enter his front door and slam it behind him. In a long, stormy interview, in which Webster made his views on Boucicault quite clear in language 'more tinged with Billingsgate than choice Italian', as Jefferson recalled,[8] the actor persuaded the manager to allow the play to go ahead and it duly opened, as scheduled, on 4 September. It was fortunate for Webster that, however reluctantly, he permitted Jefferson to make his début, for *Rip van*

Winkle ran for 170 nights and restored the Adelphi's ailing fortunes. It also made Jefferson's name. Although Boucicault's play was, in many ways, unremarkable, his ability as a constructor of dramatically effective scenes, allied to Jefferson's talented playing and the extra pieces of business the actor introduced to the title role, gave Jefferson a part in which he could continue to appear for the rest of his life. Linked irrevocably with Jefferson, *Rip van Winkle* became one of the most popular successes of the second half of the century, and Jefferson need never have played another role. Indeed, although he did appear in other plays, nothing matched *Rip* in the public's estimation, and he was still appearing in it more than thirty years later, after Boucicault was dead. The most galling aspect of the play for its creator was that, having agreed to write it for money, it took nearly ten years for Jefferson to pay up.

After a visit to Paris in the spring of 1866 to set up and supervise a production of *Arrah-na-Pogue* in French, during which he left rehearsals to give evidence in London to a Parliamentary Commission on the theatre, Boucicault wrote a new vehicle for Jefferson, *The Parish Clerk*. Produced at the Prince's Theatre, Manchester, on 30 April, it lasted only a week. Jefferson thought it a beautiful play and blamed its failure entirely on his inability to get the leading character right, but he was not really to blame; it was a poor piece which never stood any chance of success.

Boucicault was now forty-five. He had always been a prolific writer (according to his evidence to the Parliamentary Commission that April he was already the author of between 180 and 200 pieces),[9] and he had no intention of letting up. With the successes of *The Streets of London* (in its many versions), *Arrah-na-Pogue* and *Rip van Winkle* completely obliterating the failure of Astley's, he embarked upon a sustained phase of creative writing. At a dinner party the question of the literary merit of a recently produced play was discussed, and it was maintained by some that the literary element in a drama was an impediment rather than an assistance to popular success. 'Gentlemen,' said Boucicault, 'will you permit that this question be settled practically? I propose to write three new pieces: one a society drama, relying mainly on its literary treatment; the second a domestic drama; and the third a sensation drama. The pieces shall be produced at the same time, and I guarantee that the success of each shall be in reverse ratio of its merits.'[10]

The three pieces were duly written, and the first, the society drama, *The Two Lives of Mary Leigh* (later renamed *Hunted Down*), was produced at the Prince's Theatre, Manchester, with Boucicault directing, on 30 July. The play was a well-written melodrama in three acts (probably taken from a French source) with an interesting cast: playing the part of Mary Leigh, the devoted mother whose past haunts her, was Kate Terry, grandmother of the distinguished actor Sir John Gielgud, who had first met Boucicault when she had played Prince Arthur, at the age of eight, in Kean's production of *King John* at the Princess's in 1852; and playing Rawdon Scudamore, the polished, villainous adventurer who returns to persecute her, was Henry Irving, the man who had played Hardress Cregan for Boucicault two years before. The part suited Irving to perfection, and although, as Boucicault had predicted at the dinner-party, reaction to the play was only lukewarm, the praise for Irving was unbounded. Also in the company was Lydia Foote, an actress to whom Boucicault was greatly attracted. Although Agnes was still an attractive woman of thirty-two, the years of touring and raising four children were beginning to take their toll on her looks and she was starting to become matronly. Boucicault, as he grew older, responded by turning his attention more and more to young actresses. He had known Lydia for some months before the Manchester engagement. On 14 February, St Valentine's Day, he had written her an anonymous poem, 'From A Devoted Dog',[11] containing some excrutiating puns on her surname Foote (which was a stage name; her family name was Legge). She was a moderately talented actress who was more than happy to use Boucicault's infatuation to her own advantage, and when the older playwright took her under his wing, furthering her career as best he could, it is more than probable that they became lovers.

From Manchester, Boucicault returned to London to

appear in the second of his three plays, the domestic drama, *The Long Strike*. Based loosely on episodes from *Mary Barton* and *Lizzie Leigh*, two novels by Mrs Gaskell, it opened at the Lyceum on 15 September with a strong cast that included Agnes, Boucicault, Sam Emery and J. C. Cowper. Charles Dickens, a close friend of the producer Charles Fechter, attended some of the rehearsals and helped the production with advice and comments.

It is unnecessary to say that the play is done with a master's hand [he wrote to Fechter]. Its closeness and movement are quite surprising. Its construction is admirable. I have the strongest belief in its making a great success. But I must add this proviso: I never saw a play so dangerously depending in critical places on strict natural propriety in the manner and perfection in the shaping of the small parts. Those small parts cannot take the play up, but they can let it down. I would not leave a hair on the head of one of them to the chance of the first night, but I would see, to the minutest particular, the make-up of every one of them at a night rehearsal.[12]

As Boucicault had predicted, *The Long Strike* proved a much more attractive proposition at the box office than had *The Two Lives of Mary Leigh*. It is one of the earliest examples of a play centred on a labour dispute, and the use of the telegraph for the first time on stage proved to be an attractive novelty.

The third of his plays, the sensation drama, was an out-and-out melodrama, and demonstrated, as Boucicault had said it would, that the public appetite for such plays was insatiable. *The Flying Scud*, a racing drama, produced a vogue for such plays and pandered unashamedly to popular taste. It opened at the Holborn Theatre on 6 October and ran for 207 nights, much to the consternation of the critics, who shook their heads and declared that Boucicault, whatever they might have said about him in the past, was called to higher things. The climax of the play, of which they so heartily disapproved, was the Derby at Epsom, run at the back of the stage by

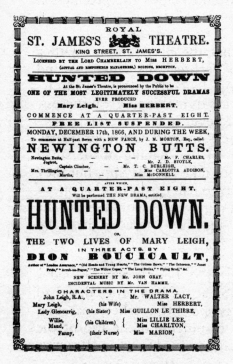

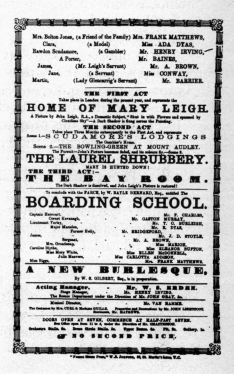

Hunted Down, the play in which Boucicault brought Henry Irving to London in 1866 following his success in Manchester where the play was called the *Two Lives of Mary Leigh*. Irving, who made his name as the villainous Rawdon Scudamore, was also the production's stage manager, responsible for 'directing' the play.

cardboard horses, with the winning horse, the Flying Scud, being led on to the stage at the end.

On 5 November, *The Two Lives of Mary Leigh*, renamed *Hunted Down*, opened in London at the St James's Theatre. The novelist Charles Reade, with whom Boucicault was contemplating writing a novel, had been to Manchester for the play's first night and had been so struck by the power of Irving's acting that he straightway offered to present him and the play in London; but Boucicault, not permitting his friendship with Reade to encroach upon the making of money, concluded a better deal with Louisa Herbert, manageress of the St James's. Miss Herbert wanted to play the part of Mary Leigh herself, so there was no place in the production for Kate Terry, but Boucicault insisted, as a condition of giving her the rights, that Irving be retained in the role of Rawdon Scudamore. It has been suggested that this was Irving's own stipulation, that he had only agreed to play the part in Manchester if he could be in any future London production, but since he had been going through a very bad patch when he first took the role, having lost his job at the Theatre Royal as a result of his refusal to continue with the Davenport brothers' send-up, it seems unlikely that he would have dared to antagonize Boucicault, and risk losing a part which was a life-saver, by making such a demand. Work was too precious to turn down or away, and in later years Irving was to acknowledge his debt to Boucicault for having 'discovered' him. He had tried to make it in London once before, but had been forced to return to the provinces where, despite his unwavering belief in his own ability, he was in danger of becoming another of the many actors doomed to play out their lives in the relative obscurity of the provinces, until the role of Rawdon Scudamore came up. It was, he knew, his last chance to make a name for himself.

Many years later he was to tell actor Joe Graham how he had got the London engagement.

He also confided in me [remembered Graham] that his first London engagement – as Rawdon Scudamore in *Hunted Down*, at the St James's, then under the management of the beautiful Miss Herbert – was the result of his previous selection for the part by the author, Dion Boucicault, on its original production under another title in the provinces. As the result of an interview, which had involved an expensive journey from Manchester, the great Dion was graciously pleased to signify his approval and definitely promise him the part, but fixing the date for rehearsal without breathing a word as to 'terms'. A diffident mention of this not unimportant item was met by a vigorous slap on the shoulder and the reassuring words: 'Mr Irving, I never haggle with an artist. Three pounds!' 'However,' recalled Sir Henry, 'he promised I should play the part in London – if good enough,' and so far he kept his word, the salary, alas! remaining the same.[13]

Rehearsals for the London production of *Hunted Down* began in the autumn, and Irving, who had been appointed stage manager, which, in effect, meant he was directing the play – a measure of Boucicault's confidence in him – found himself in distinguished company. Apart from Miss Herbert, others in the cast included Walter Lacy, Frank Matthews and Edward Addison. It soon became apparent that the production was not going to be got ready in time for its projected opening on 6 October, and Miss Herbert decided to substitute *The Belle's Stratagem* in its place. Irving, who found himself cast as Doricourt, was heart-broken. He was hardly noticed in the reviews and his longed-for first appearance in London as a leading actor turned out to be a very damp squib. His hopes of making an impact were still pinned firmly on *Hunted Down*.

The first night, on 5 November, was a star-studded affair. Boucicault had publicized his protégé well and the audience was full of distinguished and influential people, Charles Dickens, George Eliot, George Henry Lewes and Lord Stanhope, founder of the National Gallery, among them. As the curtain fell on the last act, the theatre rang with cheers for Irving. His style of acting, free from exaggeration and convention, had surprised and puzzled the audience at first, but by the end of the play he had been accepted completely. 'When he is seedy,' wrote one critic, 'his seediness is not indicated by preposterous rages or by new trousers with a hole in them; his clothes are clothes that are well – but not too well – worn . . . The finest piece of undemonstrative acting that I have seen since I saw Mr Hare as Prince Perovsky.'[14] After the last curtain call, George Eliot asked Lewes what he thought. 'In twenty years,' he replied, 'he will be at the head of the English stage.' 'He is there, I think, already,' murmured the novelist.[15] Charles Dickens was equally impressed. 'Mark my words,' he said, 'that man will be a great actor.'[16]

Boucicault had good reason to be proud of his protégé that night, for he had given Irving the chance to show what he could do and Irving had seized it completely. Never again would he have to return to the provinces, praying for the opportunity to be allowed to demonstrate his talent before a London audience. The seal was set on a friendship that was to last until Boucicault's death.

Hunted Down ran at the St James's for four months until 8 February 1867, and demonstrated once more that Boucicault was the total master of his craft, that he had his finger on the public pulse, and that he could, almost at will, turn out a drama to satisfy public craving. In 1866, in addition to revivals of his earlier dramas, productions in France and the United States, he had four new plays on in the West End, provoking a writer in the *Illustrated News* to parody Watts's famous poem:

> How doth the busy Dion B.
> Improve the present hour
> And place on every stage a play
> From Drury Lane to Bower.

Not all the plays Boucicault touched turned to gold by any means. *A Wild Goose Chase* by Lester Wallack, which he edited for E. A. Sothern to star in at the Haymarket in April 1867, was slapdash by his standards and was quickly dropped, and when *How She Loves Him* was given its London première by Squire Bancroft at his newly opened Prince of Wales Theatre, its failure surprised everyone, except perhaps Boucicault, who directed.

I regret that my comedy was caviare to the public [he wrote to Marie Wilton, Bancroft's wife]. I doubted its agreement with their taste and stomach, and so told you before it was played . . . The public pretend they want pure comedy; this is not so. What they want is *domestic drama*, treated with a broad comic character. A sentimental, pathetic play, comically rendered, such as *Ours, Caste*, the *Colleen Bawn, Arrah-na-Pogue* . . . Be advised then; refuse dramas which are wholly serious or wholly comic – seek those which blend the two.[17]

Since the play had failed to live up to expectations, Boucicault refused to accept a penny in payment, a generous gesture when one considers his reputation and how hard he pursued any person who produced his plays without permission.

The preceding two years had not, of course, been without their litigation. In March 1867, at the same time as he was presenting a petition to Parliament on behalf of the French Society of Authors (of which he had been elected a member), asking for a copyright agreement to be drawn up between the two countries, Boucicault, who had probably 'borrowed' more French plots than any other writer in English, was busy suing managers in America and Britain for pirating his dramas and playing them illegally. He, too, was being sued, this time by Antonio Trentanove, an Italian sculptor, for whom he and Agnes had sat in 1860 at the height of their fame in *The Colleen Bawn*. Boucicault hadn't been happy with the two busts and had refused to pay the fee of £300, but had given Trentanove £55 on account since the sculptor was going through a difficult time financially. For five years Trentanove tried to get the rest of the money he was owed, and in 1865 he persuaded Agnes to sit for him again, assuring her that the new sculpture would be acceptable. It wasn't, Boucicault still refused to pay, and Trentanove began an action to recover his fee. The case was referred to John Foley, a senior member of the Royal Academy, for adjudication, and Boucicault was ordered to pay half the amount demanded, less the £55, or else to sit for a new bust and pay the full £300.[18] There is no record that he did either.

On 27 February 1867, the Boucicaults' fifth child, Nina, was born at 326 Regent Street. Like two of her brothers, Nina was to choose the stage as a career, and with her mother's good looks and not a little of her talent, she was to become very successful, creating the role of Kitty Verdun in *Charley's Aunt* and, the part for which she is best remembered today, *Peter Pan* in the first production of the J. M. Barrie classic. She made her last appearance in *Waste* in 1936, and died in West London in 1950.

In May 1867 it appears that Boucicault was again contemplating running his own theatre, for it was announced that he planned to transform the St Martin's Hall into a theatre, but, wisely perhaps, the project was abandoned. However, a growing family, on which he lavished presents, the purchase of a new house in Brighton, and Lydia Foote, who had to be kept in dresses and entertained, meant he could not afford to forgo work for long, nor did he have any wish to be out of the public eye. In September, one year after his and Agnes's last appearance on the London stage in *The Long Strike*, he revived *Arrah-na-Pogue* at the Princess's for them both to appear in their original roles. The public showed they had not been forgotten, and the play ran for three months, playing to packed houses. Many years later both Boucicault and Agnes were to recall this revival as if it had been the first production. The night of the first production, he said, was the night of the Clerkenwell explosion. He was wrong; it was two years before, and *Arrah* was not even being played on the night the explosion took place. Although the play could have run into 1868, Boucicault grew tired of it and decided to give *The Colleen Bawn* its first London airing for five years, opening at the end of November. The Clerkenwell explosion, an attempt to release Richard Burke from prison, took place on Friday, 13 December. Again, according to Boucicault, the Prince of Wales was in the house: that evening the Prince was out of town and Boucicault was taking his running header as Myles.[19]

In February 1868, *The Octoroon* replaced *The Colleen Bawn* and brought the Princess's season of revivals to a very profitable and successful conclusion. At the same time, *Foul Play*, the novel on which Boucicault had been collaborating with Charles Reade, started to appear in twenty-five weekly parts in the magazine *Once-a-Week*. Charles Reade was a man of striking personal appearance. Over six feet tall, he was boisterous, impatient, genial, impulsively generous and a good friend. He and Boucicault, who were in many ways similar, hit it off immediately when they first met, and Reade became a constant visitor to Regent Street, being one of the people who had attended the Davenport brothers' séance in 1864. During one of their many convivial evenings together, it occurred to them that their combined names could produce a work that would make them both fortunes. First they would write a novel, then turn it into a play, and clean up on both sides of the Atlantic. They approached a publisher with their scheme, and were given an advance of £2,000, at that time one of the highest amounts ever advanced in England for a work of fiction.

As soon as *Foul Play* started to appear, the cry of plagiarism went up. *The Mask* published cruel caricatures of both writers and accused them of stealing their plot from a French play, printing extracts from the play alongside parts of the novel. Boucicault, who had heard the accusation too many times before to be affected or concerned, refused to comment and it was left to the indignant Reade to defend their integrity. Rather unwisely, for Reade was not so innocent himself when it came to filching other people's ideas, he rushed at their adversaries like a bull at a red cape: Boucicault's contribution had consisted of writing two or three complete chapters and suggesting invaluable incidents, plot details and colouring; twenty-three of the chapters had not a single idea in common with the French play and a careful analysis of the remaining two showed that although there were superficial similarities, their treatment of the events depicted was completely different. In spite of the vehemence of his denials, Reade must have known that the plot of *Foul Play* (satirized in *Punch* as *Chicken Hazard*) was taken from a French play. The idea may have been suggested by Boucicault, but Reade was clearly not the innocent party he made himself out to be, for it is impossible for him to have been in ignorance as to the source, and his own dramatization of the novel shows that he knew the French work well. As for Boucicault, he just sat back and let the controversy generate sales for the novel, which it did nicely.

When it came to the second part of their scheme, to dramatize the novel, the two writers found they could not work with each other, and each decided to produce his own version. Boucicault's was the first ready, and he got it on at the Holborn Theatre on 28 May, where it proved to be a dismal failure. Reade's version, which was in every respect superior, was produced three days later in Leeds, and then in Manchester, but because of the failure of Boucicault's play, no London manager would touch it. Nine years later, Reade revised the play as *The Scuttled Ship* for the Olympic Theatre, but it sank without trace. The incidents following the publication of the novel and his failure to get his play on in London in no way affected Reade's friendship with Boucicault, nor did it alter Reade's opinion that Boucicault was the greatest dramatist of his generation.

The controversy aroused by *Foul Play*'s source did not prevent Boucicault from incorporating the sensation scene from another play into his next new piece, *After Dark*. The year before, in New York, Augustin Daly had written and produced a play called *Under the Gaslight*, an unremarkable work except for one well-conceived and well-staged scene in which the hero was bound to a railway line and escapes just before the express rushes past. The 'sensation' had the desired effect upon the audience, even though, on the first night, the 'train' parted in the middle to disclose the legs of the man propelling it, and the play ran for two months. It was too good an idea for Boucicault to pass over, and, as he so often did, he began to work on his new piece by plotting back from the sensation scene he wanted to show, in this case, an escape from an oncoming train. He found the story-line he wanted in a French play by D'Ennery and Grangé, and because he knew he was treading on dangerous ground, he was careful to get their permission to adapt the play into English and he also altered a few details from Daly's scene. But when *After Dark* was produced at the Princess's Theatre on 12 August, a year to the day after *Under the Gaslight* had first been seen, the similarities were obvious. *After Dark* was the smash hit of the London season and it was not long before American managers were negotiating to present it in New York. Palmer and Jarrett secured the rights and announced it for production at Niblo's Theatre on 16 November, just two weeks after Daly proposed opening his revival of *Under the Gaslight*. Using the copyright laws that Boucicault had been instrumental in putting on the statute book, Daly applied for and won an injunction to prevent *After Dark* being staged, and the case came to court in December. Daly's lawyers argued that the success of their client's play was due entirely to the railroad scene, that it was entirely original to Daly, and that Boucicault had stolen it. Palmer and Jarrett did not deny the charge of plagiarism – indeed, they were well aware of what Boucicault had been up to, for they had advertised *After Dark* as being 'derived from a melodrama by Messrs d'Ennery and Granger [*sic*] with their permission'. Their defence was based on attacking Daly's claim of originality: the incident, they said, had been used in a magazine story published four months before Daly's play had been produced. It was, at best, a shaky line of defence. In the magazine story, the hero had been tied to the main line, then under repair, and the train had passed by harmlessly on a siding. In Daly's version, the hero was rescued at the last moment by the heroine. Realizing the weakness of their argument, Palmer and Jarrett then tried to use the 1856 Copyright Act. They claimed that since Daly's effects relied upon stage business, it was not a literary product, but mechanical, and therefore did not fall within the scope of the Act. Both arguments were dismissed by the judge. As a last fling, the defendants claimed that Daly had forfeited his copyright by virtue of the fact that the play's subtitle in the printed version was different from that filed with the court for copyright. This, too, was rejected, and Palmer and Jarrett were forced to pay Daly a royalty for every performance of *After Dark* that was given in the United States. They were hardly the losers, for the play had been given such publicity by the trial that, with the notice added to the playbills that 'The Great Railroad Scene is presented', it played to packed houses.

Boucicault was never called to account for his actions, though the case did have one unexpected benefit by helping to clarify the law; and, through the judge's ruling that Daly could have a copyright in stage directions, many new areas of theatrical activity were brought within the scope of the Act.

While Palmer and Jarrett were in a New York court room, arguing for his play, Boucicault and Agnes were in Dublin, where they had returned to appear in the revised version of *Arrah-na-Pogue*, for its first production in his native city. The houses were full and appreciative for their three-week engagement, at the end of which Boucicault went in front of the curtain to thank the public for its patronage and to announce that he and Agnes were both retiring from the stage. He was forty-eight and the years of constant toil, the obsession with making money and the high living had conspired to cause him a nervous breakdown earlier in the year. Since his wife had finally decided that she had had enough of acting and wanted to stay at home with her family, the stage no longer held any attractions for him. From then on he intended to devote himself exclusively to writing.

10

RETIREMENT AND COMEBACK

For the next two years, Boucicault was as good as his word. He and Agnes returned to London at the close of their Dublin engagement, and while she took care of the children and the house, he settled down to a long period of sustained writing. On 1 May 1869, his adaptation of Sardou's *Seraphine* (a play for which he wrote to Sardou offering to pay a royalty even though he did not have to) opened at the Queen's Theatre, but the subject-matter – a mother who forces her illegitimate daughter to become a nun as a penance for her own sin – was not considered suitable for theatrical portrayal, neither was it enjoyed, and so the play failed. Nine days later, on 10 May, *Presumptive Evidence*, yet another version of the ever-popular, much-adapted *Le Courrier de Lyon*, replaced *After Dark* at the Princess's, lasting for two and a half weeks until the close of the season; and in August, *Formosa; or, The Railroad to Ruin*, appeared at Drury Lane, to be met by a storm of protest. It was a typically well-constructed, effective Boucicault sensation drama, culminating in the rowing on stage of the Oxford *v.* Cambridge Boat Race, for which *The Times* predicted a long run in spite of, or more accurately because of, its setting, for many of the events leading up to the boat race took place in the salon of 'Formosa', a professional woman of low birth who was using her considerable charms

175

to make money. The existence of such high-class whores as Mabel Gray, on whom Formosa was supposed to be modelled, was well known, and in reflecting the public interest in the goings-on of members of high society, Boucicault had again picked a winner. What upset most of the critics was not just the depiction of a harlot on stage, immoral though that was considered to be, but that such activities should be portrayed on the stage of a theatre that was still considered to be the shrine of English drama. 'Not only is a harlot the heroine of the piece,' wrote an indignant reader to *The Times*, 'but her harlotry is made one of its most prominent features. To assist the effect, there were three or four subordinate harlots.' There were even objections to the play on the grounds that Tom, the hero and Oxford stroke, was approaching the eve of the race in 'the very vortex of dissipation', and that, first, he would not be permitted to do this, or secondly, if permitted, he would be simply incapable of rowing[1] (in the play the Oxford boat had, of course, won). While joining in the general condemnation of the play's morality, the public rushed to see it and kept *Formosa* on the boards of Drury Lane until 18 December, a run of 117 nights which made Boucicault and Frederick Chatterton, the theatre's manager, more than £12,000 between them.

Much of the success of *Formosa* was directly attributable to the violence with which the critics attacked it and the interest Boucicault and Chatterton were able to generate by their carefully placed letters defending it: the public just had to see such an immoral piece for itself. Throughout his career, Boucicault had frequently been castigated for the immoral, unhealthy and, at times, offensive tone of much of his writing, but he'd rarely been attacked with the vehemence that greeted *Formosa*, and he was astute enough to realize that the play was receiving more publicity than would ever have been possible from paid advertisements. So, whenever interest in it looked like flagging, he renewed it with anonymous letters to the press attacking himself. Not for nothing was it said that he could always be relied upon to start a controversy in the papers if ever there was a lull in news. It was in one of their replies to an attack on the play that Chatterton signed his name to the aphorism, written by Boucicault, 'Shakespeare spelt ruin and Byron bankruptcy.'

Reading *Formosa* today, it is hard to understand how the innocuous dialogue and innocent action could have brought so much censure upon the author for writing it and Chatterton for presenting it, and it would seem that, apart from any vicarious pleasure the audiences may have taken in the setting, the evening was really made by the superb playing of Henry Irving as Compton Kerr, the villain, and Katherine Rogers, the beautiful young actress who was to become another of Boucicault's mistresses, as Formosa.

On 23 June, Aubrey, the Boucicaults' sixth and last child, had been born, and Boucicault's urge to wander while Agnes was in confinement had reasserted itself. Although he had given up acting, he had not given up the role of distinguished dramatist, and he was a constant backstage visitor in many West End theatres. The musical comedy star, Emily Soldene, recalled his visits to the Lyceum with delightful naïvety. Henry Farnie, manager of the Lyceum, was, she wrote in her autobiography,

> generally to be found in one of the upper entrances very much engaged with the chorus – the feminine chorus. He never allowed anything in the way of a deputy or anything else, if he could possibly help it, to come between him and the chorus. He had a very keen feeling for the beautiful and most especially affected the Burne-Jones style of beauty, but was not bigoted. Indeed, I may mention, as showing the broad and catholic view he took of these aesthetic differences, that the best-looking girls in the theatre, even if they were a little plump, were never allowed to appeal to him in vain. As a rule, their intelligence was not on a par with their physical perfections, but this did not affect the benevolence of his intentions. He would call a rehearsal at any extraordinary hour, and if the girls were very good-looking indeed would stop with them any length, or even give them lessons privately one at a time . . . Of course this sort of thing was a great tax on his time and patience, and sometimes he would be assisted in the work by Dion Boucicault who

came to the theatre pretty frequently, and was understood to take a good deal of paternal interest in the young ladies' progress; of course purely from an artistic point of view. But Mr Farnie must have had a real regard for Mr Boucicault, and would not allow him to be worried with the woes of the chorus, for no sooner did the girls surround this charming author-actor, and the most interesting man of his day, than Farnie would clap his hands together violently, and cry out, 'Now girls, to your places.'

Boucicault never allowed his interest in chorus girls and young actresses to interfere with his work; his writing came before everything. The month after the opening of *Formosa*, a revision of his friend Tom Robertson's play *Dreams*, undertaken at Robertson's request, was produced in New York. Just what part Boucicault had in the revised version isn't known since it hasn't survived, but with his name on the playbill it was doomed to failure, for the American critics and public were scornful of any man who could write a play as disgusting as *Formosa*.

> It is safe to assume [wrote one critic], since this play deals with sweet, gentle, and sacred feelings, that all the good in it is Mr Robertson's, and the bad in it Mr Boucicault's. The latter person has placed his intellectual condition in a strong light lately; and if there be anything which he is manifestly incompetent to teach it is the pure passion which they feel who truly love. *Dreams* is fraught with this. Possibly Mr Boucicault worked in the stage-effect – of the duel-scene – which closes act fourth. This is felicitously melo-dramatic, and quite in the line of an inspired stage carpenter who fancies himself to be a man of genius.[2]

It was to take a long time, and many new plays, before Boucicault was forgiven for *Formosa*. Not that he was unduly worried, for the only verdict of which he took account was the one at the box office, and the play was still clearing over £1,500 a week. 'Public opinion,' he once wrote, 'is the highest and sole court of jurisdiction in literary and artistic matters.'[3]

His next play, *Lost at Sea*, opened at the Adelphi in October and suffered a similar fate to *Dreams*. A lurid melodrama, written in collaboration with Henry J. Byron, it attempted, with a fire scene and spectacular panoramas of London and the River Thames, to cash in on the success of plays like *The Poor of New York*, which it strongly resembles, and produced the comment that the authors had 'depended on stage arrangements, and saved themselves the trouble of even aiming at the least degree of literary excellence'.[4] But in spite of some clever writing and some effective staging, the novelty of 'sensation drama' was beginning to wear off and the play failed to attract an audience. Boucicault began to cast around for stories to suit the changing taste.

On 7 March 1870, two plays, both announced as new, were given as a double-bill at the Princess's, replacing *Formosa*, which had transferred there from the Adelphi when Chatterton had refused to put it back on after the pantomime, much to Boucicault's disgust. Neither was a new work, both being revisions of plays Boucicault had written for Webster twenty-five years earlier. *Paul Lafarge* was a revision of *Victor and Hortense*, while *A Dark Night's Work* had been seen previously as *Giralda*. His next play, *The Rapparee*, which appeared at the Princess's in September, was an Irish romantic drama set in the time of James II, and was again drawn from his earlier work without any of the inspiration of a *Colleen Bawn* or an *Arrah-na-Pogue*.

We are all familiar with the matter of the drama itself in the former works of the author [commented the critic of the *Illustrated London News*]. He has, indeed, repeated the incidents and character of his previous productions, and even the dialogue is only colourably varied from that of any of his antecedent plays. But, it must be confessed, it is so carefully manipulated that there is scarcely a redundant line in the composition.

The Rapparee, in which Shiel Barry made his London début, failed to run. In December, *A Christmas Story* at the Gaiety and *Jezebel* at the Holborn, also failed to make any impact;

After which at 8.30 a New Drama, in Three Acts, entitled

JEZEBEL !

OR, THE DEAD RECKONING.

WRITTEN BY DION BOUCICAULT,

The Author of " The Streets of London," " Collen Bawn," " Flying Scud,"
" Arrah-Na Pogue," " Rip Van Winkle," " After Dark," "The Willow
Corpse," " The Corsican Brothers," " London Assurance," &c., &c.
**The subject of the First and Second Acts of this Play is to be found in
a Work by M. MASSON.**
Entirely New Scenery by Messrs. HAWES CRAVEN and JULIAN HICKS.
Dresses by Mr. S. MAY and Mrs. JAMES. New Music by Mr. G. RICHARDSON.
Appointments by Mr. A. LLOYDS.

CHARACTERS.

George D'Artigues ... (a Wealthy Merchant of Bordeaux) ... **Mr. H. NEVILLE**

Alfred Ravel...(his Friend, a Surgeon in the French Navy)... **Mr. PHILIP DAY**

Captain Breitmann(an Old Salt in the German Merchant Service)**Mr. PARSELLE**

Cristal ... (a Gentleman in a serious Female difficulty) ... **Mr. HOLSTON**

Cottereau ... ... (a Commissioner of Police) ... ... **Mr. GARDEN**

Palma ... ... (a Mexican Vagrant) ... ... **Mr. DANVERS**

Madame D'Artigues ... ... Miss **KATHERINE RODGERS**

Gretchen ... (Niece to Captain Breitmann) ... Miss **L. FOOTE**

Lucele(Lady's Maid to Madame D'Artigues and her Confidante)Miss **N. HARRIS**

Gertrude ... ... (Servant to Gretchen) ... Miss **L. CARLYLE**

Germain ... ... (a Servant) ... ... **Mr. H. RIVERS**

Officers of Justice, Servants.

Jezebel; or, The Dead Reckoning, an adaptation from the French
which opened in December 1870. In the cast were two of
Boucicault's mistresses – Katherine Rogers and Lydia Foote.
Whether they knew about each other isn't clear; but the play failed.

seven plays since *Formosa*, and not one of them any good.

In the cast of *Jezebel* were Lydia Foote and Katherine Rogers. Whether Katherine or Lydia knew about the place the other took in Boucicault's affections isn't known, and he was careful to avoid a confrontation. The affair with Lydia had not been progressing quite as the playwright would have wished. In return for her favours she was becoming increasingly demanding, angling for him to write a play just for her. In May he had been forced to pacify her by giving her a two-year contract to appear with his companies in London and the provinces, performing only those parts of which she approved, for a salary of £750 and an agreement to provide all her wardrobe.[5] He did eventually write a play for her: *Elfie; or, The Cherry Tree Inn*, which opened, under his direction, at the Theatre Royal, Glasgow, on 10 March 1871. It was a pleasant enough comedy, better than most of his recent pieces, with an ingenious quadruple set, and Lydia scored a personal success as Elfie the maid.

> I was delighted with you last night [Boucicault wrote to her the following morning]. It will do. You must take more courage and broaden out the character a *little* more. The outline is quite correct. Give the audience your full face a little more – your profile is charming (I always admired it) but your full face is very pleasant too. You are a very good girl. Consider yourself kissed.[6]

From Glasgow they took the play to Liverpool, but Boucicault had no plans to produce it in London that season, and so he contacted his friend Squire Bancroft at the Prince of Wales to see if he would offer Lydia, who had played in the original production in 1867, a part in his revival of *Caste*. It was with considerable surprise and hurt that he discovered Lydia had been negotiating with Bancroft on her own.

> Do not think for a moment that I wish you to forgo this engagement [he wrote to her], far from it – I now urge you to accept it, if you have not already done so. I feel only hurt that you were entertaining the views and offers I made you

out of the sincere desire to be of service to you – while you were engaging yourself elsewhere. This is not returning me what I have fairly earned of you. I cannot carry and [*sic*] unpleasant feeling without ridding my mind of it very quickly and so I empty the very small vial of my wrath and have done with it.[7]

It was the beginning of the end of his affair with Lydia. He did not like to be treated so badly, and may even have been looking for an excuse to put an end to their intimacy. Although their paths were to cross and they were to work together in the future, their relationship was never again so close.

By the summer of 1871, Boucicault had recovered sufficiently from his nervous breakdown of three years earlier to be missing the stage. He had always lived beyond his means, he was generous with his money, and the failure of all his plays since his retirement, with the exception of *Formosa*, to make money had left him very short. He had been forced to sell some shares to meet his commitments (a transaction which nearly landed him in court, for he kept the £15 dividend instead of sending it on to the purchasers, and when they took him to court, paid them £12 15*s*. on the day the action was due to be heard),[8] and he needed to return to acting for the money it would bring in. Since he had no major new work ready, he decided to hang his comeback on a revival of *The Colleen Bawn*, for which he persuaded Agnes to return to the boards. After a holiday in Scarborough with his family, he and Agnes opened a two-week engagement in Manchester at the end of August, playing in *The Colleen Bawn* and a revision of George Colman's *John Bull*, in which he appeared as Dennis Bulgruddery, a good-humoured, sottish Irishman, giving a performance which confirmed him as a comic actor of genius. For the last three nights of their engagement he appeared as Kerry, an aged Irish butler (the first time he had attempted an 'old' part), in *Night and Morning*, a role he was to play successfully for the rest of his career and in which he made his final stage appearance.

As soon as it was known that the Boucicaults were back in

business, offers to present them in London began to arrive, and Boucicault accepted one from John Hollingshead, who had just taken over the Gaiety Theatre, to play a season of his Irish plays. The house was full to overflowing for their first London appearance for four years, and the season, which included *The Colleen Bawn*, *Night and Morning*, *John Bull* and *Elfie* (with Agnes playing Elfie and Lydia Foote playing a supporting role), played to capacity business for two months.

It was ironic that the public was going to see Boucicault the actor, not to see his plays, which he had always maintained were more important than the cast. As his stock as a performer rose (and he was considered to be one of the finest comic actors alive), so the estimation of his dramas fell. His instinct for knowing what an audience would want, before the audience, did seem to have deserted him, and all his attempts to find a new formula to delight and intrigue theatregoers had failed. His plans to dramatize *Edwin Drood*, Charles Dickens's last novel, first with the novelist then with Charles Dickens junior, had come to nothing, and he was having to rely on revivals of his old plays to maintain his reputation. What little success his new work had enjoyed was almost entirely due to his acting in it. Boucicault had in many senses reached an impasse. He was fifty, he had suffered a nervous breakdown brought on by constant work, he constantly needed more money than he possessed, and he seemed to be losing his touch. The death, in February 1871, of his friend, the playwright Tom Robertson, at whose funeral he was a chief mourner, also affected him deeply. Unlike Robertson, who had never sacrificed his principles but had died destitute and angry with the world, Boucicault, early in his career, chose to court popularity, to give the public the guano it wanted, instead of trying to make something of the drama. He became preoccupied with the idea that he may have been wasting his life. 'Give me,' he said, 'what every man yearns for more than a fortune – the conviction that he has done some little good in his time.'[9] As they had once before, in 1853, when he had felt he was getting nowhere in England, Boucicault's thoughts turned towards the United States as the mecca where he would be better appreciated as a playwright and the place where he would be able to recapture his missing inspiration.

In the spring of 1872, he and Agnes took *The Colleen Bawn* and *The Streets of London* (which he felt too tired to be bothered localizing) to Dublin, and then returned to the Gaiety for a second successful season, but not even the acclaim that greeted his revival of *Arrah-na-Pogue* could rid him of the idea that he must return to New York. Before he could depart, however, he had a commission to fulfil for his friend the Earl of Londesborough. The thirty-eight-year-old second Baron, ex-Member of Parliament and an enthusiastic antiquary, was also an ardent theatregoer. He had been left enormous wealth by his father – 60,000 acres of the county of Yorkshire which brought him an annual income in the region of £100,000 – and was determined to use his money to become a patron of the arts. For his first foray into production, he hired Covent Garden, appointed Boucicault his manager, and commissioned the playwright to produce the greatest spectacle ever seen on a stage anywhere, giving him a free hand to do as he wished. Boucicault did not let his lordship down. He conceived a mammoth spectacular, designed to tell the Story of Man, in which the plot was immaterial and served only to link together eighteen tableaux. The show, called *Babil and Bijou*, opened on 29 August with music especially commissioned from Jules Rivière (who conducted the orchestra), Hervé, Frederic Clay and de Billemont, and lyrics by J. R. Planché. During rehearsals, Planché found himself largely ignored by Boucicault, who slashed and cut his long rhymed speeches, and was forced to console himself with the famous witticism, delivered to an extremely tall young lady who asked him for a special song just for her, 'My dear, Longfellow is your man.'[10]

As a last contemptuous gesture against those critics who, he maintained, were causing him to leave the country, Boucicault announced that the play, which ran for four and a half hours, would start well before the customary time, thereby ensuring that they would be unable to eat before the performance. The action of *Babil and Bijou* took place in every conceivable realm, from mid-air to the bowels of the earth, and, as Townsend Walsh described, an army of men, women and children took part. There were dancers, comedians, pantomimists, Amazonian warriors and coryphees galore, together with a fantastic aquarium of pseudo oysters, crabs, cockles, seals, periwinkles, sea-lions, sea-horses, sharks, alligators, swordfish, devil-fish and lobsters – scarlet boiled lobsters at that! – at the bottom of the ocean (possibly it was the Red Sea.)[11]

The grand procession that began the third act, representing the Nine Ages of Man, produced gasps of astonishment from the audience. The scene was a mountain-top, down from which, through tortuous ravines, processed an endless army of men and women dressed in costumes of different periods, from Adam and Eve onwards, including more than twenty Amazons – tall, handsome women in glittering costumes, wearing high silver-plated helmets surmounted by white plumes – led by Helen Barry, whose attire, to say nothing of her figure, became the talk of London.

Babil and Bijou was an artistic and critical success, and ran for six months, but it could never have hoped to recover its production costs. The stage properties alone were said to have cost £17,000, and when the play closed in March 1873, Lord Londesborough was more than £11,000 out of pocket, making it the most costly West End failure of the last century. Ten days after the first night, on 7 September, Boucicault and Agnes had sailed from Liverpool aboard the steamship *Scotia* bound for New York, amid the inevitable accusations that he was running away from his responsibilities and was getting out fast. The evidence does not support this view. Boucicault had been planning his return to the States since the beginning of 1871, and he had never made any secret of his intentions; indeed, his plans for touring in America had already been announced in the press. And although *Babil and Bijou* was certainly a costly and lavish epic – 'Boucicault literally made ducks and drakes with his friend's money, and produced a quite unnecessary spectacle with reckless extravagance,' wrote the critic Clement Scott, repeating the popular view – there is no reason to suppose that Lord Londesborough was dissatisfied with it, for it was an artistic triumph, and ten years later, condensed into four acts, it was successfully and profitably revived at the Alhambra. There were some difficulties between Boucicault and his patron: Boucicault warned his lordship that costs were spiralling and did not like the earl's proposal to put a treasurer into Covent Garden to run the place after Boucicault had departed; there was also some disagreement as to how their partnership was to be terminated and who was to be responsible for the theatre; but their friendship survived the production in a way that would have been most unlikely had Boucicault defrauded him in the manner suggested in the press. When Boucicault's son Dot was twenty-one in 1880, Lord Londesborough was one among a few intimate friends invited to his party at the Star and Garter in Richmond. If anyone was left in the lurch by Boucicault's departure from London, it was his groom, who was left without pay and without money to buy feed for the children's pony.

The Boucicaults, without children, who had been left at school in London, arrived in New York on 17 September and began an engagement at Booth's Theatre six days later with *Arrah-na-Pogue*. It was twelve years since they had left the city for a brief visit to Europe, and New York turned out to welcome them back. Boucicault was genuinely surprised by the warmth of their reception. 'Time has treated him kindly,' observed the critic of the *Tribune*. 'He is a better actor than he used to be, at least in this – that his method is quieter, more refined, and more sharply intelligent; and it is absolutely precise.' With *Jessie Brown* and *Night and Morning* (renamed *Kerry*) added to the bills, they played at Booth's for eight successful weeks, and then went on a short tour to Boston and other cities before returning to New York. He was well pleased with his decision to leave England. Just as he had in 1853, he felt that he had escaped from the petty attacks of London journalists to find a land that was free, full of opportunity and appreciative of his talents. He felt he was back in his spiritual home. Just before his departure from London he had purchased the property next to his Regent Street home as an investment, and, with the children still in England, he had planned to be in America only a short time. The warmth of their reception convinced him that his future lay in New York rather than London, and early in 1873 both he and Agnes applied for, and received, American citizenship. His decision, dictated by his heart as much as his head, was understandable, for if, as he had suddenly decided, he was going to settle in the United States, there were distinct advantages, particularly in the field of copyright, for him to be a citizen. Agnes's decision was, however, puzzling. Their marriage was beginning to go through a difficult period and at the time of their naturalization they were not even living together. Katherine Rogers had followed them to New York, and she and Boucicault had set up house together. Agnes's application for US citizenship may have been a last attempt to keep her husband rather than have been prompted by a wish on her part to settle in the States, for on 12 March she left New York and returned alone to London, ostensibly to see her children, who were having problems with the establishment in which they'd been left. In reality, she realized that she was not going to win her husband back from Katherine Rogers immediately, and rather than bring matters to a head, forcing Boucicault to make a choice between them she preferred to leave until the affair had blown itself out.

Boucicault was too busy rehearsing his new play to be over-concerned by Agnes's departure; indeed, he was probably pleased she was out of the way. Five days after her departure, *Daddy O'Dowd*, a play he had started writing in England and completed in New York, opened at Booth's. Although Boucicault played the title role, the play wasn't liked and came off after only four weeks of poor business.

He was now fifty-two and beginning to feel his age. The traumas of producing *Babil and Bijou*, the exertions of appearing nightly for two and a half months as Shaun in *Arrah* (a part that would have taxed a man half his age) and the onset of gout, had all conspired to leave him feeling exhausted, and he again announced his intention to retire from acting and concentrate on writing. His resolution did not last long. A month after his 'retirement', *Mora*, a four-act original melodrama, vaguely reminiscent of half a dozen other Boucicault plays, opened at Wallack's Theatre and ran for a month, to be replaced on 1 July by *Mimi*, his version of *La Vie de Bohème*, starring Katherine Rogers – and Boucicault. The reason behind his swift return to the stage was again financial pressure. He owed money back in England, where he was overdrawn for £2,000 at the bank (he'd again had to borrow the money to pay for his and Agnes's fares to New York); he was sending back money to pay for his children's education, and was giving Agnes an allowance (out of which she refused to pay the premium on his life assurance policy when it became due). The cost of maintaining two households meant he could not afford not to act.

Mimi, which had been written especially for Katherine, played at Wallack's until the end of August, and was sufficiently well liked for them to take it on a short tour before returning to New York in time for the opening of *Led Astray* at the Union Square Theatre on 6 December. The play, which was little more than a translation of a French work, *La Tentation*, with an Irish character added, did not meet with critical approval, but the public enjoyed it and it ran for five months, saving the theatre's manager, Albert M. Palmer, from possible bankruptcy. The same month, on 22 December, another adaptation, *A Man of Honor*, was produced unsuccessfully at Wallack's.

For some time Boucicault had been wanting to visit the far west, and at the end of December he finally left New York on the eleven-day train journey to San Francisco to fulfil a financially rewarding engagement. With him went Katherine, for whom he had arranged performances in Sacramento and San Francisco. For some reason he appears to have been anticipating a hostile reception from the local press (in spite of the good advance publicity his appearances were getting and the obvious interest of the public in his trip), and he refused to give interviews when he arrived. To cut the ground from under the local journalists' feet, he opened, on 19 January 1874, in a burlesque, *Boucicault in California*, in which the playwright was seen in his hotel suite at the Occidental receiving journalists and budding playwrights, who consumed his whisky and bored him stiff, while he gave, at first hand, everything he would have said in an interview. A critic found the piece full of jokes but of questionable taste. Among the artists engaged to support his season were the Australian couple, James Cassius Williamson and Maggie Moore.

I was Murphy, his servant, with remarks on all and sundry [Williamson later recalled of the performance[12]]. Barton Hill came to tell him about the places he was going to play; then came in an actress to play the part of a débutante with a San José reputation . . . and so on. Then came in the reporters, especially W. A. Mestayer, as Bogus Push, of *The Weekly Pill* – and Boucicault talked to the reporters. He told them his opinion of everything, especially California – and left the genuine reporters without a leg to stand on. He simply said on stage everything they had to say in the papers, and left them with nothing at all to write. That always struck me as a particularly happy instance of turning the tables.

During the remainder of the month, Williamson, who was to become the major figure of Australian theatrical management, and his wife, appeared with Boucicault in *The Colleen Bawn*, *Arrah-na-Pogue*, *Kerry* and *Daddy O'Dowd*, all of which received tumultuous receptions.

From San Francisco, Boucicault travelled to Sacramento to appear with John Piper's company at the Metropolitan Theatre, arriving too late to give his first scheduled performance. He was immediately forgiven when he appeared the following night in *Kerry* and *Used Up*, for, according to the *Sacramento Bee*, 'nothing on stage could have been more perfect'. His engagement in Sacramento finished the same week with a performance in the afternoon of *The Colleen Bawn* and in the evening of *Arrah-na-Pogue*, a massive undertaking for a man of fifty-three who was suffering from gout, and it's perhaps not surprising that his playing of Shaun the Post was not considered to be very good. Two days later he was in Virginia City, Nevada, opening at Piper's Opera House, a converted gambling saloon, in *Kerry* and *Used Up*. It was here that he engaged a young actor, just starting his career, as his temporary secretary. This was David Belasco, then twenty, but destined to become one of the leading personalities of the American stage. Working with Boucicault and watching the master work was to have a profound effect upon his theatrical thinking, both as producer and as playwright. One of Belasco's best-known dramas, *The Girl of the Golden West* (on which Puccini based his opera), was a melodrama in the best Boucicaultian tradition. Belasco was a member of Piper's company in Sacramento, where he was wrongfully arrested on a charge of stealing money from the stage manager, a crime that was later proved to have been committed by someone else, and was one of the few company members who travelled to Virginia City with Boucicault. In his memoirs, Belasco recalled that one of his duties was to take dictation from Boucicault since the playwright's hands were knotted with gout.

I sat at a table, took off my coat and began act one of *Led Astray*. Boucicault lay propped up with pillows, before a blazing fire, a glass of hot whisky beside him. It was not long before I found out that he was the terror of the whole house. If there was the slightest noise below stairs, he would raise such a hubbub until it was stopped that I had never heard the like of before. Whenever he came to a part of the dialogue requiring Irish, I noticed how easily his dictation flowed. When he reached a dramatic situation, he acted it out as well as his crippled condition would allow. One thing I noticed particularly: he always held a newspaper in his hand, and gave furtive glances at something behind it I was not supposed to see. I was determined, however, to know just what he was concealing from me. The opportunity came one morning when he was called out of the room. Before he went I noted how careful he was to place a newspaper so that it completely hid the thing under it. I went quickly to the table and, turning over the pages, I found a French book, *La Tentation* [by Feuillet], from which the entire plot of *Led Astray* was taken.[13]

If Belasco's memory was correct and the play was *Led Astray*, then it must have been a revision for the London production that Boucicault was dictating since the New York production had already been a big success. He was certainly wrong about one aspect of their meeting: it was not in the fall of 1873 as he remembered, but February 1874.[14]

After four or five days in Virginia City, Boucicault moved on to Salt Lake City and then back to New York before leaving in April for London to supervise the British production of *Led Astray*, starring Helen Barry. He stayed in London until the middle of July, and then returned to New York to prepare for the opening of his next play, *Belle Lamar*, at Booth's, on 10 August. An original play, set in the Southern States, *Belle Lamar* was one of the earliest dramas to utilize the events of the Civil War as its background, but in spite of a prolonged publicity campaign, it failed to make its mark. The play with which it was replaced, a revision of Otway's *Venice Preserved*, proved to be even less popular and lasted only a week.

Although none of his recent plays had enjoyed the success of a *London Assurance*, a *Colleen Bawn* or an *Arrah*, Boucicault still enjoyed a reputation as a writer who could rescue managers in difficulty. He had worked his magic for Palmer at the Union Square Theatre with *Led Astray*, and the next manager to approach him was Augustin Daly, who had the best company in town but no plays in which to present it. Daly, who had done remarkably well out of royalties from *After Dark* and the renewed interest in his own *Under the Gaslight* following the court case of 1868, harboured no grudges towards the man who had stolen his 'Great Railroad Scene', and commissioned Boucicault to write a Western with the short-story writer, Bret Harte. Among the other ideas on which Boucicault was working was another Irish drama, set in the reign of James II, which he'd promised to Lester Wallack. The plot was to depict the struggles of a young English officer between his duty and his love for an Irish girl, and it was provisionally called *Boyne Water*. In the course of discussions with Daly, Boucicault mentioned his new play and the manager advised him to alter the period and treat the subject humorously: the public, Daly said, would feel little sympathy for distress in wigs and hooped petticoats, and, in seeking escape from the financial depression then enveloping the country, wanted to be made to laugh not to think.[15] Boucicault took his advice and began to rework *Boyne Water* while commencing his collaboration with Harte.

The partnership did not go well. Boucicault came up with a story line, which he proposed calling *Kentuck*, and set to work, but he found Harte a difficult man to pin down. He was, complained Boucicault in a note to Daly,

> dilatory and erratic. He is anxious to get the work done – but thinks we can scurry over the ground more rapidly than is consistent with safety. For your sake – as well as for ours – the piece should be carefully done . . . With some difficulty I have made Harte promise to attend here every day at 4 o'clock.

There was also the small question of payment. As the play progressed and he found more and more of the work devolving on to him, Boucicault decided that he wanted a greater share of the fee. 'I quite understand that you cannot afford to pay double price because *two names* are attached to Harte's play,' he told Daly, 'But *I* cannot afford to work for half the price.' Daly, anxious to keep him on the project since he knew Harte would never finish the play on his own, agreed to meet all Boucicault's demands, but just when it seemed as though the collaboration was at last running smoothly, Boucicault dropped the entire project without explanation. He had completed the rewrite of his Irish play, now titled *The Shaughraun*, and Lester Wallack announced it for production in November. It was with considerable consternation that Daly was to find out that, not only had Boucicault abandoned his collaboration with Bret Harte, but he had also engaged Ada Dyas, Daly's leading actress, to play the heroine in his new play.

The Shaughraun (the vagabond), a title to which Lester Wallack objected on the grounds that no one would be able to pronounce it let alone understand it, opened at Wallack's Theatre on 14 November to immediate acclaim, proving that Boucicault was far from being the spent force, living on

NEW YORK, THURSDAY, NOVEMBER 26, 1874.

WALLACK'S.

Proprietor and Manager..........Mr. Lester Wallack

DOORS OPEN AT 7.30.   PERFORMANCE COMMENCES AT EIGHT.

TO-NIGHT AND EVERY NIGHT,

Appearance of the Irish Dramatist and Comedian,

Mr. DION BOUCICAULT,

The Author of "The Colleen Bawn," "Arrah-na-Pogue," "Kerry," "Daddy O'Dowd," "Irish Heiress," "London Assurance," "Love in a Maze," "Rip Van Winkle," "Mimi," "Old Heads and Young Hearts," "Woman," "Octoroon," "Jessie Brown," "Love and Money," "Formosa," "Jezebel," "Lost at Sea," "Jessie Deans," "The Corsican Brothers," "Hunted Down," "After Dark," "Belphegor," "Janet Pride," "Don Cæsar de Bazan," "Napoleon's Old Guard," "Sixtus the Fifth," "Dot," "The Life of an Actress," "Used Up," "Vanity Fair," "Smike," "Flying Scud," "Babil and Bijou," "Eily," "Belle Lamar," "Foul Play," "Mora," "The Knight of Arva," "The Long Strike," "The Willow Copse," "Andy Blake," "Genevieve," "How She Loves Him," "Louis XI.," "Pauvrette," "Streets of New York," "Man of Honor," "The Phantom," "Faust and Marguerita," "Led Astray."

In an entirely New and Original Play, in 3 Acts, illustrative of Irish Life and Character, entitled

THE SHAUGHRAUN.

The action of the play takes place in the County Sligo.
Time—The Present.

CHARACTERS IN THE PLAY.

CAPTAIN MOLINEUX, a young English Officer, commanding a detachment at Ballyraggett......MR. H. J. MONTAGUE
ROBERT FFOLLIOTT, a young Irish Gentleman, under sentence as a Fenian, in love with Arte O'Neale, MR. J. B. POLK
FATHER DOLAN, the Parish Priest of Suilabeg, his tutor and guardian......MR. JOHN GILBERT
CORRY KINCHELA, a Squireen......MR. EDWARD ARNOTT
HARVEY DUFF, a Police Agent, in disguise of a peasant under the name of Kinch......MR. HARRY BECKETT
CONN, THE SHAUGHRAUN, the soul of every fair, the life of every funeral, the first fiddle at all weddings and patterns......MR. BOUCICAULT
SERGEANT JONES of the 41st......MR. LEONARD
MANGAN,......MR. JOSEPHS
REILLY,......MR. E. M. HOLLAND
SULLIVAN, } Peasants {......MR. C. E. EDWIN
DOYLE,......MR. PECK
DONOVAN,......MR. ATKIN
ARTE O'NEALE, in love with Robert......MISS JEFFREYS LEWIS
CLAIRE FFOLLIOTT, a Sligo Lady......MISS ADA DYAS
MRS. O'KELLY, Conn's Mother......MADAME PONISI
MOYA, Father Dolan's Niece, in love with Conn, MISS IONE BURKE
BRIDGET MADIGAN, a Keener......MRS. SEFTON
NANCY MALONE, a Keener......MISS BLAISDELL

Peasants, Soldiers, Constabulary.

THE ACTION OF THE PLAY.

ACT I.—SCENE 1—SUILABEG. (Gehrwood.) The home of two Irish girls—the visit. Molineux seeks a days sport, and finds game he did not expect. The two guardians. Father Dolan gives Kinchela a piece of his mind. The Police Agent. The unexpected visitor.

SCENE 2—THE BLANKETS. (Morris.)—Conn's Cupboard. The Fugitive. Two lovers. A ring at the bell.

SCENE 3—THE EXTERIOR OF FATHER DOLAN'S. (Clare.) The Shaughraun. Conn goes hunting. Moya and her Sweetheart.

SCENE 4—THE HOME OF THE PARISH PRIEST. (Clare.) Conn makes a clean breast of it. The Fugitive's Return. The Priest's Fireside. Home again. The knock at the door. The arrest.

ACT II.—SCENE 1—A ROOM IN BALLYRAGGETT HOUSE. The counter plot. The murder planned.

SCENE 2—FATHER DOLAN'S. (Clare.) Claire and Molineux find each other out.
SCENE 3—THE BARRACK-ROOM. (Morris.) How Robert Ffolliott fell into the trap and played into the hands of his foes.
SCENE 4—MRS. O'KELLY'S CABIN. (Gehrwood.) Conn gets a letter and is bothered; he breaks away from his mother's apron strings.
SCENE 5—THE GATE TOWER. (Matt. Morgan.) The ambush and the escape.
SCENE 6—THE BLANKETS. Conn and Robert hunted. How Conn played the fox.
SCENE 7—RATHGARRON MEAD. How Claire Ffolliott played decoy-duck and saved the Captain.

SCENE 8—THE RUINS OF ST. BRIDGET'S ABBEY. (Matt. Morgan.) The love tryst. Arte and Moya at the appointed spot. The bait and the trap. Harvey Duff makes a mistake and gives a signal. The Shaughraun takes a rise out of him and gets a fall.

ACT III.—SCENE 1—MRS. O'KELLY'S CABIN. The canopy. A light breaks in upon Molineux. An unexpected interview.

SCENE 2—THE WAKE OF CONN, THE SHAUGHRAUN. Great news. Conn hears a good deal of news about himself. A surprise. Two unwilling guides.

SCENE 3—THE SHANTY. Arte and Moya in prison.

SCENE 4—THE COOT'S NEST. Harvey Duff gets into a warm corner. Kinchela comes to a bad end. Father Dolan gives his consent.

During the evening, the Band, under the direction of Mr. THOS. BAKER, will perform the following selections:

OVERTURE. "Shaughraun,"......BAKER
Introducing Old and New Irish Airs: "Irish Wail," "Caleb is me Chree," "You remember Ellen," "Willie Reilly," "The Jolly Ploughboy," "Arven More,"—Solo Cornet. "The March," "Green Girls," "The Joy of Peace," "The Coolin," "Soll Clarionet and Oboe," "Tad Red Fox," "Jig—St. Patrick was a Gentleman."
PANTALOON (new). "Komarine Kojo."—(on Knock Melodies).
WALTZ (new). "Da Da,"......STRAUSS

reputation, that some people claimed. In it, Boucicault again exploited the territory he had explored in *The Colleen Bawn* and *Arrah-na-Pogue*, and the similarities between the three plays are obvious. Set during the Fenian insurrection of 1866, *The Shaughraun* contains young lovers, a priest, an English gentleman and Conn, 'the soul of every fair, the life of every funeral, the first fiddle at all weddings and patterns'. Many of the highly effective and dramatic scenes in the play have their counterparts in earlier Boucicault dramas, but in most respects *The Shaughraun* was an original composition and by far the best and greatest of his melodramas.

The part of Conn, the most important character in the play, was played by Boucicault and gave him his most successful role ever, confirming him as an actor of the first rank and as a comic writer of brilliance. He was fifty-five, had suffered from gout and exhaustion, but he threw himself into the part with all the gusto of a young man. 'It was my good fortune to see Mr Boucicault in the title part of his own play, *Shaughraun*,' recalled the actress Helena Modjeska, 'and I did not know what to admire most, the wonderful originality, wit, and clever construction of the author, the perfect production of the stage manager, or the finish and truth of his exquisite acting. He looked eighteen on the stage, and was simply irresistible.'[16]

Boucicault was so intent on getting perfection into the production that he forgot to pick out a costume for himself and only realized his oversight on the opening night. He rushed to the property room, picked up an old coat that had been used for *Tony Lumpkin* and a pair of battered boots, and put them on. His dress became inseparable from the part. In spite of other mishaps on the first night – the moon in act two exploded just before the curtain rose, leaving a black hole in the set, yet silver ripples continued to play on the water – *The Shaughraun* became the hit of the season. When it finished its run four months later at the end of March, it had grossed nearly a quarter of a million dollars, and the receipts for the Thanksgiving Day matinée were $2,250, the highest ever recorded in New York. On the last night Boucicault was given an official presentation by the Irish community of New

York for his services to Irish drama, a gesture that touched him deeply.

From New York he took the play to Boston, where it continued to attract full houses, and in four weeks he personally made almost $30,000 at an average of $600 a night. When he appeared in San Francisco, the pattern was the same and he took more than $9,000. For the next few years *The Shaughraun* was to play to capacity houses wherever it was presented and to earn Boucicault more money than any of his other dramas – half a million dollars in the United States alone. What he proposed doing with his money was a constant worry to his mother in England.

> Dion has had great success with his new play at N. York [she wrote to his cousin soon after the play had opened], but he is so fearfully extravagant and indulges the same tastes so frightfully in his *children* that it deprives *me* of all hope as to his and their future to say nothing of ourselves who are I may say – *almost* wholly dependent on him. He has the heart to be the best of sons but with all his talents he sadly wants common sense, the best gift man or woman can possess.[17]

With the proceeds he bought himself a steam yacht, which he christened *The Shaughraun*, planning to use it as a retreat where he could write and to house his companies when touring the Eastern seaboard. He also contemplated sailing it to England and running up the rebel Irish flag in the Solent. His interest in the boat, however, which cost him $75,000, was short-lived: on one of his first trips in her, she developed engine trouble and he refused ever to sail in her again, eventually selling her at a loss. He also took to hiring special railway carriages with his name emblazoned on the side, to transport his companies around the States. If he had never written another play after *The Shaughraun*, Boucicault's stock among his contemporaries would have been considerably higher than it became, for with each successive drama he now produced, he proved conclusively that he had written his last major work.

For his engagement in Boston, Boucicault contracted a new

company which included the young Maurice Barrymore, father of Lionel, Ethel and John, who had just arrived in America from England. During rehearsals, Boucicault's eye fell on Ida Savory, a young actress, for whose affections he had a rival in Barrymore. He did his best to belittle Barrymore in front of the rest of the cast, but the animosity quickly turned to interest and then friendship, and Miss Savory had to be content with sharing her two suitors on the rare occasions when they were not out together drinking or wenching.[18] Boucicault also found another compensation for not winning the undivided attention of Ida Savory in the shape of Clara Rousby, an English actress of considerable charm and figure who was also appearing in Boston at that time.

After his successful tour of the States, Boucicault returned to London in the middle of August to present *The Shaughraun* at Drury Lane for Chatterton. The actress who was cast to play Moya dropped out at the last moment and, much against Boucicault's wishes, his wife Agnes was engaged to take her place. Despite their marital difficulties off stage, their partnership worked its magic in the theatre and the play ran from 4 September until 18 December, netting £14,000 for Boucicault and Chatterton, and was only withdrawn because Drury Lane had been booked for a pantomime. With a few minor cast changes (one of which brought in Lydia Foote to the company), the production moved to the Adelphi for another month.

Moved by the reception the play had been given and by the emotions aroused in him as an Irishman, Boucicault was prompted on 1 January 1876 to write an open letter to Benjamin Disraeli, the British Prime Minister, demanding, in the name of the thousands who had seen *The Shaughraun* (and who had by so doing, according to Boucicault, expressed their sympathy with the cause of Irish Home Rule), that the British government should release the many Irish political prisoners then languishing in gaols in Britain and Australia. Disraeli ignored his appeal, refusing to become involved in an episode he considered to be nothing more than a publicity stunt to advertise Boucicault's forthcoming tour. A short while after, when Boucicault's name was mentioned in his presence, Disraeli turned to his secretary: 'Boucicault!' he said. 'Strange name; I think I've heard it before. Is it someone in the conjuring business?'[19]

It is probable that Boucicault wrote his letter for motives other than financial gain (although the free publicity for his tour cannot have been far from his mind), for the older he became the more he saw himself as being in a position to take positive action on the Irish Question. He was, however, determined to leave the Adelphi when the play closed on Saturday, 22 January, in a blaze of publicity, and since the Prime Minister was not prepared to assist him, he arranged for the house to be filled with his supporters. The news of his move was quickly conveyed to Chatterton, who anticipated a seditious speech or a demonstration against the government, and was determined to prevent either. He put his own men in the remainder of the house and awaited the evening with some trepidation. The events of the night were to take a quite different turn from those expected by either Boucicault or Chatterton.

When the curtain rose [Chatterton recalled[20]], the house was crowded, the audience fervid and demonstrative. At the end of the first act, there was a double call, and a laurel wreath with green ribbons was cast at Boucicault's feet. At the end of the second act he was called for again and again, and pelted with shamrocks. At nine o'clock I arrived. I had barely got inside the theatre when an inspector of police came up. The man was pale and livid, and could scarcely gasp out his awful intelligence. There had been an accident on the Great Northern Railway, near Huntingdon, in which poor Willie, Boucicault's eldest son, had been killed.

Willie, not quite twenty-one, was Boucicault's favourite child. Unlike his brothers and sisters, he had no wish to go on the stage and wanted to be a farmer. He had been to stay with friends in Lincolnshire, and had caught the southbound *Flying Scot* at Peterborough, bound for King's Cross, London, on the Friday evening. Twenty minutes after the train had pulled out of the station, at Abbot's Ripton near Huntingdon, in a violent snowstorm, the *Flying Scot* had ploughed into the back of a coal train. Eleven minutes later, a northbound express, unable to stop in time, had hit the wreckage. Twelve people were killed instantly, two died in hospital and many were seriously injured. Willie's body was found among the wreckage and taken to Huntingdon County Hospital, but a series of mishaps delayed identification and it was not until late on Saturday that the first details of the accident were telegraphed to London. The first person to identify Willie had been the surgeon Christopher Heath, a family friend, who had travelled to Huntingdon to attend to the brother of another friend involved in the crash. Arriving back in London in the early evening, Heath hurried round to Regent Street only to find that both parents had already left for the theatre. They had heard about the accident and were worried about Willie. From his dressing room, Boucicault sent a short note to the General Manager of the Great Northern at King's Cross. 'I expected my son to return from Lincolnshire yesterday. Having received no news of him I am greatly distressed by the intelligence of the accident yesterday . . . Among those hurt by the accident is there any one answering this description?'

This was the situation that faced Chatterton when he reached the Adelphi to find the police inspector about to go in search of Boucicault to break the news. He refused to allow the man to go backstage and undertook to tell Boucicault himself.

One thing was quite certain, the tidings must be kept from Dion and his wife till they got home. So, giving imperative orders that no one was to be admitted behind the scenes, I made my way on to the stage, where, the very moment I entered, I encountered Boucicault face to face. He accosted me somewhat defiantly with: 'So you've turned up at last.' 'Yes, I've come to do honour to the occasion,' I replied. I had a bad time of it for the next hour, for I had to keep up a smiling face and try to talk upon indifferent subjects, thinking all the while of how the news was to be broken. Willie had been the apple of his father's eye. If there was one human being that Dion Boucicault loved in the world besides himself, it was that poor boy. At last, with the end of the play and the customary calls and recalls, came a roar from Boucicault's partisans: 'Boucicault! Speech! Speech!' This was responded to by a counter-roar from my myrmidons of 'No! No! Chatterton!' I remained in the prompt entrance, prepared for all emergencies. At last the uproar in front culminated in a tumult, during which it seemed as if the house was coming down about our ears. Boucicault, who had gone to his dressing-room, came down, and, meeting my stage manager, remarked in the most ingenuous manner: 'Dear, dear, this is dreadful. Where is Chatterton?' 'There,' replied the stage manager, pointing to me; whereupon Dion came up and inquired: 'Don't you think I'd better go on?' 'No,' I said, sturdily. 'I don't think anything of the kind.' 'I really must,' he said. 'You really musn't,' said I. 'But they'll tear the house down.' 'It's my house, not yours, so that's my look-out.' 'By god, I will go on!' snarled Boucicault, savagely. 'Then you'll have to walk over my body first, and when you've done that my carpenters have their orders to prevent your going on. Now look here! Let's talk common-sense; you've had your little innings; you've had all the compliments, all the honours that any actor or author could desire, but your engagement is over. So it's no good kicking against the pricks.' With that we glared at each other. Then there was a lull in the storm in front. After a minute's reflection he simmered down and said in his pleasantest manner: 'Very well. Come to my room, have a glass of wine, and let us shake hands anyway.' So that difficulty was over, but 'the greatest was behind.' Dion was now at his best, and was as jolly as he could be; and when he was jolly he was one of the pleasantest fellows breathing. Mrs Boucicault was – as she always was – charming. The difficulty was, how to tell them of their bereavement.

Chatterton could not find the words to break the news, and learning that Boucicault's brother William was in the front of the house with his doctor, went in search of them to ask them to do it. He arranged to get the Boucicaults back to Regent

Street as quickly as possible, where William and the doctor would be waiting. Returning backstage, he found Lydia Foote and another actress in tears, waiting for Agnes to appear so that they could offer their condolences. He bundled them out of the theatre,

for which, of course, I was put down as an unsympathetic brute. I had a cab waiting at the Royal entrance in Maiden Lane, and when Mrs Boucicault came downstairs, I packed her into it, saying that Dion had gone home and wished to see her immediately. She turned pale and looked at me dubiously. 'There's nothing wrong, Mr Chatterton – nothing about Willie?' she inquired. I hadn't the heart to tell her so I said, 'Nothing particular; only Dion has a friend or two to supper, and he wants you at once.' With that she drove off . . . God knows how the father and mother passed that night. I only know I never closed my eyes till morning, for thinking of the poor lad who lay dead in Huntingdon.[21]

The following Monday, Boucicault's brother George travelled to Huntingdon to attend the inquest and delivered a blistering attack on the railway authorities for their tardiness in identifying Willie and failure to notify the parents sooner. The funeral took place on the afternoon of Wednesday, 26 January, and by general consent shops in the town were closed and blinds drawn as a mark of respect. Agnes was still too shocked to make the journey, and Boucicault travelled up with his brothers George and William, and his son Dot.

Mr Boucicault exhibited no outward sign of emotion while the coffin . . . was lowered into the grave [reported a local paper]. After the last words of the minister had been pronounced, he approached the grave and passed round it. After intently gazing down upon the coffin, he took from his pocket a letter and cast it into the grave, and then, his long-sustained fortitude appearing suddenly to desert him, he threw his arm around the neck of his son and quickly walked away.[22]

11

OUT OF FASHION

WILLIE'S DEATH was a bitter blow to both parents and, for a while, their shared grief brought them closer than they had been for some time. Deeply touched by the sympathy shown to him at the funeral by the people of Huntingdon, Boucicault wrote to the town's mayor, offering to pay for a suitable memorial to Willie to be erected locally. Huntingdon council considered two schemes: either a drinking fountain, to be placed in front of the hospital or in the market place, or else help with the restoration of the grammar school, a dilapidated medieval building which had itself once been a hospital. The idea of the fountain was eventually vetoed by those councillors who were opposed to a public monument being erected by a Catholic (they assumed Boucicault, being Irish, was Catholic), and who disliked his choice of a quotation from his play *Effie Deans* for the inscription, and instead they settled on rebuilding the school. The idea of restoring the school fired Boucicault's imagination, and with a donation of £900 from the playwright, work began. While the council had been deliberating, he had also given £25 to the funds of the local hospital. The new school was reopened in December 1877 and continued in use until 1939 when, after further restoration, the building became a museum commemorating Huntingdon's most famous son, Oliver Cromwell. The fact that Boucicault, who had made so much out of being Irish and campaigning for a free Ireland, should have been most responsible for the restoration of the school attended by, for Irishmen, that most hated and despised of Englishmen, was an irony the papers were not slow to point out.

The production of *The Shaughraun*, with which Boucicault and Agnes had intended touring after the end of the Adelphi run, went on without them, opening the rebuilt Theatre Royal in Edinburgh on 27 January, the day after Willie's funeral, with Eveleen Ryan as Moya and Hubert O'Grady as Conn. A second company assembled by Boucicault also took the play on a tour of Northern England, and at the end of each engagement, he ordered that a special benefit should be given for the dependants of Fenian prisoners.

While Boucicault had no wish to return to acting (both he and Agnes staying out of the cast when *The Shaughraun* moved to Glasgow in March), there was one engagement he did not want to cancel, directing a Paris revival of *Arrah-na-Pogue* at the Porte Saint-Martin in April. The brief respite he and Agnes had enjoyed from their bickering was coming to an end and he was eager to get away and be on his own. Thoughts of death preoccupied him even in Paris, and while he was there he drew up a will leaving everything to be divided between his five surviving children and asking Dot (Darley George, his seventeen-year-old eldest boy since Willie's death), to take the name Dion. He made no provision at all for Agnes, on whom he claimed to have settled enough property in the United States to give her an income for life (property which, incidentally, had been bought mostly with her money and which, at the time of his 1863 bankruptcy, he had claimed was producing nothing but taxes).

Returning to London, he revised *Louis XI* (the play in which Charles Kean had scored a success in 1855) for Henry Irving to open his new season at the Lyceum, and on 29 July left for New York alone, leaving behind Agnes, his children and a country which meant only pain and grief to him. Being back in America and reunited with Katherine Rogers revived his flagging spirits and helped lift his depression. He began to act again, and started to write. On 3 October, *Forbidden Fruit*, a three-act farce, opened at Wallack's. A tale of errant husbands in search of a night out with the girls, it is a well-crafted but artificial piece, a precursor of the dialogue comedies of Oscar Wilde, and although it drew large audiences, it never quite became a hit.

Two months before Boucicault had returned to the States, in May, the Australian couple J. C. Williamson and Maggie Moore (who had appeared with him in San Francisco), had started a season at the Adelphi Theatre in London in revivals of *The Colleen Bawn* and *Arrah-na-Pogue*. Both plays proved to be enormously popular, making their leading players into stars and reminding Boucicault that the two Irish dramas were among the best plays in his prolific output. He had raised no objection to the Williamsons appearing in either play – they had long been public property and had been seen throughout England and America with a variety of actors and actresses in the leads; but when news reached him in the States in October that Chatterton was planning to present them next in *The Shaughraun*, he cabled immediately his refusal to sanction the production. *The Shaughraun*, he felt, was still very much his property, and with him in the role of Conn had a lot of mileage left in it. He did not think the time had arrived to allow anyone else (other than an actor of his own choosing) in on the part, and he had no wish to have his interpretation of the role upstaged by the mammoth success Williamson had been enjoying in *his* parts in *The Colleen Bawn* and *Arrah*. Chatterton, knowing Boucicault well, offered to pay whatever royalty the playwright wished to demand, but for Boucicault, on this occasion, that wasn't the point: he wished to reserve the role of Conn for his own next appearance on the London stage, and he didn't want Williamson to play it. By a strange oversight, Boucicault had neglected to copyright the play against free production, and Chatterton, by offering to pay a royalty, was able to proceed with his plan to produce the play in November.

Boucicault immediately took out an injunction to prevent him. Williamson, worried by this action and not quite certain what was going on, cabled Boucicault in the States to ask if the playwright was giving his permission for the production. As soon as he received the reply that he wasn't, Williamson refused to become a party to what he saw as Chatterton's betrayal of trust and would not accept the role of Conn until Boucicault personally sanctioned it. Chatterton tried all his powers of persuasion to get him to change his mind, but the actor was adamant, and ten days before the scheduled opening, Chatterton sued him and his wife for breach of contract. Boucicault repaid Williamson for taking this stand on his behalf in a shoddy way: while offering to help defray the Williamsons' legal costs (an offer that was politely declined), he superciliously disclaimed any previous association with the two Australians. 'And so,' reported the London correspondent of *The Spirit of the Times*, 'this extraordinary fight will die a natural death. In the courts of law Boucicault has been worsted by Chatterton, and in the moral courts Boucicault has certainly been worsted by Williamson, for Williamson sacrificed everything for Boucicault and was repaid by being sneered at.'

The Shaughraun went ahead at the Adelphi without the Williamsons, and played to poor houses. Two years later Chatterton's career as a manager came to an end when, in February 1879, he was declared bankrupt with assets of £2,000 and liabilities of £40,000. This quarrel, which was to be the last of the many between Chatterton and Boucicault, did have a beneficial side to it: when Williamson returned to Australia to enter management he was determined not to repeat Chatterton's mistake and, at his instigation, the entire question of the validity of English copyright in Australia was later sorted out.

Boucicault's attitude towards Williamson, whom he had known and acted with in California, seems inexplicable. He could be vain, selfish and an implacable enemy, but he was loyal and generous towards his friends and he had no reason to doubt either Williamson's friendship or his sincerity. His quarrel was with Chatterton, whom he detested, and it may have been that he thought the two were in league. Possibly he felt he was fighting to save his livelihood, since *The Shaughraun* was his only real source of income at the time; possibly the death of Willie and collapse of his marriage had in some way affected his judgement. Hurt though Williamson may have felt, he did not harbour any grudges against Boucicault and he tried to make things up between them three years later, after he had returned to Australia, by commissioning a new Irish play from him. The work was never finished, and in all probability was never started.

> Cannot understand Boucicault [wrote a puzzled Williamson to his agent in London], trying to make out that I have not acted right when all I asked was that he should deliver the play into your hands on the day agreed upon, but in a *finished state ready for production* . . . Mr Boucicault has never delivered or offered to deliver the play according to contract. I have been ready and anxious to receive the play and had my money up to pay for it, but because I wished to assure myself at my own expense that the play was really a new Irish drama and that it was in condition to be produced immediately, Mr B. abuses me to you.[1]

At the same time as Chatterton was mounting his production of *The Shaughraun* at the Adelphi, Boucicault was opening in the play in New York. Two days before the first night, Agnes had arrived in New York with the girls to attempt a reconciliation, but they were unable to settle their differences and Agnes returned sadly to London, never to live with her husband again. Whatever difficulties Boucicault was suffering in his personal life, he was never able to escape the theatre, to which he had sacrificed so much. Indeed, it was by throwing himself into his work even harder that he was able to forget his problems. On 5 December the Brooklyn Theatre was destroyed by fire with the loss of at least 300 lives, including two members of the cast. Two weeks later, at Wallack's Theatre, Boucicault was publicly demonstrating the results of his research into fireproof scenery. American theatres in particular, being built mostly from wood, had a long history of destruction by fire, a hazard that had occupied and concerned Boucicault for many years. When he had planned to build a new theatre in 1858, prior to taking over the Metropolitan and converting it into the Winter Garden, he proposed an iron structure, as he did with his unbuilt New Theatre in the

Haymarket. The last thing he wanted was for audiences to stay away because they were afraid for their safety. His demonstration was widely reported and he was inundated with inquiries about his findings.

Mr Boucicault, with a few explanatory remarks to quite a large audience interested in the matter, attempted to set fire to a scene saturated with a solution of tungstate of soda and primed with a solution of silicate of soda, suspended over the centre of the stage. A flame equal to the force of one hundred and fifty of the ordinary gas-jets on the stage was directed on the suspended canvas and held there for about two minutes. The canvas did not blaze or smoke. The portions on which the gas flame had been directed broke, fell to the ground, and crumbled into fine ashes on being touched. Several experiments of this kind were made on different parts of the canvas and always with the same result. A coil of rope was subsequently submitted to the test of fire. The flame seemed to have little or no effect upon it . . . All the managers present took a deep interest in the operation and keenly watched every phase of the experiment . . . They intend to apply it immediately, not only to all the new scenery they may be preparing, but on all the scenes at present in use in their respective theatres, as well as on the flies, wings and borders.[2]

This practical involvement with the affairs of the theatre was the tonic Boucicault needed to shake him from his depression, and he undertook an extensive tour of *The Shaughraun*, fulfilling engagements he had made two years previously.

I am touring it with the ragged old play *The Shaughraun* [he wrote to Kate Terry's husband, Arthur Lewis, from Chicago], and in 18 weeks – (the business is only so-so) I shall take a little over $30,000 (say 6,000£) (This is outside of New York and Boston.) I believe I shall be manager of Booth's Theatre here next season – it is the Drury Lane of New York – Nevertheless I stick to my old home at Wallack's (the Haymarket of the city) and play there as usual – next October. Next Monday I start for San Francisco – 2500 miles of Rail – day and night! but being *young* and *eager* I don't mind it.[3]

After his tour he returned to New York in the late spring of 1877, played Conn for a week at the Brooklyn Academy and then settled down with Kate Rogers at his apartments at 20 East 15th Street to prepare a new play for production at Wallack's in the autumn and begin a series of articles about his career and his views of the theatre for the magazine, the *North America Review*, which he intended should be the basis for an autobiography he wanted to write. His tranquillity was shattered by the news from London that, on 5 July, his eldest daughter Eve had married the actor John Clayton. He was furious.

> Dion was well when I last heard from him [wrote his mother, Anne Boursiquot, to a cousin]. I suppose, nay, I believe he is making much money (if only he takes care of it.) His daughter Eve has married without his consent and as yet has not forgiven her though he continues to allow her £300 per annum – but he never answers any of her letters. She has acted most ungratefully to him who adored her so from her infancy. She married a Mr Calthrop, a man of very good family, well-known in Lincolnshire where they have been for centuries as Squires and gentry time out of mind. But this gentleman's father, having fifteen children, the sons were obliged to exert themselves. John, Eve's husband, was intended for the church, he objected – they then got him a Government appointment in which he remained some time, but hated the routine and small pay, became stage struck and threw up his appointment and became an actor under the name of Clayton. And is now making above £2,000 a year. I hate his profession but since I have known him I like the man.[4]

It may have been because John Clayton was an actor that Boucicault was so violently opposed to the match – maybe he had thoughts of his daughter marrying into the aristocracy and completing the restoration of the family's social position – but the fact that it was Agnes who had been pushing Clayton's suit by bringing him to her house night and day cannot have helped. It took him some time to become used to the idea, and then he not only bought the couple a house near Regent's Park, but offered Clayton a job with his company in New York. The marriage was not a success. Clayton became a popular actor and was, for a time, manager of the Royal Court Theatre in Sloane Square. During rehearsals for a play there, which he was directing and in which the wife unexpectedly walks out on her husband, he returned home to find that Eve had run off with Harry Eversfield, an actor in the company and his personal secretary. She returned to him only in 1888 when he was critically ill, just before his death at the tragically early age of forty-five.

On 1 October 1877, the play Boucicault had taken the summer off to write, and his first for a year, opened at Wallack's. *Marriage* had been well advertised, with claims that it was another *London Assurance*, and it was eagerly awaited. But it proved to be a big disappointment and lasted for only a month before it was withdrawn and sent on tour. Boucicault was convinced that the play had failed because of the reviews, in particular one in the *Tribune* written by William Winter. All his loathing of the press came welling up, and he savagely attacked newspapers and the standard of dramatic criticism in general, and Winter's position as the leading New York critic in particular. After a burst of vitriolic correspondence to the *Tribune* by both men, the skirmish ended, but the idea that poor and ill-informed dramatic criticism was responsible for the poor quality of nineteenth-century drama was a theme that Boucicault was to return to, in speeches, letters and articles, more and more frequently until his death.

The failure of *Marriage* forced him back to the stage as an actor, and at the end of November he played a week at the Brooklyn Academy in *The Shaughraun* before opening in the same play for a month at the Grand Opera House, New York, at the end of December. Most of December was spent rehearsing the famous Polish actress Helena Modjeska for her Broadway début in *Adrienne Lecouvreur*.

It was an act of great kindness and a great concession on his part [she wrote in her *Memories*], and I owe him a debt of gratitude never to be repaid. He took infinite pains, teaching most of the people not only how to say their lines, but what to do, how to bow, how to enter or exit, even how to hold a snuff-box and how to brush off with a graceful gesture the snuff from their ruffled frill. The low bows and curtseys were the hardest to teach. As I watched Mr Boucicault I sincerely admired him for his authority and skill in managing each individual and his imagination in the scenic arrangements. When I tried to express my gratitude for the pains he took in directing the play, he only said he was glad to do so, because I was a stranger and he knew from experience that even the foremost actors in Europe do not trouble themselves about the stage management.

When the play opened on 22 December at the 5th Avenue Theatre, Modjeska, in spite of the handicap of a thick Polish accent, scored a personal triumph which was the platform for her to become one of the leading actresses of her generation.

Boucicault was still working hard at his writing, rising early and going to his desk before breakfast, but his output had slowed considerably, and for the first time in his career he found himself completely out of touch with the mood of the public. Nothing he attempted could recapture that mood. *The Dead Secret*, starring Katherine Rogers and based on the Wilkie Collins novel, failed at the 5th Avenue Theatre in January 1878, and *Clarissa Harlowe*, an adaptation of Samuel Richardson's novel, opened at Wallack's on 10 September to close ten days later and be replaced by Boucicault's doctored version of *The School for Scandal*. *Clarissa* was a throwback to the melodramatic, sensation plays he had been writing twenty years earlier, and had it been performed then instead of in 1878 it might well have succeeded, but playgoers had had enough of improbable plots and houses on fire.

During rehearsals for *Clarissa Harlowe*, Boucicault was approached by a reporter for his opinion on the release of the Fenian prisoner Condon. 'Franklin, my dear boy,' he replied,

'I think that now all the political prisoners are released or dead – the Government having yielded to a feeling they could no longer resist – all questions concerning them are fast dying out.' This answer was seized upon as evidence that his concern for the Fenian cause had never run deeper than the publicity he could obtain from it: 'In other words, Mr Boucicault, having obtained the advertisement he desired, has washed his hands of the matter.'[5] To a certain extent this may have been true but in Boucicault's complex character there were always more sides than the most obvious one. He was deeply proud to be Irish and genuinely pleased that his Irish plays were among the most successful he had written. He had always thrown himself whole-heartedly into raising funds for Irish causes; he gave a New York banquet for prisoners who had escaped from Australia; he had devoted the proceeds of benefit performances of *The Shaughraun* to helping prisoners' families in Ireland; he had lectured on Irish history and had been on the periphery of parliamentary moves towards Home Rule. His concern and involvement was considered to be genuine enough for him to be offered two seats in elections for Westminster, which he wisely refused, knowing that he would be unable to cope with the minutiae of parliamentary business. If he had a contribution to make, it was through his public lectures and the power of his pen. During his acceptance speech in 1874 at the end of the New York run of *The Shaughraun*, when the Irish communities in America had honoured him for his contribution to Irish drama, he made a remark that summed up his feelings: 'This, sir, is the greatest honour of my life, except one, and that was conferred upon me once, about fifty years ago, when, upon entering the world, I found myself to be an Irishman. But,' he went on, with a dig at his critics, 'as I had done nothing to deserve that compliment, I cannot claim credit for the work of which I was not the author.'[6]

Also while he was at Wallack's for *Clarissa Harlowe*, a practical joke was played on Boucicault which he was certain not to have appreciated. He had fallen asleep in the Green Room, and when he got back to his rooms he found 'Use Hail Columbia Hair Restorer' inscribed upon his bald pate.

'But then the Americans have a genius for advertising,' commented a reporter.[7]

On Friday, 13 December, Agnes arrived in New York with Patrice and Nina, hoping that Boucicault's infatuation with Katherine Rogers might have passed and that she could effect a reconciliation. Boucicault decided to turn her presence to advantage, and after he had completed a six-week engagement at the Grand Opera House, he and Agnes appeared together at Booth's for a week of Irish revivals, playing in *The Colleen Bawn*, *Arrah-na-Pogue* and *The Shaughraun*. It was her first appearance on the New York stage for five years, and her legions of fans guaranteed full houses, even though nothing could disguise the fact that her figure had become matronly and she was too old to play juvenile leads any more. Successful though they may have been on stage (the week took $12,000), Boucicault was not prepared to turn the clock back in their relationship and they were unable to settle their differences. He offered her $1,750 to go back to England and leave him alone. Sadly, and reluctantly, Agnes accepted the money and sailed for Liverpool with the children on 27 February 1879, ten days after Boucicault had opened a new engagement in Boston and three days after *Spell-bound*, his latest play, had opened at Wallack's. A reworking of *Pauline*, the play he had adapted for Kean at the Princess's in 1851, *Spell-bound* gave further proof that he was out of fashion as a dramatist. The critics were very hard on it, the public showed no interest in it whatever, and after two weeks it was withdrawn.

These failures puzzled and irritated Boucicault, for he was convinced that he was writing better than ever. Financed by his acting and the seemingly never-ending popularity of *The Shaughraun*, he was still living well, entertaining regularly and dabbling in the stock market, and he decided to go back into management himself. He paid $20,000 for a six-month lease on Booth's and spent $5,000 on redecorating the theatre completely and enlarging the balconies to hold the crowds he expected. He assembled a company of the best and most expensive actors, including his son-in-law John Clayton, and Dion junior, who was making his stage début. The season opened on 4 September 1879 with the first night of *Rescued*, a new play that he considered to be the best he had ever written.

We were fain to believe last evening that, instead of witnessing a new work, an outcome of this late and refined emotional era, we were seeing over again one of the theatrical antiquities which set man's hair on end in the Old Bowery years ago [wrote a critic, expressing most people's reaction to the play[8]]. But as Mr Boucicault is scarcely young at present, and as he probably feels a tender affection for methods which were dear to him in the past, this seeming incongruity is partially accounted for. *Rescued* is, indeed, a melodrama constructed on old-time principles, a work which is meant to astonish, to thrill, to arouse all sorts and degrees of sympathy, whether healthful or unhealthful, and, also we may add, to put a stop to reflection. It is representative throughout of its author, who, instead of being a man of genius, is simply a man of extraordinary cleverness; whose fame is built, not upon strength of imagination or strength of conception, but wholly upon a highly ingenious and polished perception of the mechanical relation of things. Mr Boucicault has never invented, though he has always contrived to obtain useful ideas from well-supplied sources; he has been a pillager of other men's brains, and as such we do not profess to hold him high in our esteem; but his rare capacity for making practical use of all kinds of material has been demonstrated over and over again, and this capacity is a talent which must be freely and fully acknowledged, before we can hope to take a fair measure of his worth.

Unable to keep *Rescued* on the boards for more than a month (and again blaming the critics' hostility towards him as the reason for the play's failure), Boucicault decided to substitute it with *Louis XI*, in which he would play the king, a part he was convinced he could do better than either Kean or Irving who had been acclaimed in it the year before at the Lyceum, while his son Dot would make his stage début as the Dauphin. The first night, on 11 October, was a fiasco, as

George Clarke, a member of the company not playing that night, recalled.

> I happened to be back on the stage, talking to some of the boys, and as I passed by the 'star dressing-room' I noticed that the door was half open and Boucicault sat before his glass making up. He caught sight of me and called me to come in. He was nervous almost to prostration, and was slapping on the greasepaint profusely and indiscriminately. 'I can't seem to get this make-up right,' he said, turning full around upon me. If it had been anyone but Dion Boucicault, I should have burst out laughing. He looked more like a Sioux or Kickapoo in full war-paint than the wily French monarch, and I felt really sorry for him. He was in genuine distress, so I volunteered to help him. He not only assented, but sat docile as a child. Snatching up a towel, I wiped off the layers of greasepaint he had daubed on. Then I proceeded to give him a quick make-up. It was a hurry-up job, but certainly a hundred percent better than he could have executed in his unstrung condition.[9]

Recovering his composure a little, Boucicault went on stage and the performance began. Clarke, who had gone to the front to watch, was amazed.

> It was weird beyond words. At first the audience sat in dumb amazement; then came titters and giggles, and finally roars. Never did monarch receive less grave and reverent treatment. Boucicault's brogue came out thick and strong . . . a French king with a Dublin brogue was too excruciating an anachronism for the audience. To make matters worse, three of the principal parts were also played by Irishmen – John Brougham, Dominick Murray and W. B. ('Billy') Cahill . . . As the tragedy – or, more properly speaking, the tragic farce – progressed, John Brougham, who loved a good joke better than anything else in the world, began to exaggerate the unctuousness of his own fine, natural brogue. Next, John Clayton, an Englishman and the son-in-law of Boucicault, who was playing

Nemours, felt in duty bound to fall in line with the others, and he too assumed a broad brogue. The rest of the company, either out of deviltry or catching the infection, became Gaelic instead of Gallic, and before the play was half over the French tragedy had degenerated into an orgy of Hibernian dialects. The audience certainly had their money's worth. Heartier laughter never resounded in a theatre. People laughed till the tears ran down their cheeks.

After only four nights, *Louis XI*, which was supposed to close the season, was taken off and *Rescued* put back in its place. What should have been a marvellous season came to a disastrous end on 25 October, on which night Brougham made his last appearance on the New York stage. Boucicault's inability to get his make-up right and his highly strung state before the opening of *Louis XI* were not the result of nervousness about his performance. The repeated failures of his new plays (another, *Contempt of Court*, had opened and closed at Wallack's during October), the constant sniping of the press, the financial losses his Booth's season were incurring (which swallowed up his savings), the death of his mother at the beginning of the year[10] and the pressures of the split with Agnes, had all conspired to throw him into a deep depression which culminated in a nervous breakdown. On 22 October, John Brougham noted in his diary, 'Dion very ill,' and before the season had ended, the playwright was on his way to Washington to relax and recover his strength. For a while his condition was serious, even though the *Washington Post* dismissed his illness sarcastically as 'overwork in stealing French plays'. He was paralysed temporarily, and unable to write or even think about the theatre, but the rest did him good, and after two weeks he was able to write to Squire Bancroft:

I doubt whether I shall ever cross the ocean again. I am rusticating at Washington for a month or two, having recovered some strength, and am waiting to know if my lease of life is out, or is to be renewed for another term. I have had notice to quit but am arguing the point ('just like you,' I think I hear you say), and nothing is settled between Nature and me.[11]

The enforced break was what he needed. Four months later, at the beginning of February 1880, he was back on stage at Wallack's and had accepted an invitation from the Gattis in London to cross the ocean and appear in *The Shaughraun* in April. Hearing of his illness, Agnes had again sailed to New York to attempt a reconciliation, but by the time she arrived he was much recovered and clearly did not want her. On Saturday, 27 March, Boucicault was scheduled to make his final performance at Wallack's in *How She Loves Him* before leaving New York for London. As he sat down in his apartment to eat his dinner before setting out for the theatre, two reporters arrived to interview him about his forthcoming visit to England, and he naturally enough invited them in. Once inside they revealed that they were not reporters but sheriff's men, there to arrest him on the instigation of Agnes who wanted a divorce and thought that if he was permitted to leave America he would never return. Lester Wallack and Theodore Moss were summoned from the theatre and paid the bail of $9,000 just in time for Boucicault to reach the theatre and make his first entrance. Doubtless the irony of the play's title did not escape him.

Agnes cited as her grounds for divorce Boucicault's adultery with Katherine Rogers and others, including Clara Rousby in Boston, during the previous nine years, during which time, she claimed, he had lived openly in New York with Katherine and was the father of her son. She took her action with reluctance to make sure he did not leave her destitute since she was without any other means of support. Boucicault, as was his usual practice, decided to conduct his side of the argument through the medium of the press and sent a long statement, in the guise of an interview, to the *Herald*, claiming that he had not lived with Agnes for eleven years, that he had always given her ample means of support but that she had dissipated his money, that she had been the one to desert him, that she had been living an impure life, entertaining disreputable people in his house, and that she had offered to withdraw her action if he would pay her off. His tone of righteous indignation fooled no one, least of all those who knew them both and had been trying to effect a reconciliation for some time. Agnes's solicitor decided to play Boucicault at his own game and issued a statement in which he, point for point, destroyed Boucicault's claims. It turned out that the 'disreputable people' Agnes had been entertaining was Boucicault's brother George, who by offering Agnes money and advice had provoked the playwright's anger.

Amidst the accusations and counter-accusations, it became clear that the main difference between Agnes and Boucicault was the question of custody of the children, three of whom were still under age. In his next statement, he went even further to try and destroy her credibility. Not only did he have proof of her infidelity, which she had confessed to him (in itself highly unlikely, since there is no evidence that she was ever unfaithful to him), but, he claimed, they had never been legally married. The news came as a bombshell: for almost thirty years they had been living together as man and wife; he had always introduced her as his wife; they had been introduced to Queen Victoria as husband and wife. Before the case could come to court and Boucicault could be asked to substantiate his claims, a court ruled that his arrest had been illegal and he left the storm behind him to sail to England in time to open in *The Shaughraun* at the Adelphi, as planned, on 24 April. Although public sympathy was all for Agnes, audiences flocked to the Adelphi to look at her monster of a husband, and the play ran for three months. The divorce proceedings dragged on for the next three years, Agnes remaining in the States, making the occasional appearance to support herself, while it was thrashed out in the courts. In June 1881, she was granted a decree *nisi* and alimony which was later reduced following an appeal by Boucicault and Agnes's determination to press for a final decree. Then, in April 1883, the suit was dropped by mutual consent. Why is not clear, though it does seem that the children may have had some bearing on the decision.

You will be pleased to hear that stupid woman has

expressed a wish to withdraw her complaint [Boucicault had written to a friend], and repudiate all her charges and drop proceedings – and asks if I will let her go back to her children – She is as mad as a Welsh rabbit!! I have not seen or heard from her – but my lawyer writes me to this effect. I am afraid she will find the children harder to deal with than their father is. She forgot that while fighting against *me* – they were receiving the blows. Ah! you are a bad lot!! – (which we can't do without.)[12]

There was little or no attempt to make the reconciliation effective; it was really nothing more than a temporary truce.

The Shaughraun's success at the Adelphi owed more to the wish of the public to see Boucicault than it did to any longing to see the play; the reviews it received showed quite clearly that it, too, was beginning to lose its appeal.

Mr Boucicault had probably by this time realized the fact that public taste in England is not now in the same condition as when stalls, boxes, and gallery applauded his Irish dramas to the echo [wrote David Anderson in his review for *The Theatre*]. This is not Mr Boucicault's fault. He acts as well as ever he did. No one could play the part of Conn the Shaughraun better than he . . . But Conn no longer satisfies an intellectual audience. As for the remainder of the characters, the knowing public have learned to look upon them as dummies, stage counters in the game of melodrama . . . Mr Boucicault, with all his ingenuity, may have outlived his age.[13]

While he was appearing at the Adelphi, Boucicault's name was used in a cruel hoax played upon the Scottish writer William McGonagall. One of Boucicault's companies was performing in Dundee for the first time, and a group of McGonagall's friends sent the 'poet' a note, supposedly from Boucicault, inviting him to lunch at Stratton's restaurant to discuss a possible engagement. McGonagall was delighted to accept, and at the appointed time went to Stratton's. The waiter from whom he inquired the whereabouts of Mr

Boucicault looked at him blankly, but an acquaintance, who 'happened to be passing', overheard the conversation and offered to take McGonagall to the upstairs room where the playwright was waiting. 'Boucicault' expressed his pleasure at meeting such a distinguished poet, discussed terms for an engagement with his company and invited the poet to run through his repertoire for the benefit of more of McGonagall's friends who had just chanced to call in. McGonagall was happy to oblige his distinguished host, gave his recitation and left his meeting with 'Boucicault' well pleased. Something, however, was worrying him, and that evening he went to the Theatre Royal and learnt from the manager that Boucicault was not in Dundee and had never been there. The manager sent a copy of the hoax letter to the Adelphi, and Boucicault sent back a cheque for £5 to comfort the distressed poet. The hoax determined McGonagall to visit London, and on his arrival he went straightway to the Adelphi to try and meet the real Boucicault. His card was returned to him and torn up in front of his eyes.[14]

In July, *The Shaughraun* was withdrawn and replaced by *Forbidden Fruit*, a play previously seen in New York and in which he didn't have to act. Three months of nightly appearances had exhausted him, but he had recovered much of his old good spirits and was enjoying being a senior, respected member of his profession. At the beginning of August he produced *A Bridal Tour* (his play *Marriage* retitled) at the Haymarket, but in spite of its clever dialogue, sharp wit and amusing situations, it failed to take off. He had also signed a contract with the Gattis to write for them, and on 19 August, *Therese; or, The Maid of Croissey*, a short piece, joined *Forbidden Fruit* at the Adelphi. It was given without announcement and without publicity, and the critics, who had been invited to attend, duly reviewed it as a play written by Mrs Gore they had seen some thirty years before. It was with mischievous delight that Boucicault was able to inform them that they had been fooled by a piece which, although taken from the same French source, he had written.

In October he returned to the stage in *The O'Dowd*, a revision of *Daddy O'Dowd* which had failed in New York seven years earlier. It fared no better in London. Audiences found his views on Irish politics unacceptable, and the play lasted only just over a month.

Mr Boucicault regrets to perceive that certain scenes in his new play, *The O'Dowd*, continue to provoke expressions of displeasure from a portion of the audience [stated a notice he inserted in the papers]. He has no wish to offend anyone. He is informed of a general opinion that the censured scenes are ill-timed, and ought to be omitted or their language changed. If the public will kindly refer to the announcement with which the production of *The O'Dowd* was prefaced, it will be seen that the features objected to are essential to the design and intent of the work. It is, therefore, in no captious spirit the author declines to alter it; but rather than lose the favour of any of his audience he will amend his error by withdrawing the play altogether.[15]

Claiming that the London press was too hostile to allow him to continue working in England, Boucicault severed his connection with the Gattis (for which they were probably glad, since their contract with him had not turned out to be as beneficial to them as they had hoped) and, at the beginning of 1881, returned to New York to form a new company to tour *The Shaughraun*, 'my bag of rags', as he called it. By early summer, after a short engagement in Boston and New York, he was back in England, embarking on another tour of his Irish faithfuls in which he was joined by Helene Stoepel (who was to become better known as Bijou Heron), daughter of his friends Robert Stoepel and Matilda Heron, and his son Dot. They played in Manchester and Liverpool, and then moved to the Standard Theatre, Bishopsgate, for twelve days, where it was noted that, although *The Colleen Bawn* was well received, 'it cannot be denied that the clap-trap with which it is plentifully furnished becomes rather tedious'.[16] The play was not helped by a poor production, well below Boucicault's usual standard. In the middle of one act the curtain was lowered, the cave scene was not ready on time, and when it eventually started a piece of scenery fell down, nearly braining

Boucicault. During the run of the play, he sold, for a penny each, copies of a twenty-five-page tract he had written entitled *The Fireside Story of Ireland*. While purporting to be an unbiased résumé of that island's history, there could be no doubting Boucicault's anti-English sentiment, and the pamphlet was duly dismissed as an advertising trick 'which must be condemned by all who believe that even in advertising good taste should be displayed by educated men'.[17]

Boucicault stayed in London to supervise the production of a revised version of *Mimi* at his son-in-law John Clayton's Royal Court, where it failed, and then took a new company to Dublin to play his three familiar Irish roles, Myles, Conn and Shaun, on what was to be his last visit to his birthplace. He then returned to the States. He was still as busy as ever with his writing, trying to find the magic formula that would bring him new success (mostly by revising old plays he felt had failed unfairly), and in order to live he was still having to act. His own financial problems did not stop him being generous with his money. While he was in Boston, in January 1882, he renewed the acquaintance of Oscar Wilde, then on an unhappy lecture tour. The lectures had been going well, but there was friction behind the scenes and Oscar was the butt of malicious gossip. He poured out his heart to the older playwright.

> He has been much distressed; and came here last night looking worn and thin . . . [Boucicault wrote to Mrs George Lewis the following day]. Oscar is helpless, because he is not a practical man of business, so when I advised him to throw over Carte, and offered to see him through financially if he did so, he felt afraid. I offered him a thousand pounds or two if he required it, but he says he will play out his contract to April . . . I do wish we could make him less Sybarite – less Epicurean . . . There is a future for him here but he *wants management*.[18]

On yet another visit to London, in the summer of 1882, Boucicault became involved with Henry Irving (for whom he was planning to write a drama on the life of Don Quixote) in trying to establish a School of Dramatic Art. On 15 May, he was one of the speakers at a meeting arranged to discuss the project, and on 26 July, at the Lyceum, he delivered a lecture on the art of acting, the proceeds of which were donated to the fund. It was a carefully thought out, well-considered lecture in which he set out to prove that, contrary to a lot of popular opinion, acting could be taught and was not just instinctive. Many of the ideas he put forward were extremely modern in concept and predated the teaching of such people as Stanislavsky. It was, however, principally for his advice on how to pronounce English correctly that his lecture was later remembered.

> He complained bitterly [recalled an eye-witness], of the way the majority of English actors pronounced the word 'war'. 'Ye prenounce the ward as if it wuz spelt w-a-u-g-h,' said the lecturer, gravely. 'Ye don't prenounce it at all as ye shud. The ward rhymes with 'par', 'are', and 'kyar', and yet ye will prenounce it as if it rhymed with 'saw' and 'paw'. Don't you see the difference?'[19]

Boucicault was by now generally regarded as an eccentric relic from a former age. The younger generation of actors, although they acknowledged his skill as a stage director and were terrified of him in rehearsal, considered him to be a has-been as a playwright. He was sixty-one, and although his health was no longer robust, he felt young in spirit and hated the thought of being dismissed as out of fashion and respected only as a venerable institution. He knew as well as anyone that what he needed was a new success. Before he had written *The Shaughraun*, it had been openly said that his powers as a writer were on the wane. Now the rumours were beginning to spread once more, he was determined to prove his critics wrong. He had done it before and he would do it again.

At the end of 1882 he returned to America with a pile of new manuscripts, including the play on which he based his hopes of making a comeback, *The Amadan*. Set in Ireland, the play opened at the Boston Museum on 5 February 1883. 'The success was very great,' he wrote to Dot. 'The play took the audience from first to last . . . I was not at my best. No one knew it but myself, as the universal opinion is that it is my greatest effort.'[20] In spite of Boucicault's enthusiasm for the piece, the play had not gone well. Some of the acting had been downright awful, certain of the stage effects had not worked, and the general critical impression was that it was far from being his best work. In the perverse way of older writers who believe their later compositions to be superior to their earlier efforts, Boucicault became unashamedly attached to the play, convinced that it would eventually be recognized as his finest. In fact, *The Amadan* merely confirmed that, while he was still a master craftsman, able to write effective scenes and clever dialogue, he really was out of touch with his audiences.

His next play, *Vice Versa*, written for Wallack and produced at Springfield, Massachusetts, in March, suffered a similar fate. When it transferred to the Star Theater, New York, with Boucicault in the lead, on 26 March, it lasted only two weeks and had to be replaced by *The Shaughraun*, which ran for a month before he tried to reintroduce *The Amadan* (which had failed at Wallack's in March). This in turn had to be replaced by *The Colleen Bawn* in which Dot played Danny Mann. Nothing could disguise the fact that, although his subject-matter was new, his technique was not, and that the style in which he had written his greatest dramas had by now become part of theatrical history. He could still, by appearing in his most famous roles, attract large audiences, but the public was not prepared to go and see him in the new plays it found to be inferior and old-fashioned. Well aware that his popularity as a dramatist was low, Boucicault published a brief résumé of his career under the name of his old school-friend, Charles Lamb Kenney, who had died the previous year, in which he emphasized his importance as a playwright.[21] The booklet might have succeeded in creating the interest in his work he wanted, if he had had the plays to offer, but he had nothing new, and throughout the last half of 1883 and most of 1884 he was forced to earn his living solely by acting. His next new play was not performed until November 1884. During a brief spell back in London during that summer he had been given the manuscript of a piece about the Irish rebel Robert Emmet. Henry Irving had commissioned the play from Frank Marshall, but when news of its production became known, he had been advised, for political reasons, to drop it from his plans. Boucicault took the Marshall play, rewrote it and produced it at McVicker's Theatre, Chicago, on 5 November.

> I produced *Emmet* here last night, with emphatic success, more *emphatic* I thought than *hearty* – [he wrote to Irving], and when I said as much I was told that the audience were disappointed that I did not play the conspicuous character in the play – and this tempered their enthusiasm. But such a group of mishaps I never witnessed – scenes bitched – properties forgotten – supers entered on scenes where they were not wanted and were absent when they were required – guns that would not go off – oh Lord! Still we overcame it all – the waits between the acts were 25 and 30 minutes long – not to speak of 3 or 4 minutes between scenes! It was awful.[22]

The play's first night coincided with the election of President Grover Cleveland, which may have accounted for the poor house, for as a drama it was not nearly as bad as its reception would seem to indicate; once more it was a question of being twenty years too late.

Although he had made several fortunes during his career (in 1875, it was estimated that the enormous sum of $25 million had been paid to witness the plays of Boucicault),[23] he was not a rich man. He had always spent lavishly, he had lost large amounts on theatrical ventures and he had given away vast sums to his family, to his friends and to those in need: few actors who approached him ever went away empty-handed. The failure of *Robert Emmet* once again placed him in financial straits, and an engagement to appear for four weeks in San Francisco for $3,500 the following spring, followed closely by an offer from J. C. Williamson to tour Australia, where he was assured he would do well, came as a godsend. By the time the tour would be over he would be almost sixty-five, and he began to think seriously of retirement.

223

I think of playing a farewell engagement in London in the spring of 1886 [he wrote to Irving]. I presume you will be at the Lyceum – if not I'd like to go there. I want to produce my whole repertoire, giving three weeks to each play, scened by Beverley, and wind up with my two new plays, for six weeks each, making five or six months in all. Then:!

And here he drew a candle-snuffer.[24]

12

A MONSTER WHO FORGETS

A T THE end of April 1885, Boucicault, accompanied by a party of six artists (including Dot, his daughter Nina, who had just started her stage career, and a young actress, Louise Thorndyke), left New York for San Francisco. They played a four-week engagement of his popular Irish dramas at the California Theatre, adding his latest play, *The Jilt*, to the repertoire on 18 May. Billed as a comedy drama, *The Jilt* was a rewriting of his highly successful horse-racing melodrama of 1866, *The Flying Scud*, but with sufficient differences to warrant its being considered a new piece. A solid piece of craftsmanship, with clever dialogue and well-created suspense, the play was his best work since *The Shaughraun* and proved immensely popular during its ten-day try-out.

On 6 June, Boucicault and his company of six sailed from San Francisco on the *Zealandia*, bound for Australia and the tour set up by Williamson.

> The voyage across the ocean was delightful [Boucicault recorded]. After one week of placid weather we reached Honolulu. Here we found my name in big letters on every fence. It was expected we should stop there and play three nights. It did not come off. After four or five hours stroll on shore, we were away again across that shimmering, pacific sea.[1]

After calling briefly at Auckland – 'enough to breed a desire to see more' – and Sydney, they arrived at Melbourne on 4 July, and a week later opened at the Theatre Royal in *The Shaughraun*, supported by artists engaged locally by Williamson. It was, Boucicault later conceded, a mistake to have taken so many of his own players with him. 'The audience there are accustomed to the local actors and prefer them to strangers. As to actresses, they like new faces but do not care to criticize much beyond that.' He advised anyone contemplating a similar tour to send out an agent in advance to hire a full local company.

'We found the theatre to be a large, dusty, primitive building,' he reported, 'with poor accommodation for the audience, and wretched arrangements for the actors behind the scenes.' He was, however, delighted to find that, even though he had a poor opinion of the local players, Williamson had spared no expense on the productions, and at the conclusion of their four weeks, playing also in *The Colleen Bawn* and *Arrah-na-Pogue*, they had taken more than £8,000, the largest sum ever made by artists visiting Australia, of which his personal share was £2,500. While in Melbourne, tragedy struck Boucicault's little company. Gerald Eyre, the juvenile lead, had been suffering from a heavy cold which developed into pneumonia. He insisted on going on stage as usual on Monday, 4 August; four days later he was dead.

From Melbourne they travelled to Sydney, where Boucicault was guest of honour at a picnic organized by Irish expatriates, and continued to play to full houses, their five weeks at the Theatre Royal producing receipts of just over £7,000. Artistically and financially, it was the most successful visit ever made to Australia, but Boucicault later calculated that, allowing for the time it had taken him to get to and from Australia and the time spent travelling between his two engagements, it had produced an average income of £34 a night, a return he felt that was hardly worth his while.

One other notable event occurred on the Australian tour: on 9 September, in a Sydney registry office, Boucicault married the twenty-one-year-old member of his company, Louise Thorndyke. He was not quite sixty-five. The witnesses were his brother Arthur and two of Arthur's children. Dot and Nina were not present, but immediately cabled to their mother in England to break the news. Straight away Agnes put an advertisement in *The World* stating that, since she was still his legal wife, the playwright was a bigamist. Quite why Boucicault should have decided to take this spectacular way to renounce Agnes as his wife isn't clear. On the marriage certificate he claimed to be a widower, and it does seem that since the breakdown of the marriage five years earlier, when Agnes had filed for divorce, he had convinced himself that they had never been legally married. Once the news of Boucicault's marriage with Louise became public, everyone, including those who had never met them, sided with Agnes and condemnation was heaped upon Boucicault's head for his despicable action. The press seized upon the announcement as an excuse to attack Boucicault the writer as a vain, insincere villain, and even his friends were shocked: '[Edmund] Yates writes to denounce Dion Boucicault and with reason as a bad old man because of his treatment of his wife after so many years – is it 26 or 36? – of married life,' wrote his schoolfriend Sir William Howard Russell, in his diary, adding cryptically, 'Poor Agnes Robertson. But she was queer too . . .'

Choosing to stay away from what he knew would be a hostile reception in the United States for as long as possible, Boucicault cancelled his plans to return and set out with Louise for a six-week tour of New Zealand. They travelled alone, without the other members of the company and without Dot and Nina, who, disapproving of a marriage that declared them to be illegitimate, had decided to sever all connections with their father and stay in Australia. Dot was to become joint-manager with Robert Brough of the Bijou Theatre, Melbourne, and the Criterion Theatre, Sydney, where, during the next ten years, his productions of plays by Robertson, Pinero, Jones and other contemporary writers were to set a standard of theatre in Australia that has seldom if ever been surpassed. Nina acted for him for a time before leaving Australia to continue her career in America and Britain, while he eventually returned to England in 1895, married the actress Irene Vanbrugh, and became a director at the Duke of York's Theatre, London, for Charles Frohman. Among his many credits was directing the first production of *Peter Pan*, starring his sister Nina.

After a triumphant six weeks in New Zealand, Boucicault and Louise returned to the United States in December and began a tour of *The Jilt*, the title of which took on a new meaning for the audiences packing every performance to look at the couple. Although the public joined the condemnation of the playwright's morality, they did not hesitate to go to the theatre to see the old man and his young 'wife'. At each venue, Boucicault hired local artists to support him and Louise, and when they appeared in Boston, in February 1886, he engaged Bijou Heron (whom he'd known when she was a child) for the role of Phyllis Welter, and her husband Henry Miller for the part of Sir Budleigh Woodstock. It was an important opportunity for the young Miller (who was to become an important director and producer himself), for it gave him a chance to study at first hand the techniques of the man he always acknowledged to be the master. Boucicault, he used to say, taught him all he knew about play production, with his unceasing command to remember that 'stage direction is nothing but the use of common sense'.

I had just left Augustin Daly's company [Miller recalled of his first meeting with Boucicault], and I was sure at that time that he [Daly] was the greatest man of the theatre the world had ever known. There was fresh in my mind one of his remedies for a lack of action created by unbroken dialogue. Whenever we had a particularly long speech to read, Daly taught us to interpolate a stroll from one side of the stage to the other, under the pretense that some object at the further end of the room had caught our attention. This was known as the 'Daly cross.' I shall never forget what followed when I introduced that bit of business to Dion Boucicault. I had a particularly long speech to read in my first role under his direction . . . Just about the middle of this speech, I shifted tranquilly from stage right to stage left and pretended to examine with keen interest a work of art on a mantlepiece against which I leaned with graceful ennui.

Down came Boucicault's fist on the arm of the orchestra chair in which he was seated. 'Just a minute,' he shouted as he rose from his place and walked to the footlights. 'Why did you make that cross, Mr Miller?' he asked. 'There is nothing in the stage directions to warrant your change of position.' Very confidently, indeed very glibly, I plunged into my defence. 'I have a very long speech at this point, Mr Boucicault,' I explained with tolerant kindness in my tones. 'So long, indeed, that it seems to me the people out in front might get restless while I am reading the lines. It occurred to me that it would be a good idea to break up the dialogue with a little action. That is why I made the cross.' Boucicault studied my face for a moment in eloquent silence. Then he delivered his ruling. 'Mr Miller,' he observed, with biting contempt in his voice, 'if I cannot hold an audience with my pen, I am sure you cannot with your feet.'[2]

After playing in Boston and New York, Boucicault accepted an offer to take *The Jilt* to London for what was to prove to be his last appearance in the city. On 29 July, he and Louise opened a successful nine-week run at the Prince's Theatre where, just as in America, audiences compelled by curiosity filled the house. By returning to London, Boucicault demonstrated his contempt for the public opinion that condemned his bigamous marriage. Untroubled by the personal antagonism towards him and the news that Agnes had again filed for divorce, he was, he claimed, happier than he had been for much of his life. 'I can truly say,' he told Albert Palmer the week before he died, 'that the only true, disinterested love that has come into my life I have found since I married Louise Thorndyke. I am a poor man now, but at last I am happy.' The feeling was mutual. 'No one else knew the sweet character of Dion,' said Louise shortly after his death. 'He was tenderness and devotion itself. A woman could not have been more thoughtful, more considerate. He never addressed a harsh or unkind word to me from the day of our marriage until his death.'[3]

Agnes filed her inevitable petition for divorce in London in May 1886. For once, Boucicault remained silent. To save

Louise from the bitter wrangling that had started once the news of their marriage became public, he refused to discuss it, or his motives, except to reiterate his claim that he and Agnes had never been legally married. Since Boucicault's marriage to Louise was not in dispute, the arguments of the divorce action revolved around whether or not he and Agnes had been married in 1853. Prompted by public opinion (which did not want Boucicault's children to be declared illegitimate), the court eventually ruled, in June 1888, that a marriage had taken place in New York in 1853, and that Boucicault's marriage to Louise was bigamous. When the final decree was made on 15 January 1889, he and Louise went through a second civil ceremony in New York.

Throughout the divorce proceedings, Agnes was awarded interim payments for maintenance which Boucicault hotly contested and refused to pay, with the result that Samuel French, the London publisher of his plays, was ordered to hand all his English royalties over to the court, but so unfashionable had Boucicault's dramas become that the money paid in failed to reach the £450 a year required. When the final decree was granted, Agnes was awarded alimony of £30 a month for the remainder of their joint lives, which, naturally, Boucicault failed to meet. The reason was not callousness on his part, but simply that he no longer had the means to pay. His last years were spent in a constant struggle trying to make ends meet. As for Agnes, she continued to act occasionally, making her last appearance in London in 1896 playing Mrs Cregan in a revival of *The Colleen Bawn*. She died in London in 1916.

After the closure of the London production of *The Jilt* in September 1886, Boucicault and Louise returned to New York to present the play for two weeks at the Standard Theater before taking it on a short tour. The novelty of seeing the couple was beginning to wear off and Boucicault was aware that he needed new works in which to appear if he was to keep audiences coming. With Louise by his side, all thoughts of retirement had been forgotten and he began to write again; new plays, articles, his autobiography. Every evening, after dinner, he would retire to his study and work,

DION BOUCICAULT'S COPYRIGHTS.

In the High Court of Justice.

Divorce Division.

BETWEEN BOUCICAULT (AGNES) *v.* BOUCICAULT (DION).

Particulars and Conditions of Sale

OF THE

VALUABLE COPYRIGHTS

(OF THE ABOVE NAMED DION BOUCICAULT)

IN

NINETEEN

WELL KNOWN & SUCCESSFUL PLAYS

Which will be Sold by Auction

BY MESSRS.

FURBER, PRICE & FURBER

(By Direction of the Sheriff of the County of London),

AT THE AUCTION OFFICES, 2, WARWICK COURT, GRAY'S INN,

On MONDAY, the 27th day of MAY, 1889,

At One for Two o'Clock.

LOT		LOT	
1	'LONDON ASSURANCE.'	10	'LONG STRIKE.'
2	'FLYING SCUD.'	11	'AFTER DARK.'
3	'RESCUED'	12	'BABEL AND BIJOU.'
4	'DADDY O'DOWD'	13	'MARRIAGE.'
5	'JEZABEL.'	14	'FOUL PLAY.'
6	'OLD HEADS & YOUNG HEARTS.'	15	'ELFIE.'
7	'ARRAH NA POGUE' with Musical Score.	16	'FAUST AND MARGARET.'
8	'STREETS OF LONDON.'	17	'FORMOSA.'
9	'JILT.'	18	'KERRY.'

19 'HUNTED DOWN.'

CONDITIONS OF SALE.

FIRST.—The highest bidder to be the purchaser, who is immediately to pay into the hands of the Auctioneers the whole of his purchase-money. The Sheriff will prepare and execute assignments of the said Copyrights upon the purchaser's request, and at the purchaser's expense.

LASTLY.—The Sheriff is to be on no account responsible for any mis-representation or mis-statement which may appear upon this Particular, but the purchaser is to be at the whole risk of his purchase; and the purchaser is not on any account nor under any pretext whatever to require the Sheriff to enter into any covenant of title, nor is the Sheriff to be called upon to refund to the purchaser the amount of his purchase-money, even should any legal objection be raised to the Sheriff's right to seize or sell the said Lot.

Printed by THOS. SCOTT & Co., Warwick Court, Holborn.

Boucicault managed to delay the sale by claiming he had already sold his copyrights to John Caddagan, his former tour manager. It went ahead eventually, fifteen plays being auctioned and realizing £586 – an average of £39 each for plays that had earned fortunes.

sleep for three or four hours, and then be back at his desk by dawn. 'Although I rise at six,' he wrote to William Winter, 'and work pretty continuously till eleven at night, the day is not long enough to enable me to include all that I would do, and that I *ought* to do before leaving much-abused but precious life.'[41] But he was growing old and could no longer produce his dramas with the same rapidity as in his youth, and more and more of his acting engagements had to be cancelled because of his indisposition. He was also failing to write anything of significance. His projected autobiography was abandoned, he failed to find a producer for his modern comedy of manners *Ourselves*, and when *Belle Lamar*, his play about the Civil War, was given in a revised version, *Fin Mac Coul of Skibbereeen*, at the Hollis Street Theatre, Boston, in February 1887, it failed to excite any interest. His next new work, *Phryne*, suffered a similar fate. Due to open at the Baldwin Theatre in San Francisco at the end of September, but postponed because of Boucicault's gout, when it was finally premièred a week late, in spite of the critics' kindness towards the author and his acting, it lasted for just two weeks.

For the rest of the year, Boucicault continued to tour, but at a much slower pace than in former years. He returned again to Boston in February 1888, for a short engagement which saw the production of *Cuishla-ma-Chree*, an adaptation of Scott's novel *Guy Mannering* completed two years earlier. The play, wrote the critic of the *Boston Journal*,

does not carry with its initial performances evidence of success. It is insufferably slow at times, and throughout has a fatal lack of vivacity and interest. In part, the dullness of last night was due to imperfect acting, but even that drawback was not accountable for the entire weakness of the play. Many of the situations are good, but several are weak so far as natural results are concerned, at least as worked upon by Mr Boucicault. The dialogue in most positions is commonplace, having little of the flavour of Boucicault's wit and brightness. Occasionally there are flashes of brilliancy when Andy or the worthy doctor utters a humorous remark or a poetic simile, but these are but beads strung on a cheap, spun twine. In short the play goes limping through its four lengthy acts.

After two weeks of playing to poor houses it was withdrawn. Boucicault had a stubborn faith in the piece, and after revising it, he tried it again in Chicago, where it was liked even less than it had been in Boston and he had to put *The Jilt* on in its place to finish his engagement.

Following the rejection of *Cuishla-ma-Chree* in Chicago, Boucicault decided to fulfil his next few weeks' engagements with *The Jilt* and *The Shaughraun*, and then, at the end of May 1888, he reluctantly decided that his touring days were over. He was sixty-seven and unable to take the strain of touring any more. He was also broke. The spiralling costs of touring, the failure of his last three plays, the lessening attraction of his old favourites, his lavishness with money, and the cost of defending the divorce action, had left him penniless. It wasn't a new situation for him to be in. He had made and lost fortunes in the past, and each time he'd been down he'd had only to write a new play for his problems to disappear. There was to be no such solution on this occasion. His facility for turning out a hit had deserted him. The man who for so long dictated public taste no longer knew what that taste was. The shift in standards and what was, or was not, acceptable confused him.

> Fifty years ago [he wrote] the dancer wore skirts reaching to her ankles – no revelation of her limb was tolerated – but on the other hand, the language in the plays was *décolleté*. Now a word susceptible of a double meaning is revolting – while women strip themselves to the skin. At one time, ladies in society uncovered their bosoms so as to leave them in full evidence, but they shrank in horror from showing their ankles. It raises the question. What is modesty? What is decency?[5]

He was also out of sympathy with the work of Ibsen and modern playwrights. In an article on Shakespeare, he observed that Constance's speeches in *King John* have no rival in drama for passionate rhetoric.

233

Yet we are told this is all wrong, false, unnatural, because unreal, and we should go to Mr Ibsen to learn in his domestic drama *The Doll's House* how an ill-used woman feels, behaves and expresses herself, according to the ethics of the modern apostle by whom the drama is to be led to salvation.[6]

Several managers tried to help him. Daniel Frohman, who had just started his successful Lyceum company, commissioned him to write a play which he intended producing on the fiftieth anniversary of the first night of *London Assurance*. Boucicault accepted the commission and agreed to make an address on the opening night.

During the progress of the play [remembered Frohman] he wrote to me: 'I am keenly sensible that I must make a ten-strike, for many reasons. Since *The Jilt* I have done nothing. Therefore I am putting all my forces into this play and have sidetracked every other work.' At another time he wrote: 'I am desirous to strike exactly what you want and I don't mind objections. They only provoke my inventive faculty to a greater extent.' Writing again later, referring to my company, then planned for serious work – 'I find you stronger – much – on the pathetic side than on the comic arm. You have plenty of shade. I am, as you know, strongest on sunlight effects.' As the play progressed I could not feel, as I told him on reading his elaborated scheme, convinced of its probable success. Later he wrote: 'I want you to be more than satisfied – for my first effort on your stage must be one of my successes; that is essential to me, for many reasons . . .' His first effort was to have been a comedy drama. This, after it was elaborated, we were constrained to discard. The second attempt was to be an effort in pure comedy . . . Alas, to my regret, the second effort was no more successful than the first.[7]

The play for Frohman was never completed. During his visits to the manager's office, Boucicault would sit and reminisce with anyone who would listen, and although he went frequently to the theatre, he would rarely stay beyond the end of the first act. He was growing old in body, but his mind was as active as ever, and having seen the first act, he knew exactly what would follow and couldn't be bothered to sit through it. On one occasion Emily Soldene recalled going to a matinée at Wallack's with Agnes and their son Aubrey.

> We sat in the front row of the stalls. Presently Mrs Dion nudged me. 'Look there,' she said, lifting her eyes to a box just above us on my left. In the box were seated Mr Dion Boucicault and his new wife, Louise Thorndyke Boucicault. We were very close, and could have shaken hands all round, but we didn't.[8]

Another manager who tried his best to help Boucicault was Albert Palmer of the Madison Square Theatre. Palmer had decided to form a drama school attached to his theatre, and wanted Boucicault to run it. With no immediate prospect of making money from writing, the playwright was happy to accept; apart from bringing in a regular salary (supposed to have been $50 a week), the job meant he would be working in the theatre and surrounded by young actresses. As soon as the formation of the school was announced, Palmer and Boucicault were inundated with applications from young hopefuls, among them Constance Morris. She was invited to attend one of the public auditions.

> Mr Boucicault sat at a long, plain, deal table [she recalled], with Mr Daly, Mr Palmer and a very handsome man who, I was afterwards informed, was Maurice Barrymore, then playing the leads in Mr Palmer's stock company . . . We were told to form a line and as each of us reached the deal table where sat the arbiters of our destiny, Mr Corbett [Boucicault's secretary] was there to interrogate us. I understand now that as we were being questioned, the others were making rapid and fugitive observations as to voice and presence: for there were floods of men and women fit and unfit, clamouring to enter. At a nod from Mr

Boucicault, some were told to pass on; others, after giving their names, were given cards, and I was one of these fortunate ones. It read – 'As You Like It. Rosalind, page 22, scene 4. Report Thursday at two o'clock. Retain this for admittance. Samuel French.'[9]

Three weeks after her audition, Constance Morris heard that she, and fifty-two others, out of a total of more than 2,000 applicants, had been selected for the school. The idea behind the school was simple: tuition would be free and the best and most talented of the students would be offered small parts with the companies of either Palmer or Daly to provide them with experience and pocket-money.

It was inevitable I suppose [recalled Constance Morris], that at this time the school should be used as a sort of parade ground for the element of society girls that had become infected by the stage virus. Almost everyone with the smallest histrionic gift has a natural dramatic fertility; but as the days went on there were found pupils so personally unfit in their conceited and feather-brained assumption of ability to act, as to be ludicrous; and out of this grew a new development. Mr Boucicault, splendidly able though he was, found it impossible to cope with so much material deficient in talent. Mr Boucicault and his colleagues decided to divide the pupils into two classes, to be known as 'internes' and 'externes'. The former, who were to be chosen by judges selected from the leading actors and managers of the day, were to be under Mr Boucicault's personal supervision and have the benefit of his admirable instruction; while the 'externes' were to be taught by Mr Corbett, directed by Mr Boucicault, and were to come into the 'interne' class only after passing successfully one of the semi-annual examinations.

One budding actress who had no difficulty in gaining admission to the 'interne' class was a pretty young Irish girl, Jessie McDermott, who was calling herself Jessica Dermot. She became one of Boucicault's favourite students, and he advised her to change her name to Maxine Elliott, the name by which she became known around the world.

Ten weeks after the school opened, the students made their first public appearance, acting a scene from *Hunted Down*, giving part of *King John*, and supporting Boucicault in his play *Kerry*. The reviews were more kind than enthusiastic. Boucicault was happy in his new life. He was secure in his love for Louise, his students admired and respected him (there could be no doubting his great ability as a teacher and promoter of ideas), and he could talk for hours about his favourite subject, the theatre. His career may have been almost over, but he had no intention of retiring. On 10 November 1888, he was guest of honour at a banquet given by the Saturday Night Club to celebrate his contribution to drama. Among the distinguished guests present were Colonel Robert Ingersoll, General Sherman, Governor Flower and Andrew Carnegie.

> Sometimes [said Boucicault in a witty speech that showed he had lost none of his genius for language], when I am passing a play-bill announcing the performance of one of my old comedies, I congratulate myself, 'Had I died forty years ago, I should be living now!' Rather Irish perhaps but it enables me to enjoy a little bit of 'everness', as Bishop Wilkins called it.[10]

Two months later, at the end of January 1889, he again proved he had lost none of his intellectual capacities when he and William Winter, the critic, debated the state of the drama for the Goethe Society at the Brunswick Hotel. The meeting was brought about by Winter (a former friend who had become an implacable enemy), who had been enraged by a series of articles from the playwright in which he blamed the moribund state of drama during the second half of the nineteenth century entirely on the press and the low standard of criticism.

Boucicault was also tempted to start writing again. He wrote to Sir Arthur Sullivan, suggesting that they should collaborate on a ballad opera, and for Palmer he rewrote the last act of Haddon Chambers's successful play *Captain Swift*, since Palmer did not think New York audiences would accept the Chambers ending in which Swift commits suicide. The play was performed, with Maurice Barrymore in the lead, at the Madison Square Theater on 4 December 1888, but Boucicault's revisions did not prove popular, and after only a week Palmer reinstated the original ending, the play running for over 150 performances.

Old age had not stilled Boucicault's keen eye nor tempered his criticisms of what he saw or thought he saw going on around him, and he still had many enemies, particularly on the press. Word started to go round that not only had his talent run dry, but that he had also slipped into senility and even imbecility. Such reports upset him greatly. Among the many visitors to the apartment at 105 West 55th Street, where he lived with Louise, was the talented young actor, Sol Smith Russell, to whom Boucicault would show the offending paragraphs repeating the rumours and mutter, 'I will show them that the brain is still there, I will show them.' One day he sent for Russell and outlined the plot of a new play he wanted to write. 'I liked it,' recalled Russell. 'I thought I saw in Jemmy Watt something that I could do justice to, and Mr Boucicault began to work on the play that was to be the answer to his critics.'[11]

During his almost daily visits to Boucicault, Russell never saw the playwright at work and began to doubt whether the old man was writing anything at all.

His wife used to say to me, 'I don't know when he writes your play, Mr Russell. He tells me it's getting on, but he never let's me see him working.' Dion Boucicault was an extraordinary man. He would work till two o'clock in the morning – shut up alone in his study – and yet be up before daylight . . . Once, I remember, I got up myself at six and went over to his house thinking to surprise him. He had already been dressed for two hours. Well, time went on, and the play was completed. He read it to me and I was delighted. He seemed confident himself. 'This will answer them,' he used to say, chuckling like a child, 'this will teach them that if Dion Boucicault is an old man his brain is as young and strong as ever.'

Several titles were suggested for the play, and eventually, against Boucicault's wishes, *A Tale of a Coat* was chosen for the try-out in Philadelphia, before it came in to Daly's in New York. Russell, Boucicault and Louise travelled on the train to Philadelphia together, and the old man was in sparkling form, talking and laughing as he had not done for a long time. But when the moment came for him to leave his hotel and set out for the theatre, he couldn't bring himself to go. During the rehearsals, which he had directed, he had suffered fainting fits (which turned out to be a mild heart-attack), and in his weak state, the excitement of the opening proved to be too much for him. 'A severe attack of sciatica deprives me of the pleasure I promised myself in witnessing your performance,' he wrote to Russell. 'I shall be there in spirit and in heart – not as author but as your affectionate and anxious friend – who has sincerely more interest in your success than in his own.'[12]

When the curtain fell for the last time there was no doubt in the minds of the audience – Boucicault was back in top form. The following morning, Russell hurried round to Boucicault's hotel without waiting to read the papers.

I found Mrs Boucicault and the dramatist taking their breakfast. 'All the papers are good,' cried Mrs Boucicault as I entered and both she and Mr Boucicault congratulated me on the success. 'There's half-a-million dollars in your play,' I said to him. 'I shall be content if it is acknowledged in New York,' was his reply. The evening papers were less enthusiastic and then, for the first time, Dion Boucicault began to be apprehensive. From then on to the production at Daly's Theatre, he was a changed man. The triumphant sparkle in his eyes died out and he waited patiently for the New York production.

A Tale of a Coat opened in New York on 14 August 1890. The reviews were less than enthusiastic, many critics pronouncing it a bad play which not even the superlative acting of Russell could save.

I hurried up to Mr Boucicault's house [related Russell], and found him sitting in a dejected manner in his study, a mass of morning papers all round him. His head was bent on his breast. His voice seemed changed as he spoke to me. 'I'm sorry for your sake,' he said, after a pause; 'for me, you know, it doesn't matter. No matter; no matter;' and he shook his head sadly. I was deeply affected, less at what he said than at the tone of indescribable despair and disappointment in his voice. I tried to cheer him up as best I could. I said, 'The public might think differently, and everything might yet go well. Perhaps I am unfitted for the part.' He made no answer, pressed my hand in silence, and I left him. Two weeks passed and the success did not come. Persons outside began to criticize the play and the business fell off rapidly. But still I persevered. At last, when the receipts at the box-office fell below the expense, my wife and my friends urged me to take off Mr Boucicault's play and substitute *A Poor Relation*. And I was compelled to yield. Now came one of the most trying things I have ever had to do in my life. I had to go and tell Mr Boucicault that I could play *A Tale of a Coat* no longer. Many times I tried to nerve myself for the dreaded ordeal before I went – and that was after four weeks of disastrous business. I dreaded telling him because Dion Boucicault had shown himself to me to be a true, unselfish, devoted friend, and I shrank from inflicting the pain I knew it would cause him. When finally I told him I should have to take it off he said sadly: 'If you think best, do so. Do not mind me. People will think differently of the play one day – they will rank it with the best I have written.'

The failure of *A Tale of a Coat* was like a hammer-blow to the old playwright, and not even the moderate success of *Lend Me Your Wife*, an adaptation which had opened at the Boston Museum on 25 August, could make up for the disappointment he felt. He loved his adopted city and desperately wanted, and needed, its approval; when that approval was withheld, it proved too much for him. The play closed on Saturday, 13 September. The following week, Boucicault went as usual to his work at the Madison Square Theatre School. On the morning of Tuesday, 16 September, a group of students, including Maxine Elliot, found him sitting in his office, morose and depressed. He went with them down to the stage to take a rehearsal, but being unable to concentrate, and complaining about the rainy weather, he soon returned to his office and after a while went home. Palmer, worried about his colleague, followed him, but was refused admission to Boucicault's apartments: the playwright had contracted pneumonia and gone to bed. Following so soon after the heart-attacks he'd had during rehearsals for *A Tale of a Coat*, it was to prove fatal. Two days later, on the afternoon of Thursday, 18 September 1890, Dion Boucicault died in the arms of his wife Louise.

Fortune has perched on my banners [he once wrote], and I have earned very large sums of money, but have reserved very little. My family have had it, and there are so many calls on one's sympathy. Besides, I do hope that I shall die without more than enough to bury me decently. It seems to me much better to give one's property to one's heirs while you are alive and can see the enjoyment it produces. Why heap it up to be wrangled for after you are gone? Postmortem prudence rarely turns out rightly. Sufficient for this life are the troubles thereof! . . . I wish I deserved such an epitaph as this: 'He lived like a prince and died worth a shilling, owing no man a penny, but leaving a record written in smiles and good humour. So do not shed a tear over him who never intentionally caused one to flow.'[13]

A career that had spanned more than fifty years, most of them at the top, that had made more money, seen more success, and produced more important theatrical innovations than any other, was over. Ibsen, Zola, Strindberg and Shaw were writing now, with Lady Gregory, Yeats, Synge and Galsworthy waiting in the wings. The last link with the great melodramas of the nineteenth century was broken, and Boucicault had, as he once joked, taken his first holiday. 'It has been a long jig,' he said shortly before his death, 'and I am beginning to see the pathos of it. I have written for a monster who forgets.'[14] In 1889, the year before his death, Agnes had announced the sale of all the Boucicault manuscripts in her possession, including *The Colleen Bawn*, *The Octoroon* and a dozen other well-known plays, any one of which had earned Boucicault a fortune in the past. Between them they fetched £586 – an average of £39 each. Although his children, in particular Dot and Nina, were to keep the Boucicault name in front of the public for another thirty years, the name of the man who had once been the most successful in the history of the English-speaking stage was about to pass into obscurity.

Boucicault's funeral took place on Monday, 22 September, at the Little Church Around the Corner on New York's 29th Street.[15]

The remains of the dramatist reposed in an oaken casket, lined with copper and covered with a black cloth, in the darkened study. The widow, alone with her grief, wept over it until the moment came for the departure to the Little Church, when the casket was sealed up [reported the *Dramatic Mirror*]. A few minutes before ten the cortège slowly moved forward toward Twenty-ninth Street. The services were announced to take place at ten o'clock, but long before that a great crowd had gathered in the yard and on the sidewalks in the neighbourhood.

The church was filled by managers, students, actors, actresses, journalists, friends and members of the public who had been his audience in life. Among the pall-bearers were Albert M. Palmer, T. Henry French, Daniel Frohman, Henry Abbey, Sol Smith Russell and Henry Miller. Of his children, only Nina (about whom there had been considerable speculation as to whether or not she would appear) was present, leaning upon the arm of Edward Sothern, son of Boucicault's friend, the actor E. A. Sothern.

After the service, the mourners and most of the pall-bearers accompanied the body to Grand Central Station where a special train was waiting to convey them to Woodlawn Cemetery. On 19 November, Louise had the body removed to its present resting place in the Mount Hope Cemetery on the banks of the river at Hastings-on-the-Hudson. When she died in 1956, at the age of ninety-two, alone and friendless in New York, she was buried beneath the same stone with the man she had loved, the greatest dramatist of the Victorian age.

NOTES AND
REFERENCES

1. Birth and Schooldays

1. Dion Boucicault, 'The Debut of a Dramatist', *North American Review*, vol. 148, April 1889.
2. Lester Wallack, *Memories of Fifty Years*, p. 175.
3. *John Bull*, 8 March 1841.
4. Anne was born in 1795, Samuel in 1769. Both dates are computed from ages given on their death certificates. A marriage licence (in the Calthrop Collection), taken out on 25 June 1813, simply states that Anne was 'a Minor under the age of 21 years'. In order to obtain the licence, which meant banns did not have to be read, Samuel had to pay the incredibly high figure of £1,000. The money was refunded when the marriage was solemnized.
5. According to Arthur Darley, a great-nephew of Anne Boursiquot, they separated in 1819 (quoted by Townsend Walsh, *The Career of Dion Boucicault*, p. 7). This was clearly not true, but does show that the rift between them was common knowledge in the family.
6. The little that is known about Samuel comes from the inaccurate reminiscences of Arthur Darley (see n. 5 above), and a letter from Florence, Boucicault's niece, to Dot Boucicault in 1899 (in Calthrop Collection). Among the items Arthur Darley passed on to Walsh was the legend 'of his being taken *flagrante delicto* and, escaping from an enraged husband, of meeting his death by jumping from the window of the bed-chamber'. Samuel must have been a remarkable old man for he was eighty-four!
7. The account of the summer at Black Rock, Anne's relationship with Lardner and the subsequent events of Boucicault's birth are in a copy of the records of the Ecclesiastical Court, Dublin, sent to London

when Lardner applied for a divorce from Cecilia in 1839 (now in the House of Lords Record Office).

8. ibid.
9. *The Literary Gazette*, 13 March 1841.
10. *The Times*, 2 February 1842.
11. According to Charles Lamb Kenney, *The Life and Career of Dion Boucicault*, pp. 8–9 (written by Boucicault himself), he went to Dr Wall's school, where his classmates included Sir William Howard Russell and Sir Henry de Bathe, in 1837. According to Russell, who is more reliable than Boucicault, they were pupils together at Dr Geoghegan's – which Russell went to from 1832 to 1837. Assuming Boucicault was correct in remembering that he went to Dr Wall's school, it must have been at this time.
12. From an article in the *World* (New York, 15 May 1887), quoted by Townsend Walsh, p. 11.
13. A questionnaire completed after Boucicault's death by Agnes Robertson, his second wife, gives Zion House as one of Boucicault's schools. In her evidence to the House of Lords in 1839, Boucicault's mother stated that she had lived in Margate. Although there are records of the school having existed there are no records of any of its pupils.
14. Clement Scott, *The Drama of Yesterday and Today*, vol. 1, p. 100. He goes on to say, 'How, with little or no education, he knew what he did know, was to me absolutely mysterious.' John Coleman in *Charles Reade, As I Knew Him*, p. 13, also writes, 'He knew something about everything.' He also adds, 'I can well believe what Charles Mathews, Walter Lacey, and John Brougham often told me – that in his *juvenilia* he was the most fascinating young scapegrace that ever baffled or bamboozled a bailiff.'
15. Records of University College School at University College, London.
16. Charles Lamb Kenney, *The Life and Career of Dion Boucicault*, pp. 4–5.
17. New York *World*, 15 May 1887, quoted by Townsend Walsh, p. 14.
18. *Strand Magazine*, July–December 1892, interview with Russell.

2. Lee Moreton, Actor and Dramatist

1. *Brighton Guardian*, 1 August 1838.
2. *The Brighton Dramatic Miscellany*, 31 July 1838.
3. *Brighton Herald*, 4 August 1838.
4. Barton Hill's recollection of Boucicault in Brighton, quoted by Townsend Walsh, p. 18.
5. *The Brighton Dramatic Miscellany*, 22 September 1838.
6. The evidence for a production of *The Legend of Devil's Dyke* comes from the dated cast list given on the printed version of the play (first printed by Dicks in 1898 – eight years after Boucicault's death) and a comment by Clement Scott in *The Drama of Yesterday and Today*, vol. I, p. 2, that it was Boucicault's first play, produced in Brighton on

1 October 1834 [*sic*], 'in which he acted and, as it is reported, made a dreadful failure as Teddy Rodent, a low comedy rat-catcher!' The evidence against a production is that it was not advertised or reviewed locally, that it is not mentioned in any records of Brighton theatre at the time, that no playbills for it have been found, and that on the night it was supposed to have been performed there does exist a playbill which has 'Lee Moreton' appearing as Rory O'More.

7. Information on Boucicault's stay in Hull is to be found in the notes kept on a collection of playbills by Leigh Murray, a fellow actor in the company (now in the Harvard Theater Collection).

8. Letter from 'Lee Moreton' in Hull, possibly to Benjamin Webster, now in possession of William W. Appleton.

9. Patrick Lynch and John Vaizey, *Guinness's Brewery in the Irish Economy, 1759–1876*, p. 234.

10. Unidentified clipping, 'Her Life With Boucicault', about Agnes Robertson, quoted by Julius H. Tolson in *Dion Boucicault*, his unpublished dissertation for the University of Pennsylvania, p. 26.

11. A highly coloured account of this time is to be found in Boucicault's 'The Debut of a Dramatist', *North American* Review, vol. 148, April 1889.

12. *The Diaries of William Macready*, entry for 6 February 1841.

13. Boucicault, 'The Debut of a Dramatist', *North American Review*, vol. 148, April 1889.

14. William W. Appleton in *Madame Vestris and the London Stage*, p. 135, gives the title *Country Matters*; *Out of Town* is the title on the original manuscript now in the Theatre Museum, London; Boucicault himself in 'The Debut of a Dramatist', *North American Review*, vol. 148, April 1889, credits Vestris with *London Assurance*.

15. *Theatrical Journal*, 13 March 1841.

16. Letter from Boucicault to Charles Mathews, dated 20 February 1841, now in Shakespeare Centre.

17. Letter from Anne Maria Boursiquot, dated 14 January 1842, now in Shakespeare Centre.

18. *New York Herald*, 18 January 1878.

19. Boucicault, 'The Debut of a Dramatist', *North American Review*, vol. 148, April 1889.

3. *Adapting to Success*

1. Letter quoted in full by Irene Vanbrugh, *To Tell My Story*, pp. 39–40.

2. Boucicault made this claim during a lecture on his life, given in New York in 1853 and reported in both the *Herald* and the *New York Times*, 29 December 1853.

3. The first playbill announcing that the play was by 'D. L. Bourcicault Esq.' rather than by Lee Moreton was for 27 March. A letter to Henry Colburn, publisher of the *Literary Gazette*, offering to contribute to the magazine, dated 15 March, says 'permit me to introduce myself as

the author of "London Assurance" ' and is signed Dion Lardner
Bourcicault (now in possession of Princeton University).

4. Irene Vanbrugh, *To Tell My Story*, pp. 39–40.
5. See 'A Night's Pleasure', one of Thackeray's 'Sketches and Travels in
London' which appeared in *Punch* between 8 January and 19 February
1848. This contains an account of a visit to one of 'Mr Boyster's
Comedies of English Life', and gives some dialogue from the drama.
6. *Era*, 13 February 1842.
7. *Era*, 24 April 1842.
8. Boucicault, 'Early Days of a Dramatist', *North American Review*, vol.
148, May 1889.
9. Boucicault, 'Decline of the Drama', *North American Review*, vol. 125,
September 1877.
10. ibid.
11. According to the evidence in his 1848 insolvency trial, Boucicault had
spent much of 1843 travelling throughout Britain. A letter from
Huddersfield this year, to Albert Smith, confirms this. Charles
Rosenberg in *You Have Heard of Them*, p. 209, states he was writing for
various provincial theatres (twenty-nine plays in one year!)
12. It has always been assumed that this was the first professional performance of *The Old Guard*; however, a playbill in the possession of
Professor F. Theodore Cloak gives a performance at the Theatre
Royal, Brighton, on 30 January 1840 (produced by Charles Hill) and
refers to it as 'the favourite petite comedy', so it had possibly been
performed even earlier.
13. *Era*, 5 November 1843.
14. Boucicault, 'Early Days of a Dramatist'.
15. 'On Actors and the Art of Acting', by George Henry Lewes, quoted
by George Rowell in *Victorian Dramatic Criticism*, pp. 88–93.
16. Charles G. Rosenberg ('Q'), *You Have Heard of Them*, pp. 206–9.
17. Letter to Webster, 27 August 1844, in National Library, Dublin.
18. Letter Mathews to Webster, 5 November 1844, in Theatre Museum,
London.
19. From Boucicault's New York lecture on his life, reported in the *New
York Times*, 29 December 1853.

4. The French Years

1. Report of the Insolvent Debtors' Court, *The Times*, 9 November
1848. The earliest dated evidence I have of him spelling his name
without the 'r' is a letter to Webster of 17 April 1846, in which he signs
himself Dion de Boucicault.
2. Undated letter in National Library, Dublin.
3. A copy of the marriage certificate is in the Calthrop Collection.
4. *The Times*, 9 November 1848.
5. Letter to Webster, dated Saturday, 13 June (1846), photocopy in
Calthrop Collection.

6. H. G. Fiske, 'Boucicault: A Memory', *New York Dramatic Mirror*, September 1890.
7. *The Spirit of the Times*, 1 February 1862.
8. *The Spirit of the Times*, 27 September 1890, obituary by Stephen Fiske.
9. Clement Scott, *The Drama of Yesterday and Today*, vol. 1, pp. 447–8.
10. *The Times*, 8 December 1848.
11. Letter to the editor of the *New York Tribune*, 23 October 1873.
12. The assertion that Boucicault was Kean's House Dramatist was made by Agnes Robertson in an article, 'In the Days of My Youth', published in *M.A.P.* in 1899. Although it is often repeated, I have not been able to find any contemporary evidence for a formal engagement as such, nor that he was paid £700 a year – indeed his letters to Kean show that he was being paid by the play. It is, however, clear that the relationship with Kean was much more than one of a writer being asked to supply a play and the term 'house dramatist' is applicable.
13. RA Queen Victoria's Journal, 26 March 1851.
14. *The Leader*, 28 February 1852.
15. RA Queen Victoria's Journal, 28 February 1852.
16. Boucicault is supposed to have given up acting in 1840 as the result of a promise made to his mother who disliked the profession. It seems much more likely that he gave it up because it was not in keeping with the social standing of a writer, which is what he wanted to be. He claimed himself, in 'Leaves from a Dramatist's Diary', *North American Review*, vol. 149, August 1889, that it was money that drove him back.
17. Agnes Robertson, 'In the Days of my Youth', *M.A.P.*, 1 July 1899.
18. *Era*, 19 September 1852.
19. Letter to Sol Smith, 15 January 1861, in collection of the Missouri Historical Society.

5. *The New World*

1. Boucicault, 'Leaves from a Dramatist's Diary', *North American Review*, vol. 149, August 1889.
2. Agnes Robertson, 'In the Days of My Youth', *M.A.P.*, 1 July 1899.
3. *Montreal Gazette*, 23 September 1853.
4. *The Times*, 22 June 1888.
5. *New York Daily Tribune*, 24 October 1853, and the *Era*, 13 November 1853, were among the papers to report that Agnes was Mrs Dion Boucicault *before* Boucicault publicly admitted their marriage.
6. Quoted by Townsend Walsh, pp. 97 and 39.
7. From the inside cover of the Samuel French 1857 New York edition of *Andy Blake*.
8. Agnes Robertson, 'In the Days of My Youth'.
9. *New York Times*, 6 November 1854.
10. *New York Times*, 12 December 1854.
11. J. B. Howe, *The Cosmopolitan Actor*, quoted by Townsend Walsh, pp. 57–9.

12. Julius H. Tolson, *Dion Boucicault*, p. 136.
13. Boucicault sold a play of this title to Robert Keeley and Charles Kean for £100 in 1851. A letter in the Theatre Museum, London, dated 11 July, acknowledges receipt of a £25 advance, the remainder to be paid on production.
14. *Memories of John E. Owens*, pp. 76–8.
15. Boucicault, 'Leaves from a Dramatist's Diary'.
16. Boucicault, 'Leaves from a Dramatist's Diary'; also Hogan, *Dion Boucicault*, pp. 105–6.
17. *Era*, 21 December 1856.
18. Boucicault has traditionally been credited with introducing the matinée. If he did, it was a joint first, for on 15 August 1857, Laura Keene also announced a three o'clock programme for her theatre in New York.
19. *Era*, 18 October, 1857.
20. Advertisement in the *New York Daily Tribune*, 16 November 1857.
21. *Era*, 10 January 1858.
22. 'Illusions of the Stage', article in *Scientific American*, 1881, supplement X, pp. 4265–6.

6. *Creating a Sensation*

1. *Era*, 21 March 1858.
2. *Era*, 31 October 1858.
3. Quoted by Montrose J. Moses, *The American Dramatist*, p. 150.
4. Quoted by William Winter, *Other Days*, p. 135.
5. Joseph Jefferson, *Rip van Winkle, an Autobiography*, pp. 159–60.
6. Letter to an unknown actor, 29 August 1859, now in Princeton University Library.
7. Jefferson, *Rip van Winkle*, pp. 160–1.
8. ibid.
9. Kate Ryan, *Old Boston Museum Days*, pp. 184–5.
10. This story is quoted by Kate Ryan (see n. 9 above), but without using names. The actor is identified as Barrymore by James Kotsilibas-Davis in *Great Times Good Times*, pp. 68–9.
11. *New York Daily Tribune*, 21 October 1859.
12. Agnes Robertson, 'In the Days of My Youth', *M.A.P.*, 1 July 1899.
13. Jefferson, *Rip van Winkle*, pp. 162–3.
14. ibid., p. 164.

7. *The Colleen Bawn*

1. *New York Daily Tribune*, 14 March 1860.
2. Agnes Robertson, 'In the Days of My Youth', *M.A.P.*, 1 July 1899.
3. Boucicault, 'Leaves from a Dramatist's Diary,' *North American Review*, vol. 149, August 1889.
4. Townsend Walsh, p. 72.

5. Bryan MacMahon, 'The Colleen Bawn', an article written for the Irish Tourist Board.
6. William Winter, *Other Days*, p. 130.
7. Quoted by Albert E. Johnson in 'Fabulous Boucicault', *Theatre Arts*, March 1953.
8. *The Spirit of the Times*, 1 February 1862.
9. Letter George Holland to Sol Smith, 7 July 1860, in collection of the Missouri Historical Society.
10. *New York Times*, 17 July 1860.
11. The details of the Boucicault–Webster relationship at the Adelphi are in the Calthrop collection and have been written up by Christopher Calthrop in 'Dion Boucicault and Benjamin Webster', *Theatre Notebook*, vol. 32, 1978.
12. Boucicault, 'Opera', *North American Review*, vol. 144, April 1887.
13. *The Spirit of the Times*, 1 February 1862.
14. Letter from Boucicault to Webster, 19 January 1861, in Boucicault's copybook, now in the Calthrop Collection.
15. Letter to George Riggs, 10 April 1861, now in Rush Rhees Library, University of Rochester.
16. *The Spirit of the Times*, 1 February 1862.
17. *The Times*, 18 June 1862. According to papers in the Calthrop Collection, Webster and Boucicault met at Astley's on 3 January 1863 to sign a formal document dissolving their partnership – as Calthrop says, a 'strangely quiet and restrained' end to the story.

8. *'Failures Don't Count'*

1. All modern accounts of the Jordan affair give Anne Walters as Jordan's wife. However, the researches of Professor F. Theodore Cloak have proved that his wife at the time was not Anne, but Emily Thorne, sister of the actor Charles Robert Thorne. A scrap of paper in the Calthrop Collection, in the handwriting of George Carew, Boucicault's solicitor, notes that Anne Walters was Jordan's first wife and that he married Emily Thorne at Hoboken, N.J., in 1857. It was her second marriage also, and she later went on to marry a third time.
2. *The Times*, 19 May 1863; an identical letter appeared in the *Daily Telegraph* on the same day.
3. Jane Frith, *Leaves from a Life*, quoted by Townsend Walsh, p. 79.
4. Jules Rivière, *My Musical Life and Recollections*, pp. 120–1.
5. *The Times*, 2 October 1862.
6. Details of the refurbishing of Astley's are in the *Daily Telegraph*, 23 December 1862. Details of the riddle project are in the Calthrop Collection. There's no evidence that the idea ever got off the drawing board, although with the advent of electricity and slide-projectors, projecting advertisements became quite common.
7. *Daily Telegraph*, 29 December 1862.
8. *Daily Telegraph*, 26 February 1863.

9. *Daily Telegraph*, 27 January 1863.
10. *Daily Telegraph*, 26 February 1863.
11. Prospectus for the New Theatre Company in the Calthrop Collection.
12. Edward Stirling, *Old Drury Lane*, vol. 2, pp. 234–6.
13. Boucicault took legal action against William Smith, Webster's manager at the Adelphi, but failed to stop the demonstrations. His application was dismissed on the grounds that although the placards and bills did not have the printer's name and address on as they should by law, only the Attorney or Solicitor General could commence proceedings under the relevant Act. See *The Times*, 11 April 1863.
14. Letter to *The Times*, 19 May 1863 (also to the *Daily Telegraph*).
15. Quoted by Townsend Walsh, pp. 91–2.
16. Quoted by Montrose J. Moses, *The American Dramatist*, p. 152.
17. Quoted by Townsend Walsh, pp. 95–6.
18. ibid., p. 94.

9. 'How Doth the Busy Dion B.'

1. The foundation stone was laid in May 1867, and the hall opened by Queen Victoria on 29 March 1871. Although Boucicault subscribed for a Grand Tier Box in early 1865, he never became a seat-holder, transferring his interest to Reuben David Sassoon according to the Royal Albert Hall records.
2. John Hollingshead, *My Lifetime*, quoted by Townsend Walsh, p. 106.
3. A letter dated Monday, 26 September, to Charles Lamb Kenney, invites him to a 'grand manifestation of spirits' on Wednesday at seven o'clock. However, a letter from Boucicault to the *Era*, 12 October 1864, gives the date, time and description of the séance I have used. Kenney's name does not appear in the list of guests present, so either the first séance was postponed or else there were two.
4. *Era*, 16 October 1864.
5. *Liverpool Daily Post*, 25 October 1864.
6. Quoted by Townsend Walsh, p. 101.
7. Papers relating to this case are in the Calthrop Collection.
8. Joseph Jefferson, *Rip van Winkle*, pp. 232–7.
9. Select Committee on Theatrical Licences and Regulations, April–May 1866, House of Lords Record Office.
10. Boucicault, 'Leaves from a Dramatist's Diary', *North American Review*, vol. 149, August 1889.
11. In the possession of Ivan F. Garnham.
12. Letter dated 4 September 1866, *The Letters of Charles Dickens*, p. 606.
13. Joe Graham, *An Old Stock-Actor's Memories*, p. 220.
14. Quoted by Laurence Irving, *Henry Irving: The Actor and His World*, pp. 132–3.
15. ibid.
16. Quoted by Townsend Walsh, p. 113.

17. Quoted in the Bancrofts' *On and Off the Stage*, p. 118.
18. The legal papers relating to this dispute are in the Calthrop Collection.
19. Agnes Robertson, 'In the Days of My Youth', *M.A.P.*, 1 July 1899, states, 'The night of the first production . . . was also the night of the Clerkenwell explosion.' She also says that when the Prince of Wales visited Boucicault backstage, he asked if Boucicault was a Fenian, to which the playwright replied, 'No, your Royal Highness, but – I love my country.' Michael Barrett, a Fenian, was hanged on 26 May 1868 for his part in the explosion – the last public execution in England.

10. *Retirement and Comeback*

1. Letter to *The Times*, quoted by Cyril Pearl, *The Girl With the Swansdown Seat*, p. 107.
2. *New York Daily Tribune*, 10 September 1869.
3. Boucicault, 'The Future American Drama', *Arena*, November 1890. Montrose J. Moses, *The American Dramatist*, p. 159, remarks, 'He was often heard to say that he preferred fifty-cent audiences to any other, since they came for legitimate amusement, and did not look upon the theatre as a kind of interlude – an indispensable accessory to dinner parties. Nor did he hesitate to proclaim, whenever the opportunity presented itself, that the drama was being kept decent only through the sincerity of this fifty-cent body.'
4. *Illustrated London News*, 9 October 1869.
5. Letter dated 31 May 1870, in possession of Ivan F. Garnham.
6. Undated letter in possession of Ivan F. Garnham.
7. Undated letter in possession of Ivan F. Garnham.
8. The papers in connection with the case of Charlotte Dence *versus* Dion Boucicault are in the Calthrop Collection. It was due to be heard in the Mayor's Court, London, on 29 October 1870.
9. Quoted by William Winter, *The Press and the Stage*, p. 12.
10. Quoted by Townsend Walsh, pp. 119–20.
11. ibid.
12. From J. C. Williamson's memoirs, quoted by Ian G. Dicker, *J.C.W.*, pp. 34–5.
13. This anecdote is related by William Winter, *The Life of David Belasco*, pp. 54–7, to whom Belasco told it. It was Winter who accepted that the meeting with Boucicault was in the fall of 1873 – and so it has been accepted ever since. Winter did, however, question whether the play Belasco worked on was *Led Astray*, and came to the conclusion that because of the date of the first production it could not have been. I tend to the view that Belasco was right and that it was a rewritten version for London, produced on 1 July 1874.
14. Leonard Lee Korf, *An Examination of Some Obscurities in the Life of Dion Boucicault*, establishes through newspaper accounts that Boucicault's visit to Virginia City was in February 1874.

15. Joseph Daly, *The Life of Augustin Daly*, p. 170.
16. Helena Modjeska, *Memories and Impressions*, p. 352.
17. Letter from Anna Maria Boursiquot to Warren Darley, 30 November 1874, in Calthrop Collection.
18. James Kotsilibas-Davis, *Great Times Good Times*, pp. 68–9.
19. John Coleman, *Players and Playwrights I Have Known*, p. 364.
20. ibid., pp. 364–9.
21. ibid.
22. *Cambridge Chronicle*, 29 January 1876.

11. Out of Fashion

1. Letter to 'My dear Buck', 20 March 1880, photocopy supplied to Christopher Calthrop by Ian G. Dicker.
2. *New York Herald*, 21 December 1876.
3. Letter to Arthur Lewis, 5 April (1875), in Calthrop Collection.
4. Letter to Warren Darley, 20 November 1877, in Calthrop Collection.
5. *The Theatre*, October 1878.
6. Speech reported in the 'Illustrated *Shaughraun* Programme', London, 1876, reprinted from the *New York Herald* of 7 and 8 March 1875.
7. *The Theatre*, August 1878.
8. *New York Times*, 5 September 1879.
9. Quoted by Townsend Walsh, pp. 154–6.
10. She died in London on 11 January 1879, aged eighty-four, and was buried in Paddington Cemetery. The inscription on her tombstone reads: 'To Anne Boucicault . . . from her beloved son Dion.'
11. Quoted by the Bancrofts, *On and Off the Stage*, p. 295.
12. Undated letter to Mrs Edward Saker, in possession of Professor F. Theodore Cloak.
13. *The Theatre*, July 1880.
14. The McGonagall–'Boucicault' meeting is chronicled in David Phillips, *No Poets' Corner in the Abbey*, pp. 107–11.
15. Quoted by Julius H. Tolson in his thesis, p. 231, from William H. Rideing, *Dramatic Notes*, p. 51.
16. *Illustrated London News*, 3 September 1881.
17. ibid.
18. Letter dated 29 January 1882, from *The Letters of Oscar Wilde*, ed. Rupert Hart-Davis, pp. 92–3.
19. Frank Frankfort Moore, *A Journalist's Note-book*, pp. 291 ff.
20. Letter to Dot Boucicault, 6 February (1883), photocopy in Calthrop Collection.
21. Nine pages of manuscript for this booklet, in the handwriting of Boucicault, are now in the University of South Florida.
22. Letter to Henry Irving, 6 November (1884), in Theatre Museum, London.
23. A calculation made by Laurence Hutton and quoted in Montrose J. Moses, *The American Dramatist*, p. 152.

24. Letter to Henry Irving, 30 December (1885), in Theatre Museum, London.

12. *A Monster Who Forgets*

1. Article by Boucicault on the tour in *Town and Country Journal*, 26 December 1885.
2. Frank P. Morse, *Backstage With Henry Miller*, pp. 107–8.
3. Quoted by H. G. Fiske, 'Boucicault: A Memory', *Dramatic Mirror*, September 1890.
4. Quoted by William Winter, *Other Days*, p. 131.
5. Letter to F. S. Palmer, editor of the *Harvard Monthly*, 22 February 1887, in Players' Club Library.
6. Boucicault, 'Spots on the Sun', *Arena*, January 1890.
7. Daniel Frohman, *Memories of a Manager*, pp. 87–92.
8. Emily Soldene, *My Theatrical and Musical Recollections*, p. 272.
9. Constance Morris, 'Dion Boucicault's School of Acting', *The Green Book Album*, August 1911.
10. Quoted by Townsend Walsh, p. 173.
11. Taken from an interview with Russell quoted in the *Dramatic Mirror*, September 1890, the week after Boucicault's funeral.
12. Undated letter to Russell in Players' Club Library.
13. Quoted by Townsend Walsh, pp. 149–50.
14. Quoted by Albert E. Johnson, 'Fabulous Boucicault', *Theatre Arts*, March 1953.
15. The Church of the Transfiguration; it got its nickname in 1870 when Joseph Jefferson was trying to arrange the funeral of the comedian George Holland. The fashionable church he went to refused to carry out the burial because Holland was an actor and Jefferson was told that there was a little church around the corner that did that sort of thing. 'God Bless the Little Church Around the Corner,' exclaimed Jefferson, and so began the church's long association with the theatrical profession.

SOURCES AND
ACKNOWLEDGEMENTS

UNPUBLISHED MATERIAL

I have been particularly fortunate for this biography in having access to the Boucicault papers now in the possession of Christopher Calthrop. These were discovered in a deed-box in the vault of a London bank in 1962. Over the years, Mr Calthrop has added material to his collection and I am indebted to him for placing it, and the results of his own considerable researches into the life of his great-grandfather, at my disposal. I would also like to acknowledge the enormous help I have derived from the researches of Townsend Walsh (from his biography of Boucicault, published in 1915, and his scrapbook of Boucicault material now in New York Public Library), Julius H. Tolson (from 'Dion Boucicault', an unpublished doctoral thesis for the University of Pennsylvania, 1951), Leonard Lee Korf (from 'An Examination of Some Obscurities in the Life of Dion Boucicault', an unpublished doctoral dissertation for the University of California, 1975), Robert Hogan (from *Dion Boucicault*, in Twayne's United States Authors Series, 1969), the late Dr Albert E. Johnson and Professor F. T. Cloak.

As well as being a prolific playwright, Boucicault was a prolific letter writer, to the press and to individuals. Many of his letters are to be found in the columns of the leading papers in Britain and America; others are now in public and private collections throughout the world, including those of the author, William W. Appleton, Christopher Calthrop, Professor F. T. Cloak, Ivan F. Garnham, the Harvard Theater Collection, the Huntingdon Library, the University of Iowa, the Missouri Historical Society, the Mitchell Library of New South Wales, the National Library of Ireland, New York Public Library, the Pierpont Morgan Library, the Walter Hampden-Edwin Booth Collection at the Players' Club, Princeton University, Rochester University, the Shakespeare Centre at Stratford-upon-Avon, the University of Texas, the Theatre Museum, London (combining the collections of the British Theatre Museum and the Enthoven of the Victoria and Albert Museum), Yale University and Robert Young Jnr. Boucicault's letter to Mrs George Lewis about Oscar Wilde's American tour of 1882 and a letter to Clara Morris are in *The Letters of Oscar Wilde*, edited by Sir Rupert Hart-Davis; various letters to the Bancrofts are in *On and Off the Stage*; Mary Anderson quotes a letter to her in *A Few Memories*; and Irene Vanbrugh quotes his letter to his mother, written after the first production of *London Assurance*, in *To Tell My Story*. Where I have quoted from a specific letter I would like to acknowledge the permission of the copyright holder or owner (details will be found in the 'Notes and References' section).

By far the largest collection of Boucicault material outside the Calthrop Collection is that in the University of South Florida, containing printed plays, manuscripts, documents and memorabilia belonging to Boucicault and sold as a collection by Louise Thorndyke, his third wife. The University of Kent, at Canterbury, also contains a good collection of printed and manuscript plays, while the Harvard Theater Collection, New York Public Library, and the Theatre Museum, London, also contain important original material.

The Journals of Queen Victoria, in the Royal Library at Windsor Castle, contain many interesting comments about the Boucicault plays the Queen went to see, and I would like to acknowledge the gracious permission of Her Majesty Queen Elizabeth II to quote from them.

One of the most important of all documents relating to Boucicault is to be found in the House of Lords Record Office. This is the report of 'An Act to Dissolve the Marriage of Dionysius Lardner . . .' of 29 April 1839, which contains the evidence given at the Ecclesiastical Court, Dublin, in 1832, detailing the relationship between Lardner and Boucicault's mother and giving the account of Boucicault's birth. One other interesting document in the House of Lords Record Office is the report of the Select Committee on Theatrical Licenses and Regulations, 1866, to which Boucicault gave evidence.

I would also like to acknowledge the help given to me by John Hadley, a local Huntingdon historian, who supplied me with details of the Abbots Ripton train disaster of 1876 from his, as yet, unpublished manuscript, and by Alan Hankinson, who is working on a biography of Sir William Howard Russell and supplied me with all the references to Boucicault in Russell's diaries.

Much of the research for this biography has involved checking newspapers and playbills, and I am indebted to many people for helping me with this. In particular I would like to thank the librarians and staff of the following libraries and institutions: Birmingham, Blackburn, Brighton, Bristol, the British Library, Cheltenham, Dublin Public Library, Edinburgh, the Free Library of Philadelphia, Glasgow, Gloucester, Harvard,

Huddersfield, Hull, Leeds, the Library of Congress, Liverpool, Manchester, the Mitchell Library of N.S.W., Montreal, National Archives and Records Service, Washington, New York Public Library, the Theatre Museum, London, and the Westminster Reference Library.

PUBLISHED MATERIAL

These lists are not intended to be exhaustive, but to detail the most important and helpful printed sources consulted for this book. In many cases the anecdotes about Boucicault that are related (and in modern publications repeated) should be treated with great circumspection – they are excellent gossip but most unreliable as fact. They do, however, help to create an impression of the sort of man Boucicault was, how he was considered by his contemporaries, and, often, how he is considered today. For a first-class discussion of Boucicault's plays, I would refer the reader to Robert Hogan's *Dion Boucicault*.

Articles

BOUCICAULT, DION, 'The Art of Dramatic Composition', *North American Review*, vol. 126, January 1878.

——, 'At the Goethe Society', *North American Review*, vol. 148, March 1889.

——, 'Coquelin and Hading', *North American Review*, vol. 147, November 1888.

——, 'Coquelin-Irving', *North American Review*, vol. 145, August 1887.

——, 'The Debut of a Dramatist', *North American Review*, vol. 148, April 1889.

——, 'The Decline of the Drama', *North American Review*, vol. 125, September 1877.

——, 'The Decline and Fall of the Press', *North American Review*, vol. 145, July 1887.

——, 'Early Days of a Dramatist', *North American Review*, vol. 148, May 1889.

——, 'The Future American Drama', *Arena*, November 1890.

——, 'Golden Words', *Era Almanack*, 1876.

——, 'Leaves from a Dramatist's Diary', *North American Review*, vol. 149, August 1889.

——, 'Mutilations of Shakespeare, The Poet Interviewed', *North American Review*, vol. 148, February 1889.

——, 'My Pupils', *North American Review*, vol. 147, October 1888.

——, 'Opera', *North American Review*, vol. 144, April 1887.

——, 'Parnell and the Times', *North American Review*, vol. 144, June 1887.

——, 'Shakespeare's Influence on the Drama', *North American Review*, vol. 147, December 1888.

——, 'Spots on the Sun', *Arena*, January 1890.

——, 'Theatres, Halls and Audiences', *North American Review*, vol. 149, October 1889.

——, 'A Star Actor in the Colonies', *Town and Country Journal*, 26 December 1885.

CALTHROP, CHRISTOPHER, 'Dion Boucicault and Benjamin Webster', *Theatre Notebook*, vol. 32.

FAULKNER, SELDON, 'The Great Train Scene Robbery', *Quarterly Journal of Speech*, February 1964.

FIELDING, K. J., 'The Dramatization of Edwin Drood', *Theatre Notebook*, vol. 7.

FISKE, H. G., 'Boucicault: A Memory', *Dramatic Mirror*, September 1890.

FISKE, STEPHEN, obituary of Boucicault in *The Spirit of the Times*, 27 September 1890.

FOLLAND, HAROLD F., 'Lee Moreton: Debut of a Theatre Man', *Theatre Notebook*, vol. 23.

JOHNSON, ALBERT E., 'The Birth of Dion Boucicault', *Modern Drama*, September 1968.

——, 'Dion Boucicault Learns To Act', *Players*, vol. 47, December–January 1973.

——, 'Dion Boucicault: Man and Fable', *Educational Theatre Journal*, December 1954.

——, 'Fabulous Boucicault', *Theatre Arts*, March 1953.

MACMAHON, BRYAN, 'The Colleen Bawn', *Ireland of the Welcomes*, vol. 24, 1975.

MORRIS, CONSTANCE, 'Dion Boucicault's School of Acting', *Green Book Album*, August 1911.

ROBERTSON, AGNES (Mrs Dion Boucicault), 'In the Days of My Youth', *M.A.P.*, 1 July 1899.

SCOTT, GENIO, 'Mr Dion Boucicault', *The Spirit of the Times*, 1 February 1862.

Books

APPLETON, WILLIAM W., *Madame Vestris and the London Stage*, New York, 1974.

BANCROFT, SQUIRE and MARIE, *On and Off the Stage*, London, 1889.

BARNES, J. H., *Forty Years on the Stage: Others (Principally) and Myself*, London, 1914.

COLEMAN, JOHN, *Players and Playwrights I Have Known*, 2 vols., London, 1888.

COOK, DUTTON, *Nights at the Play*, London, 1883.

DALY, JOSEPH FRANCIS, *The Life of Augustin Daly*, New York, 1917.

DICKENS, CHARLES, *The Letters of Charles Dickens*, London, 1893.

DICKER, IAN G., *J. C. W., a short biography of James Cassius Williamson*, Elizabeth Tudor Press, N.S.W., 1974.

FORBES-ROBERTSON, DIANA, *Maxine*, London, 1964.

FROHMAN, DANIEL, *Memories of a Manager*, London, 1911.

GRAHAM, JOE, *An Old Stock-Actor's Memories*, London, 1930.

HOGAN, ROBERT, *Dion Boucicault*, New York, 1969.

SOURCES AND ACKNOWLEDGEMENTS

IRVING, LAURENCE, *Henry Irving: The Actor and His World*, London, 1951.

JEFFERSON, JOSEPH, *Rip van Winkle, an Autobiography*, New York, 1890.

KENNEY, CHARLES LAMB, *The Life and Career of Dion Boucicault*, New York, 1883 (written, in fact, by Boucicault).

KOTSILIBAS-DAVIS, JAMES, *Great Times Good Times*, New York, 1977.

KRAUSE, DAVID (ed.), *The Dolmen Boucicault*, Dublin, 1964.

MACREADY, WILLIAM, *The Diaries of William Charles Macready*, London, 1912.

MATTHEWS, BRANDER (ed.), *Papers On Acting*, New York, 1958 (reprint).

MODJESKA, HELENA, *Memories and Impressions*, New York, 1910.

MOORE, FRANK FRANKFORT, *A Journalist's Note-Book*, London, 1894.

MORLEY, HENRY, *The Journal of a London Playgoer*, London, 1891.

MORSE, FRANK P., *Backstage with Henry Miller*, New York, 1938.

MOSES, MONTROSE J., *Famous Actor-Families in America*, New York, 1906.

——, *The American Dramatist*, Boston, 1925.

ODELL, GEORGE C. D., *Annals of the New York Stage*, 15 vols., New York, 1927.

OWENS, JOHN E., *Memories of John E. Owens*, Baltimore, 1892.

PEARL, CYRIL, *The Girl with the Swansdown Seat*, London, 1955.

PHILLIPS, DAVID, *No Poets' Corner in the Abbey*, Dundee, 1971.

RAHILL, FRANK, *The World of Melodrama*, Pennsylvania, 1967.

REES, TERENCE, *Theatre Lighting in the Age of Gas*, London, 1978.

RIVIERE, JULES, *My Musical Life and Recollections*, London, 1893.

ROSENBERG, CHARLES G. ('Q'), *You Have Heard of Them*, New York, 1854.

ROWELL, GEORGE, *Victorian Dramatic Criticism*, London, 1971.

——, *The Victorian Theatre, A Survey*, London, 1956.

RYAN, KATE, *Old Boston Museum Days*, Boston, 1915.

SCOTT, CLEMENT, *The Drama of Yesterday and Today*, 2 vols., London, 1899.

SOLDENE, EMILY, *My Theatrical and Musical Recollections*, London, 1897.

VANBRUGH, IRENE, *To Tell My Story*, London, 1948.

VARDAC, A. NICHOLAS, *Stage to Screen*, New York, 1968.

WALLACK, LESTER, *Memories of 50 Years*, New York, 1889.

WALSH, TOWNSEND, *The Career of Dion Boucicault*, New York, 1915.

WILDE, OSCAR, *The Letters of Oscar Wilde*, ed. Rupert Hart-Davis, London, 1962.

WINTER, WILLIAM, *The Life of David Belasco*, 2 vols., New York, 1918.

——, *Other Days*, New York, 1908.

——, *The Press and the Stage*, New York, 1889.

THE PLAYS OF DION BOUCICAULT

All known plays of Dion Boucicault are listed in chronological order of production, with date and place. The list is based on one compiled originally by Christopher Calthrop (who used Allardyce Nicoll as his starting point), with some plays included in previous such lists and now known not to be by Boucicault omitted, others added, and dates corrected where evidence has been found of earlier productions. The problems of checking dates for plays which may have had a different title for their first performance, and to which Boucicault often did not put his name, are immense. This list is bound to contain some errors and omissions; it is, however, as complete as I have been able to make it.

Napoleon's Old Guard. Produced 1836, Brentford Collegiate School.
A Legend of Devil's Dyke. No record of production, though Boucicault dated his copy 1 October 1838, Theatre Royal, Brighton.
Lodgings To Let. Produced 18 February 1839, Theatre Royal, Bristol.
Jack Sheppard. Produced 26 December 1839, Theatre Royal, Hull.
The Old Guard (a revision of *Napoleon's Old Guard*). Produced 30 January 1840, Theatre Royal, Brighton. First London production 9 October 1843, Princess's.
London Assurance. Produced 4 March 1841, Covent Garden.
The Irish Heiress. Produced 7 February 1842, Covent Garden.
A Lover by Proxy. Produced 21 April 1842, Haymarket.
Alma Mater; or, A Cure for Coquettes. Produeed 19 September 1842, Haymarket.
Curiosities of Literature. Produced 24 September 1842, Haymarket.
The Bastille. A possible collaboration with Benjamin Webster. Produced 19 December 1842, Haymarket.

Woman. Produced 2 October 1843, Haymarket.

Victor and Hortense; or, False Pride (later revised as *Paul Lafarge*). Produced 1 November 1843, Haymarket.

Laying a Ghost. Produced 15 November 1843, Haymarket.

Sharp's the Word. A play given by Townsend Walsh as having been performed in London in 1843. No record of production has yet been found.

Used Up. A collaboration with Charles Mathews. Produced 6 February 1844, Haymarket.

Lolah; or, The Wreck-Light. Produced 25 March 1844, Haymarket.

Love in a Sack. Produced 22 April 1844, Haymarket.

Mother and Son. Produced 22 April 1844, Adelphi.

The Fox and the Goose; or, The Widow's Husband. One-act operetta with music by Ambroise Thomas, written in collaboration with Benjamin Webster. Produced 2 October 1844, Adelphi.

The Confederacy. An altered version of the play by Vanbrugh. Produced 2 October 1844, Haymarket.

Don Caesar de Bazan; or, Love and Honour. A collaboration with Benjamin Webster. Produced 14 October 1844, Adelphi.

Old Heads and Young Hearts. Produced 18 November 1844, Haymarket.

A Soldier of Fortune; or, The Irish Settler. A possible collaboration with Benjamin Webster. Produced 6 February 1845, Adelphi.

Peg Woffington. Produced 23 June 1845, Adelphi.

Enquire Within. Produced 25 August 1845, Lyceum.

The Old School. Produced 5 February 1846, Haymarket.

Who Did It; or, What's in the Wind (also known as *Up the Flue*). A collaboration with Charles Kenney. Produced 11 May 1846, Adelphi.

Mr Peter Piper; or, Found Out At Last. Produced 16 May 1846, Haymarket.

The Wonderful Water Cure. Operetta; a collaboration with Benjamin Webster. Produced 15 July 1846, Haymarket.

Shakespeare in Love. Produced in London during 1846 according to Townsend Walsh. No record of production.

The School for Scheming (later revised as *Love and Money*). Produced 4 February 1847, Haymarket.

La Salamandrine. Ballet for which Boucicault supplied the incidents. Produced 18 May 1847, Covent Garden.

A Confidence. Produced 2 May 1848, Haymarket.

False Colours and *The Letter of Introduction.* Two plays claimed by Boucicault during his 1848 bankruptcy hearing. No record of either being produced with these titles.

The Knight of Arva. Produced 22 November 1848, Haymarket.

The Willow Copse. A possible collaboration with Charles Kenney. Produced 26 November 1849, Adelphi.

La Garde Nationale (also performed as *The Garde Mobile*). Produced 9 January 1850, Queen's.

Giralda; or, The Invisible Husband (revised as *A Dark Night's Work*). Produced 12 September 1850, Haymarket.

A Radical Cure. Produced in London during 1850 according to Townsend Walsh. No record of production.

Belphegor. A collaboration with Benjamin Webster. Produced 13 January 1851, Adelphi.

Sixtus the Fifth; or, The Broken Vow (also known as *The Pope of Rome*). A collaboration with John Bridgeman. Produced 17 February 1851, Olympic.

Love in a Maze. Produced 6 March 1851, Princess's.

Pauline. Produced 17 March 1851, Princess's. Boucicault claimed to have written a version of this play for Kean; it is not absolutely certain that this production is of that version.

The Queen of Spades; or, The Gambler's Secret (sometimes called *The Dame of Spades*). Produced 29 March 1851, Drury Lane.

O'Flannigan and the Fairies. Produced 21 April 1851, Adelphi.

The Corsican Brothers; or, The Vendetta. Produced 24 February 1852, Princess's.

The Vampire (later revised as *The Phantom*). Produced 14 June 1852, Princess's.

The Prima Donna. Produced 18 September 1852, Princess's.

Stella. In a letter dated 18 June 1852, Boucicault acknowledges receipt of an advance on a play of this title. No record of production.

The Sentinel. Operetta with music by Robert Stoepel. Produced 10 January 1853, Strand.

Genevieve; or The Reign of Terror. Produced 20 June 1853, Adelphi.

The Young Actress. Produced 19 September 1853, Theatre Royal, Montreal.

To Parents and Guardians. Produced 28 October 1853, Burton's, New York. Claimed by Boucicault, this may have been his version of a play by Goldsmith. It is, however, more likely to be Tom Taylor's play with alterations by Boucicault.

The Fox Hunt; or, Don Quixote the Second (later revised as *The Fox Chase*). Produced 23 November 1853, Burton's, New York.

Andy Blake; or, The Irish Diamond (also called *The Dublin Boy* and *The Irish Boy*). Produced 1 March 1854, Boston Museum, Boston.

Faust and Margaret. Produced 19 April 1854, Princess's.

The Devil's In It. Produced 21 April 1854, Chestnut Street Theatre, Philadelphia.

Janet Pride. Produced 11 August 1854, Metropolitan, Buffalo.

The Fairy Star. Produced 6 November 1854, Broadway Theatre, New York.

Apollo in New York. Produced 27 November 1854, Walnut Street Theatre, Philadelphia.

Pierre the Foundling. Produced 11 December 1854, Adelphi.

Eugénie; or, A Sister's Vow. Produced 1 January 1855, Drury Lane.

Louis XI. Produced 13 January 1855, Princess's.

Agnes Robertson At Home. Produced 23 January 1855, Pelican, New Orleans.

There's Nothing In It. Produced 27 June 1855, Walnut Street Theatre, Philadelphia.

Grimaldi; or, Scenes in the Life of an Actress (also called *The Life of an Actress* and *Violet*). Produced 24 September 1855, National Theatre, Cincinnati.

The Cat Changed into a Woman. Produced 26 October 1855, National Theatre, Washington, DC.

Rachel is Coming. Produced 8 November 1855, St Louis Theatre, St Louis.

The Chameleon. Produced 20 December 1855, Gaiety, New Orleans.

Azael; or, The Prodigal Son. Produced 19 January 1856, Gaiety, New Orleans.

Una. Produced 10 February 1856, Gaiety, New Orleans.

Blue Belle. Produced 27 November 1856, Burton's, New York.

George Darville. Produced 9 March 1857, Boston Theatre, Boston.

The Invisible Husband (a revision of *Giralda*). Produced 28 October 1857, Wallack's, New York.

Wanted A Widow, With Immediate Possession. A collaboration with Charles Seymour. Produced 9 November 1857, Wallack's, New York.

The Poor of New York. A collaboration with Charles Seymour, Goodrich and Warden. Produced 8 December 1857, Wallack's, New York. (See also *The Poor of Liverpool*, 1864, below.)

Jessie Brown; or, The Relief of Lucknow. Produced 22 February 1858, Wallack's, New York.

Brigham Young; or, The Revolt of the Harem. A collaboration with Charles Seymour and others. Produced 25 May 1858, Wallack's, New York.

Pauvrette (also called *The Snow Flower* and *The Maid of the Alps*). Produced 4 October 1858, Niblo's Garden, New York.

Dot. Produced 14 September 1859, Winter Garden, New York.

Chamooni III. Produced 19 October 1859, Winter Garden, New York.

Smike; or, Scenes from Nicholas Nickleby. Produced 1 November 1859, Winter Garden, New York.

The Octoroon; or, Life in Louisiana. Produced 6 December 1859, Winter Garden, New York.

Jeanie Deans; or, The Heart of Midlothian (also called *The Trial of Effie Deans*). Produced 9 January 1860, Laura Keene's, New York.

Vanity Fair. Produced 12 March 1860, Laura Keene's, New York.

The Colleen Bawn; or, The Brides of Garryowen. Produced 29 March 1860, Laura Keene's, New York.

The Lily of Killarney. Operatic version of *The Colleen Bawn*, words by John Oxenford and Boucicault, music by Julius Benedict. Produced 10 February 1862, Covent Garden.

Lady Bird; or, Harlequin Lord Dundreary. Produced simultaneously on 26 December 1862, at New Theatre Royal, Westminster, and Wallack's, New York.

How She Loves Him. Produced 7 December 1863, Prince of Wales, Liverpool.

The Poor of Liverpool. (Adapted from *The Poor of New York*, 1857, above; also seen as *The Poor of Leeds, The Streets of Manchester, The Streets of London*, etc.). Produced 10 February 1864, Royal Amphitheatre, Liverpool.

Omoo; or, The Sea of Ice. Produced 24 October 1864, Royal Amphitheatre, Liverpool.

Arrah-na-Pogue; or, The Wicklow Wedding. Produced 7 November 1864, Old Theatre Royal, Dublin. Revised version produced 22 March 1865, Princess's.

Rip van Winkle. Produced 4 September 1865, Adelphi.

The Parish Clerk. Produced 30 April 1866, Prince's, Manchester.

The Two Lives of Mary Leigh (renamed *Hunted Down*). Produced 30 July 1866, Prince's, Manchester.

The Long Strike. Produced 15 September 1866, Lyceum.

The Flying Scud; or, A Four Legged Fortune. Produced 6 October 1866, Holborn Theatre, London.

A Wild Goose Chase (also known as *Wild Goose*). Produced 29 April 1867, Haymarket.

Foul Play. Produced 28 May 1868, Holborn Theatre, London.

After Dark; A Tale of London Life. Produced 12 August 1868, Princess's.

Seraphine; or, A Devotee. Produced 1 May 1869, Queen's, London.

Presumptive Evidence (also known as *Mercy Dodd*). Produced 10 May 1869, Princess's.

Formosa (The Most Beautiful); or, The Railroad to Ruin. Produced 5 August 1869, Drury Lane.

Dreams. A revision of T. W. Robertson's play. Produced 6 September 1869, 5th Avenue Theatre, New York.

Lost at Sea; or, A London Story. A collaboration with H. J. Byron. Produced 2 October 1869, Adelphi.

Paul Lafarge. A revision of *Victor and Hortense*. Produced 7 March 1870, Princess's.

A Dark Night's Work. A revision of *Giralda*. Produced 7 March 1870, Princess's.

The Mad Boy. Possibly by Boucicault. Produced 28 April 1870, Academy of Music, New York.

The Rapparee; or, The Treaty of Limerick. Produced 2 September 1870, Princess's.

Jezebel; or, The Dead Reckoning. Produced 5 December 1870, Holborn Theatre.

A Christmas Story. Produced 24 December 1870, Gaiety, London.

Elfie; or, The Cherry Tree Inn. Produced 10 March 1871, Theatre Royal, Glasgow.

John Bull; or, The Englishman's Fireside. A revision of George Colman's play. Produced 28 August 1871, Prince's, Manchester.

Night and Morning (later called *Kerry*). Produced 7 September 1871, Prince's, Manchester.

Babil and Bijou; or, The Lost Regalia. Produced 29 August 1872, Covent Garden.

Daddy O'Dowd (later revised as *The O'Dowd* and as *Suil-a-mor*). Produced 17 March 1873, Booth's, New York.

Mora; or, The Golden Fetters. Produced 3 June 1873, Wallack's, New York.

Mimi. Produced 1 July 1873, Wallack's, New York.

Led Astray. Produced 6 December 1873, Union Square Theatre, New York.

A Man of Honor. Produced 22 December 1873, Wallack's, New York.

A Struggle for Life. Copyrighted by Boucicault in 1873. No record of production.

Boucicault in California. Produced 19 January 1874, San Francisco Theatre.

Belle Lamar. Produced 10 August 1874, Booth's, New York.

Venice Preserved. A revision of Thomas Otway's play. Produced 14 September 1874, Booth's, New York..

The Shaughraun. Produced 14 November 1874, Wallack's, New York.

Drink. A lost play copyrighted by Boucicault in 1874.

Free Cuba. A lost play copyrighted by Boucicault and J. J. O'Kelly in 1874.

Rafael. Produced 10 April 1875, Wallack's, New York.

Forbidden Fruit. Produced 3 October 1876, Wallack's, New York.

The Dead Secret. Produced 28 January 1877, 5th Avenue Theatre, New York.

Marriage (also known as *A Bridal Tour*). Produced 1 October 1877, Wallack's, New York.

Clarissa Harlowe; or, The History of a Young Lady. Produced 10 September 1878, Wallack's, New York.

The School for Scandal. Doctored version of Sheridan's play. Produced 21 September 1878, Wallack's, New York.

Spell-bound. Produced 24 February 1879, Wallack's, New York.

Rescued; or, A Girl's Romance. Given a copyright performance 27 August 1879, King's Cross Theatre, London; produced 4 September 1879, Booth's, New York.

Contempt of Court. Given a copyright performance 1 October 1879, Marylebone, London; produced 4 October 1879, Wallack's, New York.

Therese; or, The Maid of Croissey. Produced 19 August 1880, Adelphi.

The Amadan, Produced 29 January 1883, Theatre Royal, Richmond, Surrey; then 5 February 1883, Boston Museum.

Vice Versa. Produced 21 March 1883, Wallack's, Springfield, Mass.

Robert Emmet. Given a copyright performance 4 November 1884, Prince of Wales, Greenwich, London. Produced 5 November 1884, McVicker's Theatre, Chicago.

The Jilt. Given a copyright performance 13 May 1885, Elephant and Castle, London. Produced 18 May 1885, California Theatre, San Francisco.

Fin Mac Coul of Skibbereen. A revision of *Belle Lamar*. Given a copyright performance 2 February 1887, Elephant and Castle, London. Produced 3 February 1887, Hollis Street Theatre, Boston.

The Spae Wife (later called *Cuishla-ma-Chree*). Given a copyright performance 30 March 1886, Elephant and Castle, London. Produced 20 February 1888, Hollis Street Theatre, Boston.

Phryne; or, The Romance of a Young Wife. Produced 12 September 1887, Baldwin Theatre, San Francisco.

Ourselves. Comedy written *c.* 1887. Never produced.

Captain Swift. Revision of play by Haddon Chambers. Produced with the Boucicault revisions for one week only, 4 December 1888, Madison Square Theatre, New York.

A Tale of a Coat (also referred to as *Jimmy Watt*). Given a copyright performance 1 August 1890, Elephant and Castle, London, and tried out in Philadelphia the same month. Produced 14 August 1890, Daly's, New York.

Lend Me Your Wife. Produced 25 August 1890, Boston Museum, Boston.

The Luck of Roaring Camp. Incomplete adaptation of Bret Harte's story, on which Boucicault was working at the time of his death.

99. Produced posthumously 5 October 1891, Standard Theatre, London.

Jack Weatherby. A copy of this play, signed by Boucicault, is in the National Library of Ireland, Dublin. No record of production.

Manuscripts, completely or partly in Boucicault's handwriting, of the following plays are in the collection of the University of South Florida. Some of these titles are mentioned in Boucicault's correspondence or newspaper reports of plays on which he was working but no record has yet been found of any of them having been produced:

Gabrielle, The Grass Widow, Excelsior; or, Qui Fit, Marie Antoinette, Bleak House, Joy in the House, Nectarine, A White Crow.

Two plays have always appeared on previous lists of Boucicault's plays and are now known not to be by him:

The Chaplain of the Fleet, which was granted a licence on 31 December 1890 but of which there is no record of production, was written by his son Dot (Dion Boucicault Jnr).

Norah's Vows, produced on 6 July 1878 at the Theatre Royal, Brighton, starring Agnes Robertson, was by Miss Emma Schiff.

INDEX

INDEX

INDEX